Ending Wars

Ending Wars

Feargal Cochrane

polity

First published in 2008 by Polity Press

Polity Press
65 Bridge Street
Cambridge CB2 1UR, UK

Polity Press
350 Main Street
Malden, MA 02148, USA

ISBN-13: 978-0-7456-4032-7
ISBN-13: 978-0-7456-4033-4 (pb)

A catalogue record for this book is available from the British Library.

Typeset in 10.25 on 13 pt FF Scala
by Servis Filmsetting Ltd, Stockport, Cheshire
Printed and bound in Great Britain by MPG Printers, Bodmin, Cornwall

For further information on Polity, visit our website: www.polity.co.uk

For Rosaleen

Contents

Preface and Acknowledgements   ix

Introduction   1
Focus of the Book   2
Structure of the Book   5
Conclusion   11

1 **The Changing Nature of War**   12
What is War?   13
The Social Meaning of War   15
The Limits of War   25
Modern Trends in War   27
How Do Modern Wars End?   32
Making Wars Ripe for Ending   35

2 **Third-Party Intervention**   39
What is Third-Party Intervention?   40
Different Forms of Third-Party
    Intervention   43
Chechnya and the Limits of Third-Party
    Intervention   63

3 **Negotiation or Victory?**   70
Getting to the Table: Pre-Negotiations and
    the First Steps towards Dialogue   76
Making the First Move   81

When the Talking Begins: Political Negotiations   87
The Importance of Leadership in Negotiations   95

4   **Resistance to the Peace**   101
Why Resist the Ending of War?   104
What is a Spoiler?   108
Violent Resisters   113
Peaceful Resisters   117

5   **Ending the Global War on Terror**   126
Understanding the Global War on Terror   128
Can the Global War on Terror be Ended?   138
Conclusion   148

6   **Reconciliation and Rebuilding**   150
Rebuilding through Reconciliation   153
Rebuilding through Reconstruction   167
Rebuilding Whose Peace?   169
The Need for Effective Reconstruction
    to End Wars   177
Conclusion   182

Conclusion   184

Notes   192
Bibliography   212
Index   222

Preface and Acknowledgements

This has not been an easy book to write. I have sat in front of my computer for most of the last year trying to think through the changing dynamics of armed conflicts and the patterns that exist in how they are brought to an end. When Louise Knight pitched the idea to me of writing a book entitled *Ending Wars*, I was both attracted by the ambition of such a project and at the same time horrified by its difficulty. To put it flippantly, if I knew how to end wars I would probably already have solved less difficult puzzles such as alchemy and perhaps a low-cost solution to global warming. Yet while writing the book I have tried to think through a number of questions that have confounded me for most of my life. What are the tipping points that lead *some* people both to engage in violence against others for political objectives, and to agree finally to stop doing so? To what extent do we see war as an ethical last resort, driven by our belief in the state system and the integrity of transnational organizations? Finally, how does the apparent miracle of 'peace' emerge out of these egregious acts of violence? When we consider the pain, suffering and dislocation caused by armed conflict, it is not surprising that the process of ending political violence is a difficult task, where breakdowns rather than breakthroughs are the norm.

On a more personal note, my interest in these questions comes out of the particular experience of being born and raised in Northern Ireland, where violence and politics have been regular partners in crime and where issues of the legitimacy and rationality of the use of violence for political purposes have been contested by many of those who live there. For most of my life Northern Ireland was regarded by many people as being an 'intractable' conflict, where the best that could be hoped for was an 'acceptable level of violence'.

This does not necessarily give me any particular skills for writing a book such as this one, but it does perhaps explain my reluctance to view 'official' wars through an ethical lens. My starting point is not whether a paramilitary or a politician claims to have legitimacy for the use of violence, but rather whether this was the only option available to them.

My other starting point in this book is a hopeful one. Armed conflicts are (in the main) started and perpetuated by rational actors with different sets of political goals and interests. Wars are usually ended by exactly the same people, once they determine that further violence will be counterproductive and that a political route out of conflict is the only way to secure their objectives. While it is easy to cast some actors in war as psychopaths, demagogues or 'evil-doers', who cannot be reasoned with, these are the exception rather than the rule in modern warfare. For the most part, people go to war because they think that it will work or due to other calculations such as pressure from internal political rivals or perceived aggression from external forces.

However, when this view about the productivity of war changes, real prospects for ending the violence can often emerge. All of this is easier said than done, of course, and the difficulties of getting to this point should not be underestimated. Ending an armed conflict cannot be viewed as a mechanistic exercise where the motivations and behaviour of the direct and indirect actors will conform to the same pattern. A one-size-fits-all analysis of conflict transformation inevitably risks misunderstanding the unique dynamics of individual cases in the search for simplified formulae to explain them.

The process of writing the book has been made much easier by the team at Polity, especially Louise Knight and Emma Hutchinson, both of whom guided me through the process of producing and refining the manuscript with consummate professionalism and care. I am also indebted to my colleagues in the Richardson Institute at Lancaster University, Dr Nina Caspersen and Dr Vicky Mason, whose own research has informed my thinking on several of the major debates covered within the book. I also want to thank my other colleagues in the Department of Politics and International Relations at Lancaster, in particular Professor David Denver, who provided encouragement and friendship throughout the project, and my Head of Department, Professor Chris May, who helped me to balance my responsibilities at the university with the task of researching and writing the book. I would also like to thank a number of other colleagues within and beyond Lancaster who have discussed many of the ideas within these pages and helped me to clarify my own thoughts on the wider debates, including Dr Patrick Bishop, Professor Adrian Guelke, Dr Roger Mac Ginty, Professor Hugh Miall, Professor Gerd Nonneman, Dr Graham Smith and Professor Andrew Williams.

I would also like to thank my students (past and present) who have taken my third-year undergraduate course 'Understanding Peace Processes' at Lancaster, for their enthusiasm and engagement with many of the themes at the centre of this book. The teaching has not all been one-way traffic, and I have benefited greatly from listening to their insights about how armed conflicts can be brought to an end.

A special word of thanks has to go to the anonymous reviewers of the book proposal and also the reviewers of the initial manuscript, for their constructive criticisms and suggestions. I am sure I am not the only author to think the first draft to be a work of beauty and then slowly come to the realization that the suggestions of expert readers would actually help to substantiate assertions and clarify analysis. Notwithstanding the help and guidance I have received in this process, all remaining errors of fact and analysis lie solely with the author.

My hope is that this book beats with an optimistic heart while looking at the world with a sceptical eye. It is up to those who read it to determine whether I have succeeded.

I would like to thank Greg and Kathie Irwin, Donald and Deborah McWhirter and Dr Alison Montgomery for their friendship, as well as friends and former colleagues from the Centre for the Study of Conflict at the University of Ulster, including Professor Seamus Dunn, Professor Valerie Morgan and Helen Dawson.

Finally, I would like to thank my family, Niall, Geraldine, Eamonn, Peter, Sean and my mother and father, Roisin and Gerry Cochrane, for their love and support.

The book is dedicated to my wife, Professor Rosaleen Duffy, who has had to listen to me pontificate upon the arguments within these pages since the writing began. I would like to thank her for carrying this burden with such fortitude, patience and encouragement.

Introduction

There is no such thing as a bad peace or a good war.
Benjamin Franklin[1]

This is a book about what war is, how war ends, and how this has been evolving in recent times. The starting point for this study is the view that violent conflicts are acts of human agency combined with a set of structural circumstances that trigger, cause or even encourage such acts.

War has been a familiar theme within human history which has shaped our world, geographically, politically and economically. In addition to the human death toll it has generated, it has also driven economies, caused famines, re-ordered political regimes and changed physical infrastructures. While much has been written on the causes of war, less attention has been given to the reasons why wars end. This book is aimed at understanding how wars are brought to an end and how this has been changing in line with the evolution of armed conflict over the course of the late twentieth and early twenty-first centuries.

The premise that runs through the book is that wars can be controlled and eventually terminated by human agency, given conducive structural conditions. In other words, war is not simply a force of nature, where we are all victims of violent primordial circumstances. Notwithstanding the work of Sigmund Freud on the human mind or Konrad Lorenz on the nature of aggression, we do not have to accept war as integral to the human condition. Large-scale wars and smaller low-intensity conflicts are driven by political, economic and cultural imperatives. These forms of violence emerge as a means to an end and are not normally an end in themselves, even if the causal factors are difficult to determine. As Peter Wallensteen boldly puts it: 'A strong statement is that conflicts *are* solvable. This is not necessarily an idealistic or optimistic position . . . it is a realistic position.'[2]

There have, of course, been violent conflicts that have defied termination and wars that seem to be dominated by 'ancient hatreds' that appear beyond hope. However, the view that violence is inevitable due to such enmities has often been an excuse for policy-makers to justify non-interventionist strategies until such regions burn themselves out and find a new political equilibrium.

This book argues that while there may be disagreement about how it should be achieved – e.g. realist notions of balance of power or deterrence strategies, the pacifist emphasis on the principles of non-violence, or the liberal belief in 'good governance', international mediation, constructive engagement and ultimately coercion – the contention here is that wars between states and wars within states can, under certain circumstances, be brought to an end.

Focus of the Book

A comment on terminology is important at the outset. This book deals primarily with how wars end *within* states rather than how such violence ends *between* them. There is a general consensus that armed conflict in the modern world is mainly characterized by violence within states rather than by violence between them. As a result this book focuses in particular on the processes through which these types of conflict are brought to an end. Despite conflicting methodologies, leading scholars and researchers in the area are in general agreement that the trend in modern warfare since the end of the Cold War has seen a reduction in inter-state war and a growth of intra-state violence (though this peaked in the early 1990s and has not grown consistently). As the authors of *Contemporary Conflict Resolution* explain:

> One major trend, however, shows through in almost all accounts and that is a decline in the proportion of interstate wars. . . . There were no interstate wars in 1993 and 1994, . . . only a minor border altercation between Peru and Ecuador in 1995 and a flare-up in the long-running dispute between India and Pakistan over Kashmir in 1996. . . . In 2002 there was only one interstate war. . . [though] Iraq would be added in 2003.[3]

Peter Wallensteen and Margareta Sollenberg report from their study of armed conflict during the 1990s that, while perhaps not 'extinct', inter-state wars have markedly decreased in number during the post-Cold War period. 'Of the 96 conflicts recorded for the 1989–95 period, only five were clear-cut inter-state armed conflicts, i.e. cases of two internationally recognized governments sending forces against one another over an issue of government and/or territory.'[4] The 2005 *Human Security Report* is more strident in its conclusions, declaring that there has been an inexorable shift from inter-state to intra-state conflict over time.

> Between 1816 and 2002 there were 199 international wars (including wars of colonial conquest and liberation) and 251 civil wars – one international war on average for every 1.3 civil wars over the entire period. International wars accounted for one-fifth to three-quarters of all wars being waged in the 1950s, 1960s and 1970s. . . . From the early 1980s to the early 1990s the number of international wars declined. For the rest of the 1990s and the early years of the 21st century there have been almost no international wars. The one exception was 1999, when there were three wars – two of which, Kosovo and India–Pakistan, had relatively small death tolls.[5]

Notwithstanding the war in Iraq (which might be seen as an inter-state conflict which has also become an internal one), the emphasis of this book, in a series which focuses on war in the modern world, has to be on intra-state rather than inter-state conflicts. The intention of the book is that it extends the analysis of warfare outside the boundaries of the state system, focusing on wars within states rather than on wars between them. While states remain an important point of reference when discussing the dynamics of war and strategies to bring such violence to an end, they are no longer the only one, and in some cases, where states are weak and shadow economies are strong, the state may be peripheral to the issue of whether violence continues or ends. William Reno coined the phrase the 'shadow state' in the context of sub-Saharan Africa, where conflict entrepreneurs combined across the private and public spheres to subvert the state for personal gain.[6] In the twenty-first century, states do not have a monopoly over decisions about whether to go to war, and in some instances, individual 'warlords', groups of militias, diaspora communities or transnational networks such as Al-Qaeda can play a more influential role.

The focus of this book on warfare within states is more appropriate to the conflicts of the twenty-first century and facilitates a discussion of the important roles played by transnational and civil society actors in helping to bring violent conflicts to an end. In addressing this, the chapters that follow engage with a number of current debates concerning the limits of war, the ethics of war in the modern world, the perpetrators and victims of violence, and whether it is possible for external third parties to intervene successfully in wars to help end them.

The central argument of the book is that the nature of war changed dramatically during the twentieth century in ways that make ending these conflicts more difficult to achieve in the modern world. This change has been towards a widening of the actors and victims of warfare that has accompanied the post-Cold War growth of intra-state and ethnic conflict. The pain and human suffering incurred as a result of armed conflict has increasingly been borne by civilian populations rather than by military forces in modern warfare, and this has had damaging knock-on effects in the search to end such violence. Focusing on civil wars, Roy Licklider has pointed out the obstacles in the way of bringing them to a close.

> Sustained wars produce and reinforce hatred that does not end with the violence. How do groups of people who have been killing one another with considerable enthusiasm and success come together to form a common government? How can you work together, politically and economically, with the people who killed your parents, siblings, children, friends, or lovers? On the surface it seems impossible, even grotesque. But in fact we know that it happens all the time.[7]

The decision-making process related to maintaining cease-fires, entering negotiations and implementing the terms of a settlement has been decentralized from military and political leaders to a much wider range of direct actors with less tangible mandates of support. The book examines how this change in the nature of how wars are fought (and whom they affect) has influenced the complex processes of bringing violence to an end.

Structure of the Book

The book has a thematic structure, examining the obstacles that lie in the way of ending wars and the circumstances within which efforts have been made to curtail this type of violent conflict. The purpose here is not to provide a comprehensive measurement of how many wars have ended within a given period, or to provide statistics about the number of battle deaths endured, cease-fires declared or peace agreements reached. While these issues are, of course, important, the aim of this book is to highlight a number of themes that are critical to the task of bringing modern violent political conflicts to an end. The book does not argue that the dynamics of all such conflicts are the same, or that every war can be ended through peaceful dialogue. What it does hope to demonstrate is that wars *can* be brought to an end, that conditions can *at times* be promoted which may make this more likely, and that under these circumstances, non-violent political alternatives can be pursued. While the premise here is an optimistic one, namely that violent conflict is a product of human agency, combined with malign or dysfunctional political/economic structures, it does not underestimate the difficulties inherent in ending war for those both within and beyond such conflict zones.

Chapter 1 charts the changing nature of war and includes an examination of terms such as 'war', 'conflict' and 'terrorism', explaining the way in which these terms have bled into one another as the nature of warfare has evolved over time. The academic, policy and media communities use an alphabet soup of phrases to describe warfare, including 'internal conflicts', 'new wars', 'small wars', 'civil wars' and many others besides,[8] including the more recent 'network-centric war' and 'complex political emergencies'. All of these terms have different nuances that try to capture the complexity of modern warfare and the fact that its boundaries go beyond and beneath the level of the formal state system. These changing trends in how wars are conducted are linked to the social meaning of war in the modern world and to the way in which armed conflicts are justified by those who engage in them.

The central argument put forward in this first chapter is that the process of ending wars between states is radically different to ending wars within states, where decision-making and political power are often more fractured, where civilians will often be more involved as both perpetrators and victims, and where humanitarian abuses may have been more extreme. In cases such as Bosnia, Kosovo, Rwanda and Liberia, the act of killing itself was often so traumatic that it added to the difficulty of ending the violence. It is important to recognize this evolution in how wars have been fought since the latter part of the twentieth century in order to understand the process though which such violent conflicts are brought to an end.

Chapter 2 examines the role of international and local third-party intervention aimed at ending war. In many armed conflicts, external third parties have played a role in bringing violence to a halt. This chapter explores the history of third-party intervention and looks at the various roles, from fact-finding and mediation to peace-keeping and peace-enforcement. This will illustrate the vast range of tasks often undertaken by third parties in efforts to promote negotiations, cease-fires, demilitarization and post-war reconstruction. In addition to looking at a number of high-profile external interventions aimed at ending violence, the chapter looks at examples such as Chechnya and Darfur where such intervention has not taken place. It considers why this has not happened and what this tells us about the international political system and its capacity to intervene to end armed conflict. One of the key features of this chapter is an assessment of the record of external agencies in helping to end war, highlighting the dilemmas facing humanitarian intervention and the failures of transnational actors in regions such as Rwanda and Bosnia.

Chapter 3 focuses on the role that political negotiations play in the task of bringing warfare to an end and examines the complexities and setbacks that often accompany such processes. Once it is clear to the conflict parties that military victory is unlikely (or that defeat is inevitable), the process of looking for a political route out of war will intensify. While many of these negotiations often end in failure, this chapter looks at the dynamics of the negotiating process and at the techniques that can help move such dialogue out of political stalemate. The chapter highlights the difficulties associated with negotiating the journey out of warfare and focuses on contemporary examples, including South Africa, Northern Ireland and the Middle East. These case studies illustrate the way in which military and political stalemates evolve over time, leading to informal talks and formal negotiations aimed at ending violence and achieving political settlements. It connects to the previous chapter by examining the differences between negotiating an end to inter- and intra-state warfare: William Zartman declared that 'internal conflicts – civil wars – are the most difficult of conflicts to negotiate. Only a quarter to a third of modern civil wars (including anticolonial wars) have found their way to negotiation, whereas more than half of modern interstate wars have done so.'[9]

Chapter 4 explores the manner in which certain groups have tried to resist or undermine efforts to negotiate an end to war. Groups who may have an interest in violent conflict continuing, or who disagree with the political conditions under which the war is being ended, may try to destabilize efforts to bring the war to a close. This is particularly relevant within intra-state warfare, where some actors have political and economic interests in its continuation and may lose out if the conflict is brought to an end. The chapter proposes refinements to Stephen Stedman's concept of 'spoiler' groups who seek to undermine political efforts to end warfare.[10] While Stedman seeks to differentiate between various categories, such as 'limited spoilers', 'total spoilers' and 'greedy spoilers',[11] it is argued here that such labelling too easily collapses supposed spoiler activity with support for, or actual involvement in, continued violence. However, some of those who resist political efforts aimed at ending warfare or managing conflict may do so because they feel that these political processes are so seriously flawed that they will lead to the re-emergence of violence, or that they seek to prioritize order over justice by imposing inequitable political and economic arrangements on one or more of the conflict parties. There is a danger here that this too easily equates spoilers with opponents of peace and implicitly identifies the 'peace process' itself as being equivalent to moderation and any opposition to it as extreme.

Chapter 4 therefore seeks to separate out those who have resisted the ending of war and the reasons why they have done so, ranging from military and political leaders with political, economic and personal self-interest in perpetuating the war, to those who see cease-fire agreements or treaty agreements as being 'peace at any price' which will ultimately lead to the re-emergence of violence at a later date.

Chapter 5 moves on to examine the global war on terror (GWOT) and the extent to which this represents a new form of warfare with different implications for termination. In his agenda-setting address to a joint session of the US Congress on 20 September 2001 in the immediate aftermath of 9/11, US President George Bush claimed that the attack opened up a new departure in conflict. War had gone global, and bringing this violence to an end required a co-ordinated global response between two mutually exclusive parties: those who valued freedom and tolerance, on the one hand, and the purveyors of fear and terror, on the other. This chapter engages with the debates surrounding the new security environment post-9/11 and focuses in particular on the newly identified paradigm of violent conflict represented by sub-state warfare. It has been suggested by some commentators that this represents a departure in traditional notions of how wars are conducted, whom they impact upon and how they can be managed or resolved. The chapter explores the dynamics of sub-state warfare and assesses the difficulties associated with bringing these violent conflicts to an end. It also challenges the claim that a new paradigm of warfare opened up after September 11, 2001. It is argued here that many of the techniques and practices believed to be new departures in war (attacks on civilians; no-warning, maximum-impact bombings or 'spectaculars'; the use of fear and terror for political leverage; the use of legal mechanisms by security forces – detention/expulsion, use of military intelligence, torture – aka 'extraordinary renditions') are in fact well-worn practices in war and in attempts to control it. What has changed since September 11, 2001 is that war has been extended to the point where it now impacts much more directly upon Western civilian societies than was the case in the past, as do the symptoms of modern warfare such as refugee flows, the extension of emergency laws and the sur-veillance of civilian populations. It is also argued that the GWOT cannot be won by military means and can only be ended in conjunction with a strategic review of US foreign policy in the Middle East.

Chapter 6 turns its attention to the importance of reconcilia-tion and reconstruction in rebuilding war-torn societies. The main focus here is on the complexities of the efforts that have been made towards these ends and at the structures and agen-cies that have been set in place to achieve them. The chapter examines the difficulties faced by ethically divided societies (and external third parties) in the process of dealing with the political, economic and personal traumas that are the inevitable consequence of war. Using examples including Rwanda, Bosnia, South Africa, Northern Ireland and Iraq, this chapter outlines the array of tasks that face shattered societies after the physical violence has been brought to an end. It is argued here that while justice is an inherent requirement for reconciliation to occur, it is difficult to devise political institutions capable of delivering this within the highly sensitive context of a shattered society. In addition, while reconstruction is needed to help the victims of violence reconstruct their shattered lives, this is often more than a neutral or technical exercise, and is frequently embedded within the liberal ideology of powerful Western interests. In circumstances where these Western states and transnational organizations were part of the war itself, attempts to engage in post-war reconstruction have inevitably been accompanied by allegations of bias and political self-interest, which have hampered the rebuilding effort.

Conclusion

This book argues that the ideology and sinews of war are the products of aggressive human interactions, enabled and driven by particular sets of political, economic and social conditions. The task for students of international relations and those seeking to play a positive policy role within violently divided societies is to understand the combination of structure and agency that produces and escalates this violence and to determine whether strategies are available to de-escalate and terminate it. The chapters that follow are an attempt to illustrate the challenges and opportunities that exist in the effort to end armed conflict in the modern world.

CHAPTER ONE

The Changing Nature of War

> Through much of history, war has been the norm rather than
> the exception in relations among nations.
>
> Joseph Nye[1]

All of us are familiar with the concept of war and are aware of
the heavy cost it brings in terms of death, injury and destruction to the world in which we live. As the journalist Robert Fisk
has eloquently remarked, '[W]ar is primarily not about victory
or defeat but about death and the infliction of death. It represents the total failure of the human spirit.'[2] While most readers of this book will thankfully not have been exposed to the
full horrors of warfare, we all have at least a working knowledge of some of the larger-scale 'hegemonic' wars that have
been documented through recent human history and know
something of their causal factors and how these violent conflagrations were eventually brought to an end. However, much
less attention has been paid to the fact that wars have been
evolving and mutating in three inter-connecting ways: firstly,
in how they are conducted; secondly, in terms of the people
affected by them; and, thirdly, in the challenges and opportunities this presents for bringing wars to an end.

Violent conflict in the twenty-first century is a different phenomenon to its ancient relation, described by Thucydides in
his *History of the Peloponnesian War* in the fifth century BC, or
more recent examples such as World Wars I and II during the
twentieth century. Contemporary conflicts are often mobile
and fluid, with complex arrays of direct and indirect actors and

uncertain timelines. As a consequence, decisions about *why* to go to war, *when* to go to war, *whom* to go to war with, *how* to engage in battle and *when* to stop are more complicated now than they were in the past. It is important to account for and understand the changing nature of warfare, as this is directly connected to how such conflicts can be brought to an end in today's world.

What is War?

Before discussing how the practice of war has changed, it is sensible to provide some definition about how war is understood. This book prefers an inclusive definition of armed conflict that treats war as an issue of scale, rather than as an inherently different form of physical violence. War, therefore, is defined here as being a period of organized violence between at least two parties, who may come from transnational, state or sub-state sources. As the impact on the victim remains the same (death, injury, displacement), little effort is made here to distinguish between levels of legitimate authority in the act of violence. As Quincy Wright has remarked in his classic analysis *A Study of War*: '[W]ar is only one of many abnormal legal situations. It is but one of numerous conflict procedures. It is only an extreme case of group attitudes. It is only a very large-scale resort to violence.'[3]

Categorizations of violence can easily lead to justifications of it for the purposes of national defence or in pursuit of that increasingly hollow phrase within international affairs, 'international peace and security'. Thus, acts of violence up to and including acts of war committed by states are easily deemed to be acts of 'reasonable force', while those committed by paramilitary factions are categorized as 'acts of terrorism'. However, it is important to ensure that arithmetic categories do not become moral ones and that violence from undeclared wars gets its share of attention alongside the violence authorized/legitimized by the state and powerful international institutions.[4] To focus on large-scale war at the expense of undeclared or smaller-scale (but more numerous) conflicts within states would risk taking an unnecessarily state-centric view of violent conflict in the contemporary world. Worse still, to engage in the binary logic of state-driven 'force' versus non-state-based 'terror' is of little comfort to those who experience and suffer such violence in their lives.

While many commentators (and perpetrators) agree that war is horrific, painful and costly in human and economic terms, there remains a belief that states (and their elite actors) can be absolved from the responsibility and guilt of the act of killing if such violence is organized along certain lines, or if it is sanctioned by a 'legitimate' authority. As a consequence, the treatment of war is not limited in this book to inter-state conflict, or to a particular threshold of casualties, but is taken to include intra-state and sub-state conflict of the type high-lighted in the post-9/11 era, with the global war on terror. The purpose here is to extend the analysis of warfare outside the boundaries of the international state system and focus on wars within states rather than on wars between them. This framing is more appropriate to the conflicts of the twenty-first century and facilitates an integrated discussion of the important roles played by state, sub-state and transnational actors in both the conduct and termination of warfare.

Several different approaches have been taken by conflict researchers in order to define, categorize and quantify warfare, most of which attempt to analyse the patterns and frequency of armed conflict over time. While plenty of information has been collected to define, map and quantify the intensity of armed conflict, its power as an explanatory tool is less certain. As Dennis Sandole points out, '[N]ot only do we not know much, if anything, about the sources of influence on decisions to go to war, but what we think we know could be challenged by other (contradictory) findings.'[5] One of the central reasons for the debate surrounding the limits of war, the precise figures that surround its frequency and intensity, and whether its causal factors can be understood and controlled relates to the varied methodologies that have been used to gather such information. However, another more fundamental issue is pertinent here, namely that armed conflict is not a closed system that lends itself easily to quantification. The edges of measurement in the gathering (and interpretation) of these data are often blurred and subject to different techniques. These different methodologies can produce alarming variations in assessments of war frequency and intensity and diverse interpretations about what these figures mean for future trends in armed conflict and possible strategies that might be pursued for ending it.[6]

The Social Meaning of War

While quantitative researchers have spent some time defining what wars are,[7] less attention has been given to the changing meaning of war as a social descriptor of armed conflict. In the past, the act of war was indelibly connected to statehood, and decisions about going to war, the conduct during war and when to end the conflict were taken by the elite political and military groups within states. This, together with the organization of the international political system which recognized the rights of states, served to connect the concept of 'war' with the legitimacy of states, and to render the act of warfare as being, on certain occasions, 'just'. The use of armed conflict from non-state sources, on the other hand, has generally been regarded as unwarranted and illegitimate 'terrorism' (e.g. the Tamil Tigers, the Provisional IRA and, of course, Al-Qaeda) or the more recently coined 'insurgency', to describe the actions of various groups of militant Sunni nationalists in Iraq. This is not to say that the actions of paramilitary groups have not been deadly and to deny that many people have been (and continue to be) killed or injured in horrifying ways by such groups. However, as Fred Halliday has pointed out, '[T]he great mass of criminal activities against civilians and others are carried out not by rebel groups, but by states.'[8] It might also be argued that not all of this death and destruction is carried out by states that we might describe as being 'rogue', 'weak', 'collapsed' or otherwise dysfunctional regimes within the neo-liberal paradigm of 'good governance'.

The ending of the Cold War witnessed the curious phenomenon of the 'democratic peace' and its close associate, 'humanitarian war'. These are at the heart of the distinction between war as being a regrettable but essential and even reasonable social phenomenon, on the one hand, and war as unnecessary and pernicious, on the other. Advocates of the 'democratic peace' advance the neo-liberal view that international peace and security can only be achieved through the promotion of the values and structures of Western democracy and liberal market reform. The logic goes that as democracies do not wage war on other democracies, then the world will be a safer place when the values and practices of democratization are extended from the Global North to the Global South. One of the leading thinkers behind democratic peace theory is Michael Doyle, who argues that, for all of their flaws, inconsistencies and selfish motivations, liberal states have the capacity to tame the anarchic nature of the international system and produce greater peace and stability. 'Even though liberal states have become involved in numerous wars with nonliberal states, constitutionally secure liberal states have yet to engage in war with one another. . . . A liberal zone of peace, a pacific union, has been maintained and has expanded despite numerous particular conflicts of economic and strategic interest.'[9] Todd Landman outlines the case for the democratic peace in the following summary of academic literature on the subject.

> In the international sphere, the very large literature on the democratic peace has shown that since the late 1800s pairs of democracies (i.e. dyads) do not go to war with one another . . . . Some commentators have argued that this empirical finding is the closest thing to a law that political science has established . . . . Further research argues that democracies are less conflict-prone than non-democracies . . . and that democratizing countries that have well-managed transitions are less likely to be engaged in interstate warfare . . . .[10]

Critics of this view would argue that while democratic states might have demonstrated a reluctance to go to war with one another, they seemed more enthusiastic about going to war with those whom they felt did not live up to their standards of governance. In fact, those at the policy end of the democratic peace have been zealous – even evangelical – in their desire to bring war to a host of countries in the developing world. As the 2005 *Human Security Report* suggests, '[T]he UK, France, the US and the Soviet Union/Russia top the list of countries involved in international wars in the last 60 years.'[11]

In his challenging book *At War's End*, Roland Paris makes an important distinction which he claims advocates of the democratic peace model fail fully to appreciate. 'Although well-established market democracies may be more peaceful in their internal and international affairs than non-democracies, the policy of promoting democracy necessarily involves *transforming* a state into a market democracy.'[12] For Paris, it is not so much the pursuit of democratic norms and market liberalization that is the problem, but rather the *means* of getting there that creates the difficulty. This transition, often forced at an unreasonable pace within societies still dealing with the trauma of war, is likely to exacerbate rather than end conflict in the region. David Keen, writing about the role of international financial institutions and their promotion of liberal market reforms in Sierra Leone, remarks that

> one can certainly point to many western countries with relatively free markets where democracy is well established and where the risk of war (or at least internal war) seems minimal. However, an apparent correlation between (relatively) free markets, democracy, and peace within developed countries tells us little about how less fortunate countries might best arrive at this enviable state of affairs.[13]

Roger Mac Ginty has critiqued what he terms the hegemonic dominance of democratic peace theory, and points out that 'correlation is not the same as causation. . . . The precise reasons for the seeming association between democratic states and warlessness are unclear and are likely to reside in such a complex matrix of reasons (enduring alliances and patterns of trade, etc.) that it is difficult to promote one war-resisting factor such as democracy above others.'[14]

The assumptions behind the democratic peace have even led some to extrapolate beyond the bounds of reason. The *New York Times* journalist Thomas Friedman, for instance, famously expounded the 'Golden Arches Theory' in his book *The Lexus and the Olive Tree*.[15] This theory put forward the notion that no two countries with a McDonald's restaurant have ever gone to war with one another and that most of their franchises are in democratic states. Thus to follow the theory through, the more McDonald's outlets there are around the world, the fewer wars there will be (though perhaps the more deaths from obesity). The one problem with the Golden Arches Theory, of course, is that it is super-sized nonsense (e.g. the fact that Panama had a McDonald's did not prevent a US invasion in 1989). However, if nothing else, it illustrates the hegemony of democratic peace theory within contemporary Western discourse as a way of bringing wars to an end.

Justice in War

The argument put forward in this book is that the state does not have any superior moral authority compared to non-state actors when it comes to using violence for political purposes, even if it claims the legal authority to do so. The modern nation-state was, of course, carved out of violent conflict, and so should be circumspect about staking any claims in the area of political morality. While the state certainly has the ability to deliver death on a massive scale and has demonstrated its capacity to do so for many centuries, we no longer live in a Hobbesian world where the sovereign is granted tyrannical powers, including those of life or death, in return for delivering stability and order to anarchic communities. The belief that there is a 'legitimate authority' for killing has been an integral element of Just War Theory (JWT) for many centuries, but is frequently in the eye of the beholder, or the mob, and has been used by everyone from Oliver Cromwell to former British Prime Minister Tony Blair to argue that society will be improved through the use of regrettable, but necessary, acts of violence. While states have and will continue to use violence in pursuit of various political, economic and ideological ends, they should not boast about it or try to justify it. More importantly perhaps, we as citizens of these states should not encourage it.

Assessments about the legitimacy of war will vary depending on the context involved and the political perspectives of those engaged in such debates; the point here is that the rules for the use of violent force have been changing in subtle but important ways since the end of the twentieth century. There are several areas where this can be observed, which intersect with modern readings of classical JWT. As Stephen Chan has suggested, the concept of the just war has become embedded within the transnational foundations of the international system, such as the Geneva Conventions and the UN Charter, which 'give the modern world its universal laws of war'.[16]

Several of the main pillars of JWT remain central to the justification of armed conflict today, but have mutated in interesting ways since the concept was devised by St Augustine in the fourth/fifth century and refined by St Thomas Aquinas in the twelfth century, Hugo Grotius in the seventeenth century and Michael Walzer in the twentieth.[17] Three of the traditional tenets of JWT (having a 'legitimate authority'; possessing a 'just cause' for going to war; and avoiding the direct targeting of civilians in the activity of war) illustrate both the elasticity of the theory and the way it has managed to encompass not only the logic of *realpolitik*, but also the neo-liberal prosecution of the democratic peace. Clearly, there is confusion and disagreement today about who (or what) represents a 'legitimate authority' in matters of war. This disagreement has allowed sub-state groups to declare their legitimacy on the grounds of being unrecognized states with *de facto* (if not *de jure*) authority, or political movements representative of the will of the people seeking to overthrow the repressive rule of hegemonic authority. While issues of legitimate authority are contested in the contemporary globalized world, so too is the notion of the 'just cause' as a rationale for the use of war. Practically everyone who goes to war claims to have a just cause, and this has also been complicated by the move from the assumed certainties of the realist and neo-realist era, to the evangelism of today's neo-liberal order. Thus, while a just cause for the use of war in traditional inter-state conflict may have been cast as being a response to a threat to a state's territorial integrity, economic resources or political interests, the just cause of the democratic peace is often articulated in terms of a threat to core *values*.

In recent years, the use of war by powerful Western states (and by transnational agencies such as the UN and NATO) has been justified on the basis of values such as democracy, freedom and the pursuit of international peace and security. This change is linked, of course, to the current post-Cold War confusion which pervades the international political system. This confusion is summed up in the following question. Is the purpose of the United Nations (and other transnational organizations such as NATO) to recognize and protect the territorial integrity of states, or to protect individuals within those states from brutal or inhuman treatment by their own governments? The answer to this question has been evolving since the end of the Cold War and has paralleled the policy shift within the international arena from realism to neo-liberalism ushered in by the growth of humanitarian intervention. Thomas Weiss shines a powerful light on this post-Westphalian tension in his own insightful contribution to this book series. 'The [UN] Charter contains a seeming contradiction between the intervention-proscribing principle of state sovereignty (especially in Article 2) and the intervention-prescribing principle of human rights (especially in Articles 55–6). This clash is especially evident when push comes to shove over humanitarian intervention.'[18] The *values* of the democratic peace have witnessed a deadly and inconsistent ping-pong taking place between these two principles, in line (critics would suggest) with individual economic and geo-political interests of powerful Western governments. Put more starkly, such governments pick and choose between issues of state sovereignty and human rights standards when it suits them to do so and invoke Just War Theory and an articulation of shared values to mobilize political support for their actions. In 1999 former British Prime Minister Tony Blair gave a speech in the United States which claimed that NATO military intervention in Kosovo was about such core values: 'No one in the West who has seen what is happening in Kosovo can doubt that NATO's military action is justified. . . . This is a just war, based not on any territorial ambitions but on values. We cannot let the evil of ethnic cleansing stand. We must not rest until it is reversed.'[19] This defence of armed conflict in pursuit of wider ethics such as democracy, freedom and international peace and security, rather than narrowly defined state-driven pre-occupations of self-interest, has become the hegemonic discourse of international policy-making in the justification of war in the twenty-first century. As David Rieff has warned, however: 'A war of values . . . is, almost by definition, a crusading venture.'[20] David Welch identified this move from interests to values in his 1993 book *Justice and the Genesis of War*, where the 'justice motive' acted as a catalyst for political leaders to seek redress for gaps between their perceived entitlements and their benefits.[21]

The third frequently cited defence of the just war, avoiding direct attacks on civilians, is also worthy of consideration. The changing nature of war in the modern world has allowed advocates to point towards technological advances as illustrative of a low-cost war. The development of advanced surveillance capabilities and air superiority (especially by the US, but also by transnational bodies such as NATO) has led to a doctrine often referred to as the Revolution in Military Affairs (RMA). This emerged during the 1990s in response to the growing interventionism encapsulated above in Tony Blair's speech. This twin-track use of intelligence-gathering techniques and mobile military forces, combined with the capacity for the use of overwhelming force which could be delivered from a remote distance, changed the view (among some) that war could be targeted more directly at the guilty, while sparing the lives of the innocent. As Fred Halliday remarks; RMA 'allowed for the spectre of a war in which combat troops would not be used and in which casualties would be minimal'.[22] The political implication of RMA for the justification of war is that the ability to target the guilty and spare civilian suffering has augmented the ethical envelope within which the use of war can be used with a clear conscience. Thus Blair could legitimize (however reluctantly) the spilling of blood in Kosovo, Afghanistan and Iraq, while supporting peace processes in other contexts such as in the Middle East or Northern Ireland.

The point here is not to rehearse ongoing debates relating to the legitimacy of recent wars in Kosovo, Afghanistan and Iraq, so much as to point out that these illustrate the ways in which the social meaning of war has been changing during the latter stages of the twentieth and the early twenty-first centuries. The main policy drivers of the democratic peace are now having to defend their use of violence in terms of protecting international peace and security and base this on values such as freedom, liberty and democracy. This is a change in the defence of the need for war, as articulated by the likes of Machiavelli, the father of political realism. While state-driven excuses for the necessity of resorting to armed conflict have moved from interests to values with the advent of the democratic peace, the concern here must be that the ability to interpret the ethics of war has stretched the elastic of Just War Theory to breaking point. If we cannot agree about what authority (state, sub-state or transnational) is legitimate, what causes are overwhelmingly important, or who civilian non-combatants and legitimate targets are in the fog of today's intra-state ethnic conflagrations, then existing doctrines on the ethics of war require urgent updating.

Jus Post Bellum

An attempt at such an updating of JWT has been provided by the emergence of the concept of *jus post bellum*. In response to the growth of humanitarian intervention since the end of the Cold War, JWT has evolved to consider the ethics of war *after* the immediate violence has come to an end. As Gary Bass, among others, has indicated, while the rules about going to war and subsequent behaviour in war have been widely debated, 'Much less has been said about what happens after a war. But the aftermath of war is crucial to the justice of the war itself.'[23] This connects the principles underlying the legitimacy of war to the practice of reconstruction after it has ended. A number of critical issues present themselves here, perhaps the most central being the extent to which outside parties retain a responsibility for rebuilding after the violent phase of a war has ended. Assuming for a moment that the *jus in bello* and *jus ad bellum* categories of JWT can be satisfied, how long do external parties have to stay involved in these regions to ensure *jus post bellum* – justice after war? This is a difficult question to answer, both in ethical and in practical terms. It requires those who advocate violence to demonstrate not only that the decision to go to war and their conduct in that war was legitimate, but that their actions *after* the war were also ethical. Brian Orend has written about these complex issues in some detail, providing what he calls 'a plausible list of propositions regarding what would be at least permissible with regard to a just settlement of a just war'.[24] These criteria offer a useful starting point and revolve around reversing aggression, protecting human rights and punishing those deemed to be guilty of abusing these human rights. As always with JWT, however, the devil is very much in the detail, and Orend's starting point presupposes, firstly, that the other principles of JWT are viable and, secondly, that those responsible for delivering on *jus post bellum* are not themselves implicated in aggression, or other ethical misdemeanours linked to *jus in bello* or *jus ad bellum*. Alex Bellamy has suggested, meanwhile, that for *jus post bellum* to operate successfully, a fine line must be pursued by external third parties between helping indigenous communities rebuild the region while not imposing a political or economic blueprint on the society which does not match internal wishes. 'The failure to demonstrate commitment [to *jus post bellum*] casts serious doubt on an intervener's humanitarian intent and, where this was the principal justification for going to war, the legitimacy of the intervention itself.'[25] The later chapters in this book, which focus on the wars in Afghanistan and Iraq and the efforts to rebuild these societies after violent conflict, would suggest that the conditions of *jus post bellum* have not been met in these cases. Nevertheless, the changing nature of war and of external intervention in war has produced the concept of *jus post bellum* to help us think through the difficult questions surrounding the ethics of war. While these criteria will always be subject to debate, disagreement and revision, the development of *jus post bellum* is a welcome and overdue addition to JWT and to the challenging task of determining the legitimacy of war.

The Limits of War

The case that the nature of war and the complexity of international responses to it have been changing in recent years is not a difficult one to make. Another element in this evolutionary process is that it is also more difficult to determine when war has actually ended today than it was in the past. In the time of Thucydides, and in the modern realist era of Hans Morgenthau, or his intellectual offspring Henry Kissinger, it was relatively easy to determine when wars were over. This was connected, of course, to the fact that it was also reasonably straightforward to determine whom wars were being fought between and why.

This became less obvious with the advent of hegemonic neoliberalism within the international system. Ironically perhaps, this very point was highlighted by George W. Bush shortly after he became US President. In a speech to the Radio and Television Correspondents dinner in March 2001, he outlined his foreign policy agenda (before 9/11). 'When I was coming up, it was a dangerous world and we knew exactly who they were. It was us versus them. And it was clear who them was. Today, we're not so sure who they are, but we know they're there.'[26] What these rhetorical stumblings were pitching at was the idea that even before the events of September 11, 2001, the international political environment had become much more complicated since the rigid certainties of the Cold War period.

In today's world, of course, it is not *only* states that go to war and it is not *only* the leaders of those states who have the capacity to declare or end wars. In the modern era, the direct and indirect actors in warfare have multiplied to the point that ending armed conflict has expanded beyond simple state control. This poses problems in determining when a war has ended, as quite often such conflicts stagger towards peace with multiple declarations (and breaches) of cease-fire agreements and many false dawns where political agreements falter or break down altogether. This has been amply demonstrated in the on-again-off-again low-intensity conflicts in the Middle East, Sri Lanka and Northern Ireland, as well as in larger-scale conflagrations such as in Bosnia prior to the 1995 Dayton Accord. Roger Mac Ginty has illustrated the limbo lands of contemporary political conflicts represented in the phrase 'no war, no peace', where regions have experienced a reduction of direct physical violence but no sustained conflict transformation process where the causes of the conflict have been satisfactorily addressed.[27] As we no longer live (for the most part) in a world where wars are fought by the military forces alone, on a narrowly specified geographical battlefield, and ended by heads of state signing peace treaties or terms of surrender, determining the end point of war is usually an inexact science. As the NGO International IDEA has pointed out, '[I]ncreasingly in today's wars, civilians are targeted directly; the historically sharp line between military combatants and civilians has become distinctly blurred.'[28] This is especially obvious in the growing number of intra-state ethnic conflicts that characterized the 1990s. War and peace in the modern world is a messy and unpredictable business, and determining when a war has ended can be extremely difficult to assess without an adequate passage of time. Some leading commentators, such as Peter Wallensteen and Margareta Sollenberg, use the methodology of the University of Uppsala Conflict Data Program, which requires an absence of violence for a period of twelve months after the conflict. However, as others have pointed out, this must be a vague measurement at best and is more viable as a theoretical performance indicator than in the complex and messy reality of regions emerging out of violent political conflict.[29] In reality, violence by some groups against other groups often evolves in form, duration, intensity and causation. Determining whether or not an act of violence was committed against a victim because of their ethnicity (as opposed to non-conflict-related reasons) is not always clear in the fog of a 'cold peace'. In the end, determining whether a war has ended is a subjective judgement that will defy the most precisely calibrated of quantitative techniques. Ultimately, we can only say that war has ended when its causal factors have been addressed through a process of observable transformative change. However, before focusing on how wars end, it is important to recognize that this is connected to the way in which they are fought.

Modern Trends in War

Several themes connect this book to the others in this series 'War and Conflict in the Modern World'. Few of them are more prominent than the fact that trends in armed conflict have changed dramatically from inter-state to intra-state violence. A number of scholarly studies and policy papers have made the point that trends in warfare over the last fifteen years have seen a reduction in large-scale inter-state violence and an increase in smaller intra-state conflicts. According to Dennis Sandole, 'Civil wars are now the dominant form of warfare.'[30] International IDEA, meanwhile, contend that 'most of today's violent conflicts are not the wars between contending states of former years, but take place within existing states. Many are inextricably bound up with concepts of identity, nation and nationalism, and many stem from the competition for resources, recognition and power.'[31] Researchers at Uppsala University have suggested that in 2005, of the thirty-one ongoing conflicts recorded around the world, all of them were intra-state.[32] This changing pattern in armed conflict has had important effects in terms of how wars are fought, who is affected by them, and how they can be brought to an end.

Scholars who focus on the frequency of armed conflict have reported on the fact that such violence rose steadily until the end of the Cold War but fell consistently after 1992. Convincing data have been provided by the Uppsala University dataset which suggest that a paradigm-shift took place in conflict types after the Cold War, from inter-state to intra-state conflicts. This changing pattern was caused by a rise of ethno-nationalist tension and emergence of secessionist movements in the early 1990s. Despite differences of emphasis provided by the varied methodologies followed by peace researchers, most are in agreement that there has been a reduction in the proportion of inter-state violence relative to intra-state conflict. As International IDEA has reported, while the good news is that inter-state war has been on the decline, '[T]he bad news is that between 1989 and 2003 . . . there were 116 significant armed conflicts around the globe of which 92 were essentially internal.'[33]

This evolution in conflict type is connected to wider changes within the structure of the international political system and in the locus of power itself within the state system. Informed commentators have frequently examined changes in the nature of armed conflict in conjunction with the evolution of the state. This led to a narrative which separated wars into different phases of history, beginning with the emergence of the dynastic state system in the fifteenth century, where sovereigns formed order out of anarchy, moving on to the primacy of popular sovereignty and struggles for national self-determination sparked off by the American and French revolutions in the late eighteenth century, where national armies formed to defend or liberate territories and peoples.[34] This evolved finally into the post-1945 bi-polar world, where, realists would contend, war was averted through the manipulation of an anarchic state system by deterrence relationships, a balance of power between states and doctrines such as mutually assured destruction (MAD). During all three of these phases, the dynamics of war were indelibly connected to the state system and to the relationships between states. The post-Cold War world has witnessed a radical shift away from the primacy of the state in war and has lessened its ability to determine its occurrence, course and outcome.

Commentators such as Mary Kaldor have emphasized the differences between inter-state Clausewitzian wars and these 'new wars', which can often exist beyond, or in spite of, the state itself.[35] Many writers on contemporary warfare have moved away from the inter-state focus of those pioneering cataloguers of war, Lewis Fry Richardson[36] and Quincy Wright,[37] in recognition that the dynamics of war have evolved over time. The central issue here is that the causes and triggers of armed conflict have become decentralized, no longer conforming to a set of agreed 'national' self-interests. While these may, of course, still exist or remain dominant in some cases, they are frequently accompanied in modern warfare by sets of conflicting or contested sub-national 'interests' such as between various identity groups within the state itself.

The direct actors in warfare have proliferated, meanwhile, to encompass a wide array of factions within and beyond the state, from ethnic groups and criminal gangs seeking political change or financial gain, to private military companies or diaspora communities, focused on either exacerbating or ameliorating violence within their former homelands.

In the context of wars in the modern world, we have witnessed a shift from violence between states to violence within them, in relation to which the coercive agencies of the state do not have full control over decisions relating to when to go to war, whom to go to war with, how to conduct the war or even when to end it. Modern wars are characterized by a cocktail of direct and indirect actors at the transnational, national and sub-national levels where the power of war is determined by the fluid relations between a complex network of individuals and groups.

Within this holistic model of armed conflict, the *way* of war has also evolved from formal declarations of hostilities between rival states for a declared set of aims, to surprise attacks such as September 11, 2001 or open-ended violence against a concept rather than against a visible enemy. These wars have witnessed an extension of the battlefield from a pre-determined geographical area separating military combatants and civilians, to an integrated conflict arena, where it is more difficult to distinguish between combatants and non-combatants. This trend is compounded by the fact that the sinews of war have also changed in modern conflict, with the proliferation of small arms, the use of child soldiers and tactics such as ethnic cleansing, famine, rape and torture all featuring prominently in late twentieth- and early twenty-first-century armed conflict.

All of this does not mean to say that Clausewitzian war is dead; the point is rather to emphasize that many of today's wars are qualitatively different in terms of how they are waged compared to previous patterns of conflict, where states had an overwhelming dominance. This different way of 'doing' war has important implications for bringing such violence to an end. In these intra-state conflicts, decision-making and political power are often more fractured than is the case in inter-state warfare, civilian populations are normally more involved, as both perpetrators and victims, and humanitarian abuses are often more extreme. In cases such as Bosnia, Kosovo, Rwanda and Liberia, the *way* of war was often so traumatic that it added to the difficulty of ending the violence. Bojicic-Dzelilovic and Kaldor have outlined this point within the context of the Bosnian war: 'Grotesque atrocities have been committed, including forced detention, torture, rape and castration.'[38] Tactics such as the killing of children, their kidnapping, indoctrination and deployment as child soldiers, and the use of rape and other forms of torture against specific communities accompanied the rise of ethno-national conflict and intra-state wars during the late twentieth century and produced levels of bitterness (and guilt) within civilian populations that are not normally associated with more traditional inter-state conflicts. Stephen Ellis quotes a Nigerian officer serving with ECOMOG as offering the following grisly account of combatants' behaviour in Liberia in the early 1990s. 'It was not unheard of to see fighters catch a member of an opposing side, especially key personalities, kill and butcher the chest, extract the heart and later eat it, either in cooked or roasted form.'[39] While informed analysts such as Ellis reject the *Heart of Darkness*-style clichés that have often accompanied discussion of warfare in West Africa, it is clear that ending intra-state violence presents different challenges and obstacles to the traditional inter-state conflicts of the Clausewitzian model. These modern wars impact on civilian populations and create greater refugee flows, problems of internal displacement and prolonged cycles of violence which political elites may find difficult to stop. 'A recent study on the effect of new internal wars on civilians in the 1990s argued that 90 per cent of fatalities in today's conflicts are civilians, as opposed to only 5 per cent in World War I and fifty per cent in World War II.'[40] While the 2005 *Human Security Report* believes this popularly quoted statistic to be a myth generated by repetition rather than quantitative evidence, it is reasonable to conclude that these internal conflicts are fought in different ways, reduce the distinction between combatants and non-combatants, often burn with greater intensity and are more difficult to end than traditional wars of the Clausewitzian type.

How Do Modern Wars End?

Ending modern warfare is inextricably linked to the ways in which such violence was conducted. The rise of ethno-nationalism, increasing involvement of civilians and internal displacement have made ending war a prolonged and difficult process. In these circumstances war is not an activity that will be terminated by the clipped pronouncements of the military leader or by the flourish of a politician's pen. Most modern wars are hydra-headed creatures with multiple causes, triggers, actors and victims.

Nevertheless, while every violent conflict has its own unique history and political dynamics, there are some generic patterns surrounding the circumstances in which these armed conflicts draw to a close. The relatively good news from those who study quantitative trends is that wars *do* actually come to an end. Data from the Uppsala project suggest that out of a total of 119 armed conflicts that took place between 1989 and 2004, ninety of them had ended by early 2005.[41] Such statistics mask a complex picture within which violent conflicts are ended. For a start, as mentioned above, defining the end of violent armed conflict is an inexact science. The Uppsala project focuses on the termination of warfare (defined, as noted, as a period of twelve months without violence), but in reality this may often be subject to a degree of yo-yoing in and out of violent conflict, and war *termination* is not necessarily the same as war *ending* in any permanent sense. As the authors of *Contemporary Conflict Resolution* have suggested, 'A war ending is not a precise moment in time, but a process. A violent conflict is over when a new political dispensation prevails, or the parties become reconciled, or a new conflict eclipses the first.'[42] For violent conflict to end, therefore, the underlying dynamics which led to its outbreak have to be addressed to the point where the direct and indirect actors are content to desist and accept a new dispensation. In the majority of cases this cannot be achieved through coercion, but must be worked for through processes of dialogue, negotiation and compromise by the parties in conflict. The circumstances for ending war are therefore multifaceted but almost always contain a combination of the following conditions:

- outright military victory or defeat to a point where the original grievances behind violence are unable to re-emerge;
- a mutually hurting stalemate (MHS) and belief among the direct actors in warfare that a military victory is unlikely and that the violent status quo is undesirable (or unacceptable) in the medium or long term;
- a 'ripe moment' for dialogue to commence and an emerging belief that a way out of violence is possible;
- a change in the external context of the conflict (e.g. levels of international support/aid) which re-orientates internal perceptions of interests and goals;
- adequate leadership from the direct actors in conflict which is capable of maintaining cease-fires, minimizing

'spoiler' activities and delivering on the promises made in negotiations;
- an inclusive process of dialogue and negotiation that deals with the underlying causes of violent conflict;
- the emergence of third parties capable of facilitating/ managing dialogue between the direct conflict actors;
- a political settlement which is acceptable to a reasonable majority of the population (and to majorities within the different identity groups); and
- processes that facilitate reconstruction and reconciliation after physical violence has ended which help to cement the peace agreement and mediate subsequent disagreements between the conflict parties.

Ending war is not, of course, a scientific exercise, and these conditions may vary in importance and intensity depending on the particular conflict concerned. Nevertheless, despite the complexities and differences from case to case, the bottom line for ending violent conflict is that those engaged in it have to want to stop. This desire will be motivated for the most part by some form of risk/benefit calculation which may (or may not) lead to a process where dialogue begins.

Obviously wars can end through outright victory or defeat, with the classic examples being World Wars I and II. However, while military victories are possible, these are rarely so over-whelming that violence does not re-emerge subsequently, or, as in the case of World War I (or the 2003 war in Iraq), that the conditions under which violence was brought to an end do not spawn further conflict at a later date. Dan Smith of International Alert has commented on the important differ-ence between the 'suspension' and the 'ending' of violence in modern warfare.

> This difference between 'ended' and 'suspended' is crucial to understanding the problem of armed conflict today. The

international political landscape is disfigured by wars that resume after not only the signing of cease-fires, but even after the conclusion of peace agreements. In the past decade alone, among the wars that have resumed after the conclusion of cease-fires or apparent peace agreements, it is possible to count those in Angola, Burundi, Cambodia, Chechnya, Croatia, Democratic Republic of Congo, Eritrea and Ethiopia, Kosovo, Liberia, the Philippines, Rwanda, Sierra Leone and Sri Lanka. Often the wars return with even greater ferocity and destructiveness, and almost always at particularly high cost for the civilian population.[43]

In modern warfare, outright victories are much less common than other outcomes, such as partial victories, wars that fizzle out then re-emerge periodically, or violence which ends following prolonged processes of dialogue, negotiation and the faltering implementation of peace agreements. Peter Wallensteen has observed that victory only accounted for around one third of the armed conflicts that took place between 1989 and 2004.[44]

Making Wars Ripe for Ending

The most critical factors among all of those listed above are the development of what William Zartman has referred to as a 'mutually hurting stalemate' (MHS), together with its stablemate, the emergence of a 'ripe moment' for violence to de-escalate and for dialogue to commence.[45] The vast majority of political conflict is conducted by rational actors who use violence as a means of securing political goals. Normally such warfare will only end when the belligerents are motivated to consider alternatives to violence. This is unlikely to happen if they believe that the war (and the political goals that lie behind it) can be won by military means. If the direct actors come to the conclusion that they have reached a stalemate and are

unable to foresee victory, and if this is combined with a perception that the status quo is hurting them or the constituencies
that they rely upon for support, then they will be more likely to
search for non-violent alternatives and the moment will be ripe
for dialogue to begin. As Zartman puts it:

> Parties resolve their conflict only when they are ready to do
> so – when alternative, usually unilateral means of achieving a
> satisfactory result are blocked and the parties feel that they
> are in an uncomfortable and costly predicament. At that ripe
> moment, they grab onto proposals that usually have been in
> the air for a long time and that only now appear attractive.[46]

Zartman highlights the case of Cyprus to indicate the lack of
a MHS and the absence of a ripe moment for dialogue to
begin.

> The basic obstacle in Cyprus was that . . . the parties never
> found themselves in a hurting stalemate at the same time, if
> they felt stalemated at all; the present situation simply did not
> hurt much, and any hurt was covered by a thick layer of right-
> eousness and wrongedness. Thereafter, neither side could
> offer incentives to the other, nor in any event could such
> incentives have been believed or reciprocated.[47]

To accept the importance of timing in an intervention to end
warfare does not mean that this is everything, or that the substantive structural issues or underlying grievances within a
violent conflict are unimportant. It is better understood as
being a catalyst which can help the conflict parties to recalibrate understandings of the need for violence and the possibilities for a negotiated settlement. From this perspective, the
dynamic for ending war is driven by a political will among the
direct actors and a transformation in the perception of their
key values, goals and interests.

Some scholars have critiqued Zartman's emphasis on hurting stalemates and ripe moments as being overly simplistic

and tautological, making it impossible to tell (until after the event) whether the conditions are conducive for ending violence or not.[48] Others, such as Ramsbotham, Woodhouse and Miall, have suggested that the complex organic evolution of violent conflicts makes it necessary to distinguish 'between ripeness for negotiations to start and ripeness for negotiations to succeed. . . . A model that sees conflicts moving from "unripeness" through a ripe moment to resolution is perhaps too course-grained to take account of the many changes that come together over time and result in a settlement.'[49] This is, of course, true, though in Zartman's defence he recognizes that the emergence of a ripe moment for the ending of violence does not mean that it will be acted upon by the parties to the conflict. 'It is not self-fulfilling or self-implementing. It must be seized, either directly by the parties or, if not, through the persuasion of a mediator.'[50] While Zartman might be criticized for placing too much emphasis on the roles of elites among the direct actors or third-party mediators, his basic premise for explaining how wars end is correct. They do so when those engaged in them come to the view that winning them is unlikely and that a way out of violence is required.

This is not, of course, a linear journey, and is likely to be subject to reversals as well as advances. The chapters that follow examine the opportunities that were missed as well as those that were seized in the efforts to bring war to an end. The political will of direct actors to seek a way out of violence may evolve at variable speeds and emerge at different times; the desire to seek a political accommodation to end an armed conflict may not be matched by the belief that a route out of violence exists or that others share the same commitment; and even when the direct actors reach a point of wanting a way out of the violence, the political process may not lead to viable negotiations or an agreed settlement.

However, war is, for the most part, a rational choice activity and a social construction of the human condition. It is, therefore, within the field of human competence to end such violence, and the next chapter examines some of the opportunities and barriers that exist in the efforts to do so.

CHAPTER TWO

Third-Party Intervention

On the flight deck of the enormous US aircraft carrier the USS *Eisenhower* in the Gulf this week, warplanes were being shot out of the steam catapults on the flight deck with engines that roared and screamed so loudly you felt it in your sinuses, teeth and jawbone.

'Listen to it,' one of the officers told me when the warplanes were launched and streaking up the Gulf to Iraq.

'It is the sound of freedom.'

Jeremy Bowen, March 2007[1]

The premise that runs through this book is that in the absence of outright victory, wars end when belligerents come to the view that their goals and interests cannot be secured through the use of violence and that political dialogue is required. In other words, they end when a mutually hurting stalemate results in a violent gridlock and a ripe moment for non-violent alternatives is produced. One factor that has made a contribution in this regard has been the role of third-party intervention by both internal and external actors. This chapter looks at the nature of such interventions and at the impacts made by these third parties in helping to reduce or transform violent political conflict. The chapter examines the boundaries of third-party intervention, focusing in particular on the differences between civil society roles (fact-finding, facilitation and mediation) and transnational third-party intervention which includes peace-keeping and peace-enforcement activities. The chapter reflects upon what the variable impacts of third-party intervention tells us about the structure of the international political system and its capacity to deliver on strategies linked to bringing armed conflicts to an end. There is a recognition here, of course, that third parties have often made wars worse, fanning the flames of violence by providing weapons and other resources to the direct actors due to vested political, economic or other strategic interests in keeping these wars going. William Zartman has noted that third parties have provided resources and sanctuary to conflict actors and have been used to provide leverage in war itself, as well as at the negotiating table.[2]

While this chapter will point to occasions where third parties have had a destructive impact, the central focus will be on the efforts made to bring armed conflicts to an end. Third-party agencies have both constructive and destructive elements to them and the question to address is not so much *can* they help in the difficult task of ending war, but, rather, *when* and *how* can they do so?

What is Third-Party Intervention?

Like many other concepts in international relations, the precise meaning of a third party is potentially vast. In their handbook for political negotiators, the NGO International IDEA have provided a useful working definition of third-party intervention that is sufficiently broad to be used here.

> A third party – a person, group, institution or country that is not identified directly or indirectly with any of the parties or interests to the conflict – can be very effective in chairing or facilitating the talks process. And a long-standing conflict, especially where there is considerable stalemate or just staleness of view, can benefit from the fresh perspective of newcomers. The first two important questions are: Do we need a third party? And, if so, who?[3]

A further question could be added to this list, namely *what* should the third party do when they intervene? The story of external third-party intervention at the transnational level is bound up with the changes that took place at the end of the Cold War period during the early 1990s. This form of third-party activity is more contentious than civil society interventions, as it includes large-scale peace-keeping and, more problematically, peace-enforcement operations. At its outer edge, therefore, third-party intervention encompasses the involvement of a state (or group of states) prepared to use violence for political ends. This is usually called force rather than violence, but the result for those unfortunate enough to be on the receiving end is the same and often includes death and injury on a large scale. Peace-enforcement operations became the cutting edge of international diplomacy at the end of the Cold War to counter the rise of ethnic conflicts during the early 1990s and the failure of peace-keeping operations to find any peace to keep in places such as Somalia, Rwanda and Bosnia.

One of the central factors in the development of this form of third-party intervention was the loosening of the international political system out of the ideological concrete that characterized geo-political logic during the Cold War period. Considerations about intervention to end wars were usually preceded by wider questions concerning the nature of the political regime and whether such intervention would strengthen the strategic interests of communist or capitalist states. This zero-sum mentality was most clearly apparent within the pronouncements of the United Nations Security Council, and in particular in the behaviour of its five permanent member states. During the Cold War, the Security Council was often ineffectual as a third-party actor due to frequent use of the veto by one or more of the permanent five. This was particularly apparent over any Chapter VII interventions that would have sanctioned coercive measures, including the threat and use of military force to compel the direct actors in conflict to change their behaviour.

Even non-coercive third-party intervention was hampered by Cold War realities and paralysis within the international political system. The statistics on the role of the Security Council in peace-keeping operations before and after the Cold War period are worth noting. Between 1948, when the UN launched its first peace-keeping mission to Israel (the United Nations Truce Supervision Organization – UNTSO), and 1978, the UN deployed thirteen peace-keeping missions. Since the end of the Cold War in 1989, however, the UN has launched forty-seven peace-keeping operations.

It is clear, then, that the UN Security Council has played a much greater role in third-party intervention since the Cold War than it did beforehand. In response to the changing nature of armed conflict outlined in the previous chapter of this book, combined with the opportunity for action afforded by the end of the Cold War, transnational agencies such as the UN began to widen their horizons and reinterpret their purpose. From this point forwards, their function as defined in the UN Charter after the end of World War II, to protect 'international peace and security', no longer meant simply monitoring and managing border incursions and other hostile acts between nation-states. The emergence of intra-state conflicts in Europe and Africa during the early 1990s required the UN to intervene as a third party when nation-states were either unwilling or unable to contain ethnic tensions, or when they were abusing the human rights of their own citizens in a way that caused a threat to neighbouring countries or to international security more broadly. Whether such interventions helped to bring armed conflict to an end in these regions is another question and one that will be returned to later in this chapter. For the moment, more needs to be said about the wide spectrum of third-party intervention, and, in particular, the differences inherent between transnational third-party interventions with a military focus and the smaller scale third-party interventions of civil society actors that emphasize non-coercive functions.

Different Forms of Third-Party Intervention

Third-party intervention aimed at ending armed conflict involves a potentially vast array of agencies and actors at micro and macro levels, from the smallest non-governmental organization to the top table of international governance such as the United Nations, NATO and the EU. These interventions may involve the use of consensus-building, carrot-and-stick diplomacy or even the direct use of violence by third-party actors in their efforts to enforce military cease-fires or settlements on the warring factions. While it is impossible here to cover every aspect of such a widespread phenomenon, this chapter looks at some of the different techniques that third-party agencies have adopted from the micro to the macro levels and assesses the successes and failures of each.

There are many examples where international and local third parties have played a vital role in the infrastructure within which the direct actors in conflict operate. This often includes acting as a go-between or conducting shuttle diplomacy for those unwilling to engage in direct dialogue with one another and generally acting as a conduit for information to flow between groups before sufficient trust has been established for peace talks to begin. Third parties may also act as fact-finders or mediators between warring factions, helping to establish a degree of trust on all sides that the peace process might have the potential to result in an agreed settlement that could end the need for violence. An example of this was provided by former UN Secretary-General Kofi Annan's intervention in Kenya in January 2008 when he attempted to broker talks between the government and main opposition party to end violence that had resulted in around 1,000 deaths and 250,000 internally displaced people following the disputed election of 27 December 2007.

These various interventions by internal and external third parties can be a critical factor in ending violence when the direct actors in conflict have reached a point of MHS, where they no longer believe that they can win the war or secure their objectives through violent means. At the same time they may be unable to see a political route out of conflict, or determine whether their enemies also want to look for alternatives to violence. In such circumstances, third parties can play a vital role in helping to negotiate cease-fires and political dialogue.

Micro Interventions

Third-party intervention in violent political conflict at the micro level has mainly focused upon efforts to engineer cease-fire agreements, support political negotiations and prevent the re-emergence of conflict during the fragile peace that often accompanies political settlements. While international non-governmental organizations (INGOs) such as International Alert and the Search for Common Ground have often played constructive roles in these efforts, the focus here will be on the roles of individuals and internal civil society organizations in the two separate cases of Northern Ireland and South Africa. These conflicts both had unique and complex histories and direct comparisons risk reductionist analyses. Nevertheless, in both of these cases third-party interventions from civil society actors played a significant role in the political processes that led to negotiations and subsequent agreements. While it would be an exaggeration to claim that these third parties *caused* the end of violent conflict in the two cases, it is reasonable to suggest that they *facilitated* and *enabled* the direct actors who wanted to find a political alternative to violence to do so. Within this context, third parties can be viewed as being an indispensable element in the difficult process of ending armed conflict.

In Northern Ireland, third-party interventions did not change the minds of those active within paramilitary organizations or those caricatured by Irish republicans as the 'securocrats' within the British state. However, what these individuals and groups did very effectively was to facilitate dialogue, illustrate the public desire for political alternatives to violence, deliver vital services to those caught up in conflict and support the political elites in their efforts to negotiate their way towards paramilitary cease-fires and, ultimately, a political settlement. While these multilateral third-party interventions did not *cause* the conflict in Northern Ireland to end, the claim that the peace process would not have taken place without civil society intervention is a reasonable one to make. This case fits neatly into William Zartman's belief that there is often a 'ripe moment' for third-party intervention to occur. From this perspective, such interventions will only be productive when the internal parties are ready for it and when the direct actors have reached a point where they are ready to sit down and discuss political alternatives to violence. This does not mean that third parties are necessarily condemned to thumb-twiddling while they wait for the ripe moment to arrive. A lot can (and has) been done by third parties to make these conflict-ridden places more responsive to interventions aimed at bringing the violence to an end.

Northern Ireland is a small, though politically complex, region with a sophisticated, politically literate, relatively well-funded and vibrant civil society. Many of its constituent elements – NGO activists, educators, Church organizations, the media, business leaders and trade unions – played their part in advocating their opposition to sectarian violence and the need for a political settlement to be reached through dialogue and negotiation.

The republican and loyalist paramilitary cease-fires declared in 1994 were mediated by third-party intermediaries from the Catholic and Protestant Churches, and the foundations of the entire peace process in Northern Ireland were assisted by the 'good offices' of Father Alec Reid, a Catholic priest based in the Clonard Monastery in Belfast, who acted as a link between the leaders of the moderate nationalist Social Democratic and Labour Party (SDLP) and Sinn Fein. Father Reid is regarded by many informed observers as having played a crucial role in the Northern Ireland peace process. His account of how he became involved in the genesis of this process is a textbook example of how third parties can act as a catalyst and assist ripe moments in becoming self-fulfilling prophecies. 'The SDLP and the Dublin government wouldn't talk to Sinn Fein unless the IRA stopped [violence], so you were in a Catch-22 situation. And the Sinn Fein people could do nothing about creating or developing an alternative unless they could talk to the Irish government and the SDLP.'[4] Reid's intervention came in a letter to John Hume (leader of the SDLP) in 1985, suggesting dialogue between the SDLP and Sinn Fein to break this impasse. A series of secret meetings subsequently took place over eight months between the two parties at Clonard Monastery, which began the slow process of re-evaluation within the republican movement in Northern Ireland about their objectives, and the violent strategy they were using to obtain them. Two of the region's leading journalists have remarked that this intervention 'was a dialogue which was to prove to be one of the most important wellsprings of the peace process. . . . Over the next few years the fighting would continue, but so would the talking.'[5] A line can certainly be drawn between this intervention and the eventual IRA cease-fire in 1994, which in turn opened the way for formal political dialogue and eventual political agreement in 1998.

In addition to the interventions of courageous individuals such as Father Reid, other elements within civil society played third-party roles that helped to facilitate dialogue and movement during the peace process in Northern Ireland. While the business sector was initially wary of expressing views on the political situation, it became more vocal during the early 1990s in response to progress in the wider 'peace process' and after the paramilitary cease-fires were declared. Although most business organizations shied away from aligning themselves with particular political viewpoints, many business groups were eager to point out the economic opportunities that political stability offered to Northern Ireland, and issued warnings about the negative impact on jobs and inward investment that violence and political instability would cause. In 1994, the Northern Ireland Confederation of British Industry (CBI) published a document entitled *Peace – A Challenging New Era*, which became coined by the media as the 'peace dividend' paper. This was an influential document that spelled out in detail an economic rationale for peace based upon stability, investment and economic prosperity due to the reduction of security costs, and the increase in tourism and external investment.[6] The publication of this paper by the CBI provides a good example of the virtuous circle that civil society can help to generate, as the phrase 'peace dividend' was taken up both by the media and by politicians, and has been used extensively ever since as a reference point for civil society interventions in the peace process. By the mid-1990s, the CBI in Northern Ireland had already established firm links with the Irish Business and Employers Confederation in the Irish Republic as a means of promoting economic co-operation between the two parts of the island. These organic connections proved useful as the peace process began to gather momentum during the 1990s. The CBI's logic expressed in the 'peace dividend' paper – that economic resources being soaked up by security spending could be more usefully deployed on tourism and to generate external investment – gained increasing credibility as the peace process developed. Following the 1994 cease-fires, tourism in the region rose by 20 per cent, while unemployment dropped to 11.5 per cent (a fourteen-year low), and $48 million of new investment was announced.[7] As one fascinating account of the role of the private sector in peacebuilding puts it: 'Thanks to the CBI the idea of a peace dividend became integral to the vocabulary of peace in Northern Ireland. . . . By approaching peace from a business angle, the CBI changed the terms of the debate and helped infuse new momentum into the peace process.'[8] In the Northern Ireland case, the business sector went a step beyond providing an economic assessment of the impact of violence on the local economy. They became directly involved in the politics of the peace process and joined up with other elements within civil society, such as the media, the trade union movement and the main Churches, to sell a political message. They supported the formal negotiations, provided their 'good offices' for meetings between the political parties, urged the direct actors to maintain their cease-fires and dialogue with one another, and advocated a 'Yes' vote in the referendum on the Good Friday Agreement reached on 10 April 1998. The conflict studies theorist John Paul Lederach has written about the need to 'build a peace constituency' within societies that are attempting to come out of violent political conflicts, and in Northern Ireland the multilateral third-party interventions of civil society actors made a major contribution to this difficult process of turning vicious circles into virtuous ones.[9]

Third-party interventions by civil society actors in Northern Ireland had an indirect rather than immediate role in the peace process, but were nevertheless critical to ending the political violence and devising a political settlement for the region.[10] As a member of one of Northern Ireland's largest

NGOs has observed: '[I]t is clichéd, but nonetheless true, to say that over the past 35 years, the voluntary and community sector has provided much of the glue that held Northern Ireland society together.'[11] It contributed to the 'mood music' prior to the 1997–8 negotiations which helped to create a climate for constructive discussions to take place, it acted as a resource for individuals who had been directly affected by the conflict, and it helped to support the political parties in the risky business of searching for a settlement. Civil society could only make this contribution because of wider changes in the context of the peace process, linked to evolution within the strategies of the paramilitary groups and third-party intervention from external mediators, notably the Clinton administration and Senator George Mitchell. As Chair and (formally speaking) the chief mediator in the negotiations that led to the Good Friday Agreement in 1998, Mitchell used what Joseph Nye has referred to as 'soft power'[12] to build consensus and trust between the negotiators, which widened the space available for a political settlement to occur. Unlike the intervention of his American counterpart, Richard Holbrooke, in the Bosnian war and Dayton agreement of 1995, George Mitchell focused his interventions on building internal consensus and mutual respect (if not trust) between the negotiators in Northern Ireland. Thus, it was within the framework of other contextual changes in the peace process that civil society managed to make a positive impact. While much of this contribution was indirect and intangible, it was nevertheless a vital ingredient of the peace process and played an important part in ending political violence in the region.

In the case of South Africa, third-party intervention by civil society actors also played a major role in ending the conflict and helping to ensure a stable transition to democratic government in 1994. While South Africa might not fit within the quantitative researcher's definitional nodes of 'war', it was one in all but name between the minority white government, which was increasingly desperate to cling to power, and an increasingly frustrated and emboldened non-white population hungry for change. Rupert Taylor has outlined the way in which the conflict had come to a head during the 1980s and the levels of political repression which existed. 'By the end of 1985, the South African Defence Force (SADF) had deployed over 32,000 troops in ninety-six of the country's townships. . . . Between 1985 and 1988, over five thousand people were killed in political violence in South Africa and approximately fifty thousand people were detained. By the end of 1988, thirty-two non-violent anti-apartheid organizations had been banned.'[13]

Civil society in South Africa was well ahead of the National Party government in the peace process in the early 1990s. The business community, for example, became convinced ahead of the government that apartheid was not working, that it was wrecking the economy and that it would have to be reformed. As a result, it held talks with the African National Congress (ANC) long before the government did. Church leaders meanwhile became increasingly agitated at the rising level of violence and increasingly vocal in their condemnations of state brutality. In addition to this, the work carried out by individual peace groups in South Africa created a focus for opposition to the government and for international support, and this also forced the National Party to come to the negotiating table with the ANC and accept reforms.

These third parties all became involved in the peace process in South Africa at different times and at varying levels. The business community established contacts within the leadership of both the ANC and the National Party in the late 1980s, stressing the need for some form of negotiated settlement. In 1988, following a meeting of business leaders in Broederstroom, the Consultative Business Movement (CBM) was formed, which began to establish links with the ANC and the Inkatha Freedom

Party. The CBM linked up with the South African Council of Churches at the beginning of the 1990s and helped break the impasse between the National Party government and the ANC over the need to open direct negotiations aimed at securing a peace settlement. The importance of the CBM in the South African peace process is indicated by the fact that they were asked to provide the secretariat and administrative support for the Convention for a Democratic South Africa (CODESA) meetings in the early 1990s that led eventually to the constitutional settlement and democratic elections in 1994.[14] After the unbanning of the ANC and release of Nelson Mandela at the beginning of the 1990s, trade union groups and the main Churches also began to act as shuttle diplomats between the two sides. During the formal negotiations between the ANC and the National Party, business groups intervened when deadlocks and difficulties emerged, their most important role being to help convince the Inkatha Freedom Party to participate in the election on the eve of the poll in 1994. This helped to unite the country in the election and avoided having a significant group outside the peace process as a classic 'spoiler' trying to destabilize it.

This high level of involvement by civil society in the South African peace process was accompanied by informal low-level activities carried out by the numerous community-based peace groups and individuals working at a local level. These NGOs provided a focus within South Africa for the anti-apartheid movement. They also grew into a highly professional, well-resourced and skilled sector, highlighting abuses and advocating change based on non-racial democratic politics. As Colin Knox and Padraic Quirk have commented: 'Between 1990 and 1994, the NGO "peace" network facilitated, mediated, monitored, trained and reported on the unfolding events of the transition to democracy.'[15] Perhaps the best way of summarizing the role of civil society in South Africa was that the various groups within the community, at various levels, both formal and informal, intervened at appropriate moments to 'oil the wheels' of the transition to democracy. While they did not *cause* an end to this era of violent conflict, they were a fundamental part of it. Returning to Zartman's metaphor, they helped to bring the conflict to the point of 'ripeness' and facilitated movement between the conflict parties once that had been achieved. The former leader of the parliamentary opposition in South Africa, Fredrick van Zyl Slabbart, played an important third-party role by convening a secret meeting in Senegal in 1987 between fifty influential Afrikaners and seventeen leading officials of the ANC. This was at a time when the organization was still banned and its leaders where either in exile or in jail in South Africa. Slabbart's metaphor for explaining the role of civil society in bringing the conflict to an end seems appropriate: 'Chaos theory says that the flutter of a butterfly's wings eventually ends up in a hurricane. Does it cause a hurricane? No, but it was part of it.'[16]

In El Salvador, meanwhile, micro interventions from the business community helped to bring an end to a civil war that had lasted for twelve years between the government and the FMLN in which 75,000 people died with two million displaced. The emergence of a modernizing business elite and formation of the Salvadoran Foundation for Development (FUSADES) was crucial to the peace negotiations between the government and the FMLN and to the implementation of the eventual Chapultepec Peace Accords. In essence, FUSADES became convinced that the civil war was damaging the economy and that a settlement would produce a 'peace dividend' capable of dealing with many of the grievances underpinning the conflict. When the pro-business party the Nationalist Republican Alliance (ARENA) won the Presidency in 1985, its leader, Alfredo Cristiani, opened talks with the FMLN immediately over the terms of a peace settlement. These talks were facilitated by FUSADES and the Catholic Church and provide a further illustration of the potential for civil society to contribute positively to emerging peace processes.[17]

While such micro interventions are less visible than formal peace negotiations conducted by political elites, they are nonetheless important in the general infra-structure of bringing wars to an end. It is these types of interventions that make peace visible to people in an everyday sense, in a way treaties and formal agreements cannot.[18]

Macro Interventions

Third-party interventions aimed at reducing or ending armed conflict are not restricted to micro-level engagements, and significant roles can be seen at the international level, with attempts being made by the UN, NATO and the EU to prevent, contain or end warfare, using a range of political, economic and military strategies. As the authors of *Contemporary Conflict Resolution* have pointed out, third-party interventions, while far from being a panacea, 'are often important catalysts for peacemaking'.[19]

Underlying the story of transnational third-party intervention is the post-Cold War evolution of the United Nations – more specifically, the shift in its focus from the relations between states to (or as well as) relations within states. Peter Wallensteen asserts boldly that 'the UN is the primary international body for peace and security.'[20] But here's the rub: some believe that the UN has lost its credibility due to failures such as Rwanda and Sudan, due to the selectivity of its interventions, which often seem based on the political/economic interests of its most powerful members, and due to its emasculation in the recent US intervention in Iraq, where the UN Security Council was largely ignored.[21] A flagship report from the independent International Commission on Intervention and State Sovereignty entitled *The Responsibility to Protect* (R2P) comments on the credibility problem for external third parties such as the UN following its most well-known failure of modern times.

> Rwanda in 1994 laid bare the full horror of inaction. The United Nations (UN) Secretariat and some permanent members of the Security Council knew that officials connected to the then government were planning genocide; UN forces were present, but not in sufficient number at the outset; and credible strategies were available to prevent, or at least greatly mitigate, the slaughter which followed. But the Security Council refused to take the necessary action. That was a failure of international will – of civic courage – at the highest level. . . . In the aftermath, many African peoples concluded that, for all the rhetoric about the universality of human rights, some human lives end up mattering a great deal less to the international community than others.[22]

However, the authors of this report together with other commentators counsel us not to throw the UN baby out with the third-party bathwater, and claim that in terms of moving into an era where something can be done about large-scale human suffering due to wars within states, it is all we have got. The authors of *Contemporary Conflict Resolution* are sympathetic to this position: 'It is true that the UN has also faced some dreadful failures in the post-Cold War world, including Bosnia, Rwanda and Somalia. Nevertheless, as the instrument through which the international community arranges ceasefires, organizes peacekeeping, facilitates elections and monitors disengagement and demilitarization, the UN has an acknowledged corpus of knowledge and experience to bring to bear.'[23]

The changing nature of war during this period, together with the increased impact on civilian populations, led to a recalibration of notions of international peace and security. As

Thomas Weiss has remarked in his book *Humanitarian Intervention*, 'A remarkable development of the post-Cold War era has been the routine use of military force to protect human beings trapped in the throes of war.'[24] The problem here is that sometimes the cure has been worse than the disease, and third-party interventions that have used coercive force have, on occasions, resulted in greater numbers of people dying faster and more horribly than might have otherwise been the case. Nevertheless, there have been occasions when coercive third-party intervention has brought armed conflict to an end and at least provided a cold peace within the region. An obvious example was provided by the intervention of the UN and NATO in the war in former Yugoslavia in the early 1990s. The Dayton agreement and the military deployment of UN and NATO military forces eventually brought the armed conflict to an end, though this intervention did little to deal with the underlying causes of conflict in the region and was unable to prevent the re-emergence of war in Kosovo in 1999. This case suggests that coercive third-party intervention can bring wars to an end so long as there is sufficient coherence and political will within the third parties involved, which was certainly not the case within the early stages of the Bosnian intervention. As Karin Fierke has pointed out, before the US used aerial bombing in 1995, neither it nor NATO was taken seriously by the direct actors involved. 'But this was preceded by years of failure to follow through on successive threats, which severely damaged the credibility of both the UN and NATO as institutions.'[25] This was compounded by instances where the UN presence was patently impotent due to the remit and terms of engagement of its peace-keeping troops. The case of Srebrenica in July 1995, where 7,000 civilians were massacred by Bosnian Serbs despite the presence of UN peace-keepers, was a tragedy for those involved and a very public humiliation for the UN.

During the Cold War, however, the spotlight remained trained on protecting the sovereignty of states and the integrity of their borders. During the 1990s the UN and other transnational agencies, such as NATO, turned the spotlight onto the violent behaviour of people *within* states as a way of reinterpreting their remit, especially in terms of their Chapter VI and Chapter VII responsibilities. This has led to a sustained debate about the legitimacy of international intervention and the balance between the rights of states to their sovereignty and the rights of individuals who live within them. The former UN Secretary-General, Kofi Annan, used his position to encourage the Security Council (and the member states) to move beyond traditional patterns of action which treated state sovereignty as sacrosanct. In an agenda-setting article in the *Economist* in September 1999, Annan talked of 'two concepts of sovereignty', the inference being that if states wantonly abused their own citizens or were unable to control widespread conflict within and across their borders, then the international community had the right and the responsibility to intervene to restore order.[26] This doctrine was already well established through what has become known as 'humanitarian intervention', a phrase which denotes external third-party intervention within the borders of a state without its prior invitation, for humanitarian purposes. This short phrase encapsulates the shift in emphasis from the sovereignty of states, to the experiences of human beings *within* them. When the degree of human suffering within states is considered so heinous, or so destabilizing to neighbouring countries, transnational agencies such as the UN and NATO have intervened to either keep a peace, or enforce one by military means. In Gareth Evans' foreword to Thomas Weiss's book *Humanitarian Intervention*, he outlines the operational product of this change, which has become known as the 'Responsibility to Protect' (or R2P).

> The core idea of Responsibility to Protect . . . is that the perspective that matters is that of suffering human beings: states have the primary responsibility for protecting their own citizens from human-made catastrophe, but when a state abdicates that responsibility – through either incapacity or ill-will – it shifts to the wider international community, to regional and global organisations . . . and to the governments and citizens of other countries.[27]

Some commentators have seen this as a worrying development, opening a Pandora's Box of third-party intervention activities that confuse the purpose of the international community to keep the peace *between* states rather than attempting to keep the peace *within* them. Others see these types of interventions as the emergence of the UN as it was meant to be when the UN Charter was conceived after the end of World War II. Despite failures such as Rwanda, Somalia and the early intervention during the Bosnian war, at least the international community was making an attempt, however tentative, to deal with large-scale human suffering within states, rather than sitting on its hands, as the permanent members of the UN Security Council largely did during the Cold War. This agenda of transnational third-party intervention to protect massive losses of human life within states was highlighted by former UN Secretary-General Kofi Annan in 2004 on the tenth anniversary of the conflict in Rwanda when he announced a new 'Action Plan to Prevent Genocide'. His summary of the failure of third-party intervention efforts in Rwanda was stark.

> We must never forget our collective failure to protect at least 800,000 defenceless men, women and children who perished in Rwanda 10 years ago. Such crimes cannot be reversed. Such failures cannot be repaired. The dead cannot be brought back to life. So what can we do? First, we must all acknowledge our responsibility for not having done more to prevent or stop the genocide. Neither the United Nations Secretariat, nor the Security Council, nor Member States in

general, nor the international media, paid enough attention to the gathering signs of disaster. Still less did we take timely action.[28]

By 2008 these high ideals look rather jaded in the context of the failure of international third parties to intervene in the Sudan over the conflict in Darfur, which has resulted in over 200,000 deaths during the last four years. A report from the United Nations Human Rights Commission on Darfur, published on 12 March 2007, claimed that the Sudanese government was 'orchestrating' and 'participating' in war crimes (including mass rape and kidnapping) while international organizations looked on. The leader of the commission, Jody Williams, claimed that the reaction of the UN and other international third parties illustrated the emptiness of the 'Responsibility to Protect' doctrine and the 'pathetic' failure of the international community to intervene in the conflict effectively. 'There are so many hollow threats towards Khartoum, that if I were Khartoum I wouldn't pay any attention either. It is more than a tragedy. It was after Rwanda that people said "never again", and here we are again . . . and the world sits by.'[29] Thomas Weiss's condemnation of the failure of international third parties does not pull its punches:

> [I]t is appalling that after three and a half years, the Security Council was still dickering over the consent of a government that is responsible for the deaths of hundreds of thousands of people and the flight of millions from their homes. . . . The repeated failure to come to the rescue mocks the value of the emerging R2P norm, and ultimately may further erode public support for the United Nations.[30]

Of course, there is much more to international third-party intervention than coercive engagement, and the carrot has been used as well as the stick. There have been a number of armed conflicts and emerging crises where third parties such as the UN and the EU have helped end the violence or prevented it from re-igniting. Non-coercive international third-party intervention can cover a range of activities, such as the provision of shuttle diplomacy, fact-finding missions, good offices and even mediation and arbitration, where a peace process reaches a relatively advanced stage of development. These functions are laid out in the UN Charter under Chapter VI regulations, which focus on the peaceful settlement of disputes. These interventions can help bring warring factions into contact with one another, provide the mechanisms for the first faltering dialogue to begin, help maintain these contacts in the face of the inevitable distrust that will exist between the conflict parties, and facilitate the peace process as it evolves. In the real world of international politics, of course, this line between *enabling* the internal conflict parties and *coercing* them can be a fine one, and sometimes where a powerful international third party such as the US plays a leading role, its function in practice often goes beyond its theoretical remit. The point at which encouraging a conflict party to accept political or economic reforms in return for aid, investment or entry to the European Union moves from being helpful and enabling to becoming coercive blackmail may be in the eye of the beholder. It is undeniable that the most powerful political and economic transnational agencies, the UN, EU, NATO, IMF and the World Bank, have increasingly tied the provision of external resources to the development of democratization and stable market economies in war-torn societies. Roland Paris is one of several analysts who have pointed out the power imbalance at the heart of many international interventions, where the powerful external third party seeks to impose its will upon local actors.

> Most international organisations engaged in peacebuilding have internalised the broadly liberal political and economic values of the wealthy and powerful industrialised democracies (which comprise the core of the current international

system), while nearly all of the countries that have hosted peacebuilding missions are located in the poor and politically weak periphery. Without exception, peacebuilding missions in the post-Cold War period have attempted to 'transplant' the values and institutions of the liberal democratic core into the domestic affairs of peripheral host states.[31]

While it is overly simplistic to view this as a purely binary relationship, where powerful third parties can impose their will on quiescent internal actors (not least because it is often local populations who call for external intervention), it is certainly the case that some of the conditional carrots used by international third parties during their interventions can have distinctive stick-like qualities to them.

One of the most longstanding UN third-party engagements has been in Cyprus, where it has been involved politically and militarily since 1964. The case of Cyprus illustrates the difficulties inherent in evaluating the success of international third-party intervention. On the one hand it stabilized the region, prevented a wider conflagration between Greece and Turkey and established a cold peace within the region, where violence has been minimized. Seen from another view, this third-party intervention has paralysed the two main groups on the island, underwritten a physical, political, social, economic and cultural apartheid in Cyprus and entrenched divisions within the region that are now more difficult to resolve. Viewed from this perspective, high fences definitely do not make good neighbours and belated political efforts to deal with ethnic divisions such as the Annan Plan of 2002 have been unable to break through the concrete which was set several decades earlier. Norrie McQueen suggests that the Cyprus case provides us with an instructive lesson of the dangers of third-party interventions which focus on restoring order and preventing armed conflict, but do not at the same time develop processes for dealing with the underlying causal factors of conflict and promote practical peace-building initiatives. 'If peacemaking is not – or cannot be – pursued in parallel with the presence of peace-keeping forces, the peacekeeping operation itself may mutate into a semi-permanent institution that hampers rather than helps the search for a permanent solution.'[32]

Third parties cannot, of course, conjure an end to war like a rabbit from a hat. At best, they can facilitate and enable those direct and indirect actors who want to find a political alternative to violence. Despite the well-documented failings of international third-party intervention that have occurred in the recent past, there are now at least a wider range of options available for those seeking external help to avail themselves of. As Peter Wallensteen reminds us: 'Parties are increasingly aware of the possibilities for settling their conflict. Therefore their decisions are now more strongly than ever related to how interested they are in achieving a settlement. The excuses for not engaging in a peace process are becoming increasingly limited.'[33]

Non-coercive diplomatic interventions have been a feature of UN involvement in conflicts such as Nicaragua, Mozambique and El Salvador, and these interventions made a significant contribution to the ending of armed conflicts in these countries.[34] In 2000, for example, after two years of fighting, Eritrea and Ethiopia signed a peace agreement (although Ethiopia subsequently reneged on it following disagreement about the border between the two countries). Nevertheless, in this case, a UN Mission in the region (UNMEE) was established to monitor a buffer zone between Ethiopia and Eritrea, which was relatively successful in terms of its admittedly limited remit.

In Mozambique, the implementation of the peace agreement during the 1990s (the General Peace Agreement of 1992) was successfully overseen by the UN operation (ONUMOZ), which concluded with the holding of multi-party elections in October 1994. Mozambique was a country ravaged by a civil war, driven in part by the political interests in what was then Rhodesia (now Zimbabwe) and South Africa within the context of Cold War geo-political logic. By the early 1990s this external context had changed substantially and the direct actors, Frelimo and Renamo, had reached something of a hurting stalemate. The role of ONUMOZ was substantial, helping to monitor the 1994 elections and demilitarize the warring factions, not to mention the mammoth task of repatriating over five million refugees. Norrie McQueen has outlined the positive impact which this intervention has had on the region. 'Mozambique now settled down to a sustained period of political stability that allowed a quite remarkable process of reconstruction to take place. Within a few years of the country being written off by many as beyond any kind of redemption, it had become something of a model for successful development in sub-Saharan Africa.'[35]

Unfortunately, however, this model was the exception rather than the rule in third-party interventions by the international community in sub-Saharan Africa and elsewhere. Nevertheless, while some might view the pitiful response of international third-party intervention in places such as Darfur as being the same old story as Rwanda, where lofty rhetoric and the rending of diplomatic garments was not met with adequate action, others would argue that we should not assess the record of these interventions by pointing to the worst cases and that much has been done by such third parties to prevent wars from breaking out, escalating or re-igniting.

Since the end of the Cold War and with the memory of failures such as Somalia and Rwanda fresh in the mind, much of the effort by international third parties was put into preventing conflict from breaking out rather than trying to deal with its aftermath. While demonstrating the impact of international third-party intervention is difficult in the context of conflict prevention initiatives, as establishing cause and effect between external interventions and events on the ground can be problematic, there are some examples that can be pointed to. Stung by its failure to intervene effectively during the early part of the Bosnian war, the UN sent its first ever peace-keeping mission to prevent war to Macedonia in 1993. This was done due to fears of spill-over impacts from Croatia and Bosnia and a view that the same conflict dynamics were present in Macedonia and could ignite in the ethnic tinderbox that was the Balkan region during the early 1990s. Owing to these concerns, the UN provided third-party support through a peace-keeping force called UNPROFOR (later UNPREDEP in 1995). At the same time, the OSCE provided its good offices and mediation functions through the High Commissioner for National Minorities. NATO troops also played an important role, its KFOR force replacing the UN operation when the war in Kosovo erupted in 1999. This was in turn replaced by an EU force, 'Operation Concordia', in 2003. This international third-party intervention was largely successful in containing the ethnic tensions in Macedonia, despite the violence that erupted around it, and without the intervention many observers believe that Macedonia would have descended into the violence experienced by its neighbours. 'Macedonia has managed to remain a unified state and to avoid an internal war. In this case the combination of cooperation between the political elites and international support has avoided what might well have been a bloody extension of the Yugoslav wars.'[36]

Chechnya and the Limits of Third-Party Intervention

Of course, there are several cases where the trumpets of the international community failed to sound anything more than a few halting notes, and where external third parties failed to intervene to protect human life as they had done elsewhere.

The lack of consistency over third-party interventions directed at containing or ending armed conflict goes to the heart of current debates surrounding the international political system. For every example where third parties intervened for humanitarian purposes, there were others where they sat back and watched while Rome burned. This very point was raised by former UN Secretary-General Kofi Annan in the context of NATO's intervention in Kosovo: 'If the new commitment to humanitarian action is to retain the support of the world's peoples, it must be – and must be seen to be – universal irrespective of region or nation. Humanity, after all, is indivisible.'[37] The case of Chechnya, however, would suggest that this is an aspiration rather than an achievement. As Thomas Weiss has pointed out: '[I]nternational dithering in Darfur, northern Uganda, and the Democratic Republic of Congo (DRC) indicates the dramatic disconnect between political reality and pious rhetoric.'[38] Some have identified an 'intervention gap' in the synapse between UN Security Council identification of a 'threat to international peace and security' and actions under Chapter VII to intervene in response to such situations. In Chechnya, the armed conflict between separatist groups and the Russian state did not even get to the floor of the Security Council despite over a decade of killing and displacement, which involved massive human rights abuses by all sides, regional destabilization and spill-over violence in the region.

The record of external third parties in Chechnya suggests that the traditional patterns of *realpolitik* familiar to realist interpretations of international politics are still very much with us. This undeclared war between Russia and Chechen fighters attempting to secede and form an independent state resulted in over 100,000 deaths since the outbreak of armed conflict in 1994 and an estimated 400,000 refugees. While Chechen separatists were guilty of many heinous acts of violence from

1994 onwards, Russian security forces hold the lion's share of responsibility for the violence that took place in the first war from 1994 to 1996 and in the second war from 1999 to 2004. 'The violations can be divided into several categories: the indiscriminate bombing of civilian areas and direct human rights violations such as extrajudicial executions, torture, massacres, and the spreading of land-mines.'[39] The battle for Grozny (the Chechen capital) in 1994–5 was compared with Stalingrad in World War II by the OSCE in 1995, and there was evidence of so-called 'filtration camps' (concentration camps in all but name) for Chechen males between the ages of 15 and 60, and even allegations of chemical weapons being used by Russian security forces against the civilian population. Despite all of this, the conflict was treated as 'domestic' by an international community anxious to secure first Boris Yeltsin's and subsequently Vladimir Putin's support for the 'new world order' and a stable (outwardly) benign Russia, committed to political and economic reform in the Western image. Put crudely, as a stable and democratic Russia was seen as being essential for peace and security in Europe, it could do what it liked in (and to) Chechnya. The conclusions of Thornike Gordadze on the lack of international intervention in Chechnya since the outbreak of armed conflict in 1994 are damning: 'The genocidal dynamic unleashed in Chechnya is supported by the silence, indeed the consent, of the "international community". Relations between the European Union, the United States and Russia are too important to be impeded by the Chechen question.'[40]

While violations of human rights have been acknowledged by external observers, there has been little agreement about what to do about the conflict and a general reluctance to pressurize the Russian government over what it likes to cast as an internal law-and-order issue. The second Chechen war which began in 1999 was defended by Russia as being a regrettable but necessary response to terrorist activity, and even as a 'peace-keeping' operation in the region.[41] This narrative fitted neatly into the international obsession with a 'war on terror' after the September 11, 2001 attacks on the United States. Seen through this lens, Russian President Vladimir Putin could claim to be at one with George Bush and Tony Blair in his commitment to eradicate the scourge of terrorism, and the threat of Muslim extremism. The actions of Chechen rebel groups in pursuit of their political goals did not make this a terribly difficult case to make. On 1 September 2004 a Chechen separatist group took over 1,200 people hostage at School Number One in the Russian town of Beslan, in North Ossetia. Following a three-day siege between the Chechen group and Russian police, a gunfight broke out which resulted in the deaths of 344 civilians, 186 of whom were school-children. International media coverage of this massacre illustrated the horrific nature of the siege and the trauma suffered by children packed into the school gym in stifling heat without food or water. After the siege, the UN Secretary-General, Kofi Annan, condemned the actions of the Chechen group as 'terrorism, pure and simple. Even without what happened in Beslan, we are all aware of the terrible toll terrorism has taken on people and nations around the world, and the need for the international community of nations to come together and work to confront this phenomenon.'[42]

While international third parties have condemned human rights abuses by the Russian security forces in Chechnya, these have been mainly rhetorical, such as the following resolution, passed in 2004 by the Parliamentary Assembly of the Council of Europe, highlighting the abuses that were taking place, yet unsupported by concrete action: 'The Assembly also strongly condemns the numerous violations of human rights such as murder, forced disappearance, torture, hostage-taking, rape and arbitrary detention committed by members of different federal and pro-Russian Chechen security forces during their "special" or "targeted" operations in the Chechen Republic and, increasingly, in neighbouring regions.'[43] Despite this and many other international declarations of concern, the policy of external third parties over the conflict in Chechnya was one of seeking constructive engagement with Russia in the hope that this might influence its policies in the region. This could be cast as being an act of prudent diplomacy, on the grounds that Western intervention might have done more harm than good, and may not have altered Russia's position on Chechnya. To others, however, it was simply an example of Western double-standards and the bankruptcy of international human rights norms. The campaigning Russian journalist Anna Politkovskaya was dismissive of the international community's reaction to the second Chechen war from 1999 onwards and its treatment of President Putin, whom she held chiefly responsible for it.

> Most of the time they forget the word Chechnya. They only remember it when there's a terrorist act. And then it's, 'Oh!' And they start their full coverage up again. But virtually nobody reports on what is really going on in that zone, in Chechnya, and the growth of terrorism. The truth is that the methods employed in Putin's anti-terrorist operation are generating a wave of terrorism the like of which we have never experienced. . . . Putin's begun to try to prove on the world stage that he's also fighting international terrorists, that he's just a part of this fashionable war. And he's been successful. He was Blair's best friend for a while. . . . It's impossible to talk on the one hand about the monstrous scale of victims in Chechnya and the spawning of terrorism and then lay out the red carpet, embrace Putin and tell him: 'We're with you, you're the best.' That shouldn't be happening. I understand, our country's a big market, it's very attractive. I understand it very well. But we're not second-class people, we're people like you, and we want to live.[44]

Many observers believe that her opposition to the Putin administration and to the war in Chechnya robbed her of that wish. Anna Politkovskaya was assassinated in her apartment building on 7 October 2006.[45]

The non-intervention in Chechnya illustrates the structural flaws inherent in the United Nations and the limits of its ability to deliver on its stated goals when these conflict with the interests of one of the permanent members of the UN Security Council. In addition, the case of Chechnya illustrates that while human rights violations that take place within states might be a concern for transnational bodies such as the UN and the EU *in certain circumstances*, they are subordinate to the wider strategic interests of those euphemistically referred to as the 'Great Powers'. In this case, the need to have Putin on board for the global war on terror, allied with the desire to continue the development of Russia as a stable market economy (Chechnya was also strategically important for the Russian oil pipeline), trumped the human rights of those living in Chechnya. While recognition that external third-party intervention within armed conflicts is selective will not be news to many readers of this book or observers of international politics, this point is significant within any discussion of the capacity of these actors to end war. It is difficult to avoid the conclusion that the case of Chechnya demonstrates the limitations of international third-party intervention, as in this instance Russia, one of the permanent five on the UN Security Council, committed human rights abuses and contributed to large-scale displacement and regional instability, rather than helping to overcome these problems. It did so under the noses and in full view of the other members of the UN Security Council and the whole international community. The conclusions of Svante Cornell on the case of Chechnya seem reasonable.

> The international might and standing of the violator of human rights thus has a strong impact on the way human

rights are dealt with in international politics. Again, it is a question of priorities: strategic considerations, although perhaps misguided, had primacy over considerations of justice and human rights. The professed goal of guiding Russia along a democratic path necessitated turning a blind eye to massive human rights violations on a genocidal scale.[46]

The metaphor used earlier in this chapter about babies and bathwater may, of course, be appropriate here, and it is certainly the case that external third-party intervention has helped to contain and end many armed conflicts around the globe. The world is not perfect and third-party interventions aimed at reducing violent conflict have been selective and inconsistent and will continue to be so. It would be facile and counterproductive to argue that because international third parties are unable to intervene *everywhere* on a consistent basis, they should intervene *nowhere*, and let wars rage despite being able on certain occasions to help bring them to an end.

However, the international policy community either has to admit that its interventions in this regard will always be selective and driven by the interests of powerful Western states, and thus ratchet down our expectations of its potential to intervene, or change the system in a way that might make Kofi Annan's ideal a reality. At the moment, in practice, and contrary to Annan's vision, 'humanity is divisible'[47] and it will continue to be so for the foreseeable future. While this will be an unpleasant thought for many, a more honest appraisal of the capacity of international third parties to intervene to end armed conflicts might help these organizations to establish coherent and consistent responses to war and gain credibility for their future policies and actions.

CHAPTER THREE

Negotiation or Victory?

This meeting represents an important step on the road to the setting-up of an Executive in six weeks' time. It has been a constructive engagement. . . . After a long and difficult time in the province, I believe that enormous opportunities lie ahead for Northern Ireland. Devolution has never been an end in itself but is about making a positive difference to people's lives. I want to make it clear that I am committed to delivering not only for those who voted for the DUP but for all the people of Northern Ireland. We must not allow our justified loathing of the horrors and tragedies of the past to become a barrier to creating a better and more stable future. With hard work and a commitment to succeed, I believe we can lay the foundation for a better, peaceful and prosperous future for all our people.

Ian Paisley[1]

I want to begin my remarks by welcoming the statement by Ian Paisley. . . . The discussions and agreement between our two parties shows the potential of what can now be achieved. . . . Sinn Féin is about building a new relationship between orange and green and all the other colours, where every citizen can share and have equality of ownership of a peaceful, prosperous and just future. . . . We have all come a very long way in the process of peace making and national reconciliation. We are very conscious of the many people who have suffered. We owe it to them to build the best future possible.

Gerry Adams[2]

The two quotations above are an indication of what can be achieved through dialogue and negotiation. These statements by Ian Paisley and Gerry Adams following their first *ever* formal meeting represent an iconic point in the Northern Ireland peace process and a textbook example of how relations between conflict actors can evolve within a process of negotiated political dialogue. The purpose of this chapter is to illustrate how concepts of victory in political conflict evolve through processes of negotiation that are capable (despite the inevitable setbacks) of bringing violence to an end.

This book has argued that wars are not an inevitable force of nature. Wars are caused, prosecuted and terminated by a complex mixture of structural elements and acts of human agency. Some wars end because one side emerges victorious and imposes its terms on the other parties, militarily, politically and economically. Obvious examples of this are provided by the pattern of World Wars I and II in the twentieth century. However, outright victory (where a durable peace is maintained) tends to be the exception rather than the rule. It is more likely that this will remain elusive and that some form of negotiated dialogue will be required to bring a lasting end to the violence. Peter Wallensteen has shown that while 119 out of 362 conflicts ended through victory between 1946 and 2004, violence had recurred within ten years in 20 per cent of these cases and in 50 per cent of them over the whole period. The latest example of this phenomenon of course was the 2003 Iraq war, supposedly won by the US-led coalition in May 2003, yet 'by the end of 2005, 2180 American troops had been killed in a war that had seemingly been "won" two and a half years earlier.'³

When the direct actors in conflict come to the view that continued violence will not achieve their objectives, they are more likely to consider alternatives to it, including peaceful dialogue. While many of these negotiations end in failure, there are others which evolve, however haltingly, into political settlements and post-conflict reconstruction. The available evidence

would seem to suggest that despite their problems, these negotiated agreements 'were more often successful than not in
reducing violence'.[4]

This chapter looks at the ways in which armed conflicts can
be ended through political dialogue and negotiation and at
some of the sticking points and turning points in this difficult
journey. The objective here is to illustrate that wars are not
inevitably intractable or doomed to continue and that there *are*
conditions that can be fostered where constructive negotiations can take place between the direct actors that can bring
such violence to an end.

In line with the changing nature of armed conflict outlined
earlier in this book from inter-state to intra-state wars, the focus
of attention in this chapter will be on the pattern of negotiations
within three cases of intra-state conflicts. South Africa,
Northern Ireland and Israel/Palestine all experienced multi-
party negotiations during the 1990s aimed at bringing political
violence to an end. The focus on negotiations in intra-state
conflicts is appropriate not just because these are a more
common feature of contemporary violent conflict than the
more traditional inter-state wars of the past, but because negotiating an end to these civil wars is often more difficult to
achieve.

There are a number of reasons why this is the case which
relate to the way these wars are fought (the involvement of
civilian populations and dehumanizing tactics used) together
with the multiplicity of direct actors involved. Intra-state violence tends to involve a greater number of people in shallower
forms of hierarchy than wars of the past, which were controlled by states and their militaries. As a consequence, the
process of ending intra-state wars through political negotiation brings problems that are not quite as pronounced within
inter-state conflicts. These may relate to the lack of clarity over
who has the authority to negotiate within or between ethnic

groups and the multiplicity of such groups; a reluctance to recognize 'terrorists' as legitimate interlocutors; the involvement of international third parties with unrecognized groups; and, of course, the attempt to deal with identity-based as well as interest-based issues.

Difficult though such negotiations are, the fact remains that there *are* conditions when structural changes in intra-state armed conflict, in combination with acts of human agency, can facilitate and enable political dialogue and bring political violence to an end. As Stephen Stedman reminds us: '[B]etween 1988 and 1994, negotiations brought five civil wars to an end – in El Salvador, Mozambique, Namibia, Nicaragua and South Africa.'[5] While this chapter also looks at examples where negotiations have failed, it hopes to illustrate how the process of political negotiation can change the context and build trust among conflict actors in the process of peace-building as an alternative to the continuation of armed conflict.

Negotiation is far from being a soft option, of course, and it is often easier, in the short term at least, to keep on fighting rather than try to find a way out of it. The process carries risks as well as rewards, and this chapter examines the complex dynamics that lead conflict actors into the negotiating process; the barriers that exist to the reaching of an agreed settlement; the various structures and techniques used within the process; and the importance of leadership to a successful outcome.

The typical pattern of negotiations aimed at ending a prolonged period of political violence can be characterized by a series of rapid shifts, such as the declaration of cease-fires, accompanied by longer periods of inertia and stalemate where the modalities of the negotiations are discussed and debated by the conflict parties. It is very rare that a peace process which involves multi-actor negotiation and third-party intervention will go smoothly or proceed in accordance with pre-agreed timeframes. It is more usual that such negotiations will be acrimonious, with disagreements taking place over specific issues and with parties on all sides pushing the talks to the point of breakdown, or indeed past it. In successful negotiations, these sticking points will eventually be resolved and the negotiations will lurch forward again until another issue is reached that becomes a sticking point. There may well be a sustained period of pre-negotiations or talks-about-talks where the ground rules are established before the formal negotiations begin. Once the motivation for a negotiated settlement is reached, the next phase concerns how the political environment can be engineered to allow negotiations to take place. This may require the legalization of some of the direct actors, such as the African National Congress (ANC) in South Africa, or the Palestine Liberation Organization (PLO) in Israel/ Palestine. It may require the release of political prisoners from jail, a hazardous exercise packed with wider implications concerning arguments over the legitimacy of the conflict itself. Negotiations will almost always require the announcement of cease-fires by guerrilla groups, as happened in the three examples of South Africa, Israel/Palestine and Northern Ireland.

All of these activities are part of the choreography that takes place around political discussions that can subsequently evolve into formal political negotiations. William Zartman has written convincingly about the role of incentives as a dynamic in the negotiating process and about the nature of the Catch-22 situation that often characterizes this form of dialogue. Conflict parties may have reached a mutually hurting stalemate (MHS) and be persuaded that they are unable to prevail through military means alone, but at the same time may be reluctant to believe that a viable settlement can be negotiated. 'In other words, one may come to dislike the boat one is in, but there needs to be another (better) boat in the neighborhood before disembarking.'[6]

It is important to realize, of course, that the obstacles to the successful negotiation of a violent political conflict are formidable, especially in the context of the changing nature of warfare from inter-state to intra-state conflicts. The authors of *Contemporary Conflict Resolution* caution us that 'only a quarter to a third of modern civil wars have been negotiated, whereas more than half of interstate wars have been.'[7] These processes are not the same as talks to resolve civil problems such as an industrial relations dispute, where the underlying interests are the same. Negotiations aimed at ending warfare will involve at least two parties (often more), who define the other side as being a political, historical, cultural, economic or religious enemy, who might regard their underlying interests as being fundamentally separate, and who are often prepared to kill and die in pursuit of their ideological objectives. Even when some parties agree to enter negotiations, they may do so in an effort to destabilize the discussions or because they have been forced to do so by external backers, but with little interest in reaching a settlement with the other participants. These 'spoilers' will be examined in more detail in the next chapter, but it is certainly the case that there are a litany of excuses that could be given by those who are opposed to the terms or timing of negotiations aimed at bringing violent armed conflict to an end.

The parties to a violent conflict usually aim to win, and they are locked into a structure of interaction that makes them very sensitive to the prospects for winning and losing. Every event in these negotiations that takes place, every statement made, every nuance alluded to, will be scrutinized by all of the conflict parties. Concessions that involve withdrawal from long-held positions are usually bitterly resisted. One of the main reasons for this relates to the lack of trust between the parties in such negotiations. Trust and respect are rare commodities in negotiations, and it is the building of trust (for the process itself, if not between the participants) that is often the key to overcoming the sticking points that prevent political progress.

Clearly, therefore, the obstacles in the way of negotiations commencing are significant, but these need to be balanced against other factors that may provide the catalyst for talks to begin. These often relate to changes in the context of a violent conflict and the realization by the direct actors that they cannot achieve their aims without entering political dialogue. The remainder of this chapter examines the dynamics of these talks and talks-about-talks and looks at the variable fortunes experienced across a number of different cases.

Getting to the Table: Pre-Negotiations and the First Steps towards Dialogue

Political negotiations between warring factions do not happen overnight or without an important period of pre-planning and dialogue. Once the direct actors have accepted that further violence is unlikely to achieve their objectives, they may become more amenable to the search for a political route out of armed conflict. One of the central reasons for this is that these are (for the most part) political conflicts underpinned by a complex array of ideological and material issues. The use of violence is frequently a strategy used to achieve these goals and is rarely an end in itself. Thus, when the objectives cannot be attained through the use of violence, other avenues may become more attractive for the belligerents, especially if other changes in the context of the conflict (such as the emergence of a third-party mediator, or the withdrawal of support from an outside party) make this a more realistic option. As explained earlier in this book, William Zartman has written about the importance of negotiations being timed for a 'ripe moment'.[8]

The fruitless negotiations to end the war between Ethiopia and Eritrea in 1989 can be explained partly by the lack of a ripe moment. These talks were initiated and mediated by former US President Jimmy Carter and took place in Atlanta and Nairobi between the Ethiopian government and the Eritrean People's Liberation Front (EPLF). Marina Ottaway's analysis of the failure of these negotiations fits neatly within the 'ripe moment' explanation.

> The negotiations had started at an unpromising time, prompted not by favourable conditions, but by the humanitarian concerns of the mediator. From a political point of view the intervention came either too late or too early. By the time the talks had started it was too late to tackle the Eritrean conflict as a bilateral one; but the new, multilateral conflict was still too undefined, the relations among the parties were too unclear and the hopes of the EPLF for a military victory were too high for an attempt at mediation to succeed. The conflict was in a transitional stage and as a result the negotiations failed.[9]

While the timing of these initiatives is clearly important, some observers, such as John Paul Lederach, have cautioned that this can be something of a self-fulfilling prophecy which is only clear after the event. 'Ripeness is in the eye of the beholder and few who live in the settings [of protracted political violence] have the luxury of such vision.'[10]

The decision to enter political negotiations is fraught with risks for those involved. It will require leaders of states to talk to those they had previously demonized as 'terrorists' or conduct a dual policy of opening up contacts with paramilitary leaders in secret, while maintaining publicly that they will never negotiate with terrorists. This was exactly the position that former British Prime Minister John Major found himself in during the beginnings of the Northern Ireland peace process in 1993. While he had authorized secret communications with the Provisional IRA in 1990, he claimed in the House of Commons in November 1993 that he would not countenance talking to republican paramilitaries until a cease-fire was unilaterally declared by the Provisional IRA. The following exchange between Labour MP Dennis Skinner and Prime Minister Major illustrates the double-speak that political leaders are required to adopt during the pre-negotiation phase of dialogue when contacts are being established in secret between warring factions. When Dennis Skinner asked the Prime Minister why the British government would not follow the example of the Middle East and the recognition of the PLO as legitimate interlocutors by the Israeli government, John Major's response was categorical, despite the fact that he had been engaged in a similar back-channel for the previous three years.

> If the implication of his remarks is that we should sit down and talk with Mr. Adams and the Provisional IRA, I can say only that that would turn my stomach and those of most hon. Members; we will not do it. If and when there is a total ending of violence, and if and when that ending of violence is established for a significant time, we shall talk to all the constitutional parties that have people elected in their names. I will not talk to people who murder indiscriminately.[11]

While it can cause extreme political embarrassment for leaders of states to take a risk and enter dialogue with paramilitary groups, these organizations face similar worries about agreeing to engage in talks aimed at designing a negotiated settlement. This will entail both a political and personal risk to the leaders of paramilitary factions and internal political parties. Inevitably, the acceptance of the need for a negotiated settlement requires a number of shifts for those who become involved. Firstly, it will be clear that any negotiation will entail a number of trade-offs and political compromises. Secondly, the willingness to enter negotiations will require a move away from demonizing opposing conflict parties and an admission that the existing strategy is incapable of succeeding. Thirdly, it is extremely unlikely that during this phase of pre-negotiations they will be able to secure unanimous support within their organizations for opening dialogue with the enemy. Political leaders, including those within paramilitary factions, will be vulnerable in these circumstances to 'ethnic outbidding', accused by radicals within their own side of either stupidity or treachery, or both. They may also expose themselves to the risk of political assassination by those who see political dialogue as a sell-out, or who wish to take advantage of the situation and use it to remove opponents and take control of the organization for themselves. It is within these fraught cost/benefit assessments that decisions are made by the direct actors in armed conflicts about whether to pursue the opportunities for negotiations that may arise. It is hardly surprising, therefore, that the nature of any formal negotiating process often takes some time to emerge. As the editors of *Contemporary Peacemaking* outline: '[U]ltimately, the pre-negotiation phase of a peace process requires faith. It is nothing less than a high-risk gamble to ascertain the seriousness of other conflict participants.'[12]

Several months (or even years) may be spent at the pre-negotiation phase as the various protagonists tease out and try to influence the ground rules and parameters within which formal discussions will be held. These may include seeking agreements across a wide range of complex issues such as the following: Who is going to be involved in the negotiations and on what basis? This goes to the fundamental issue of political recognition of paramilitary factions as legitimate political representatives, and this in turn presents obvious difficulties for those who cast such people as terrorist criminals in the past (or indeed in the present). In the early stages of dialogue between Palestinians and the government of Israel in Madrid in 1991, the Israeli delegation refused to accept any members of the PLO on the Palestinian delegation on the basis that they were an illegal terrorist organization. The issue of *who* negotiates is often linked to the prior requirement for paramilitary cease-fires as a prerequisite for dialogue and a public recognition of principles of non-violence by such groups before they can enter the process. The Israeli government's position on non-recognition of the PLO had become untenable by the early 1990s due to the tacit recognition by the PLO of Israel's right to exist and its rejection of the use of terrorism as enshrined in the Declaration of Palestinian Independence in 1988. Following these moves, the US started talking directly to the PLO and encouraged/coerced the Israelis to follow suit. Within more top-down-driven processes, third parties may use forms of 'muscled mediation' to consolidate paramilitary factions into smaller negotiating teams in order to reduce factionalism, splintering and ethnic outbidding that can accompany such talks. This runs the risk, however, of reducing internal credibility for the process, which can come back to haunt such negotiated settlements at a later date.

The issues to be negotiated will also be a matter of debate and contestation as supporters of the political status quo may wish to take a minimalist approach and limit negotiations to issues of security. Those who have fought a revolutionary war will clearly want a much wider range of issues to be included in negotiations, including reform of the political, economic, legal and cultural institutions. Obtaining some agreement (however grudging) over what issues are to be included in the negotiations will take time and effort for all of those involved in the process. If a third party is to be involved, some discussion will be needed about who this will be and what role they will play. Finally, in armed conflicts driven by independence movements and identity-based conflicts, arguments may take place about the location of negotiations, with some groups pushing for the talks to be held outside the sovereignty of the region concerned in order to reflect the contested nature of rival claims to statehood.

Despite the unique quality of the individual cases, the pattern surrounding the process of political negotiations is strikingly similar across differing contexts. Warring parties will move from refusing to talk to one another as a matter of principle, to refusing to talk to certain groups they deem as illegitimate, despite recognizing the need for dialogue with someone. From this point there may be a reluctant agreement to enter negotiations but disagreement about the modalities concerning how these should take place (e.g. the nature of third-party mediators, sequencing of the issues to be discussed). This pattern can be seen in cases as disparate in terms of their substantive conflicts as Northern Ireland and Tajikistan, each of which nevertheless witnessed negotiations which lurched forward, despite several periods of inertia and stalemate. In both of these cases the pre-negotiation period was mediated by external third parties and was beset with disagreements over the agenda and the sequencing of when key issues would be discussed. In both cases the release of political prisoners was a key issue of the talks, while the nature of paramilitary cease-fires and the shadow of violence destabilized the negotiations and trust between those involved in them. These two cases illustrate the difficulties inherent in bringing warring factions into direct political dialogue aimed at securing a negotiated settlement.

Making the First Move

Obviously, if negotiations are going to commence, someone has to take the initiative and act as a catalyst for discussions to take place. This can be very difficult, for the reasons outlined above, and may begin in a tentative or indirect manner through third parties and back-channels to the conflicts that they provide. In the case of South Africa, Nelson Mandela played precisely this role during the 1980s while he was still in prison. The 'Mandela Initiative', as it has become known, refers to the series of letters written by the ANC leader to the government outlining the possibilities for talks between his organization and the ruling National Party. While none of Mandela's letters received a response, they were read and did inform the thinking of members of the government, so that when Mandela was hospitalized in 1985, he received a visit from the Minister for Justice, Kobie Coetsee. Pierre du Toit has commented on how this event illustrates the first significant movement in South Africa's eventual negotiated settlement between the ANC and the National Party government.

> Coetsee visited Mandela in hospital, which served as an excellent venue for pre-negotiations. First, the hospital served as symbolically 'neutral ground', not being home ground for any of the contenders. Secondly, both individuals could step out of their adversarial roles . . . for the duration of the meeting. Mandela became first, and foremost, a patient and Coetsee became a visitor. Thirdly, a *bona fide* humanitarian motive of compassion for the sick allowed both individuals to engage with little fear of losing face. At the same time, a message of huge political significance could be conveyed to Mandela: that the government was willing to reciprocate his initiatives in exploring the prospect of a negotiated settlement further.[13]

Following this event, further meetings with Mandela were held to determine the prospects for meaningful dialogue with the ANC and to ascertain whether it would be amenable to political compromise with the National Party government.

In the Middle East, the incoming Labour Prime Minister, Yitzhak Rabin, made a landmark speech following his election victory in 1992 that sent important signals to the PLO and the rest of the Arab world and attempted to set the agenda within

Israeli public opinion and prepare them for the negotiations that were to follow.

> I am prepared to travel to Amman, Damascus and Beirut today, tomorrow. For there is no greater victory than the victory of peace. . . . We must overcome the sense of isolation that has held us in its thrall for almost half a century. We must join the international movement toward peace, reconciliation and co-operation that is spreading over the entire globe these days – lest we be the last to remain, all alone, in the station. . . . The new government has . . . made it a prime goal to promote the making of peace and take vigorous steps that will lead to the conclusion of the Israeli–Arab conflict.[14]

In the context of the pre-negotiation period in Northern Ireland, Sinn Fein President Gerry Adams wrote what he called a 'Dear John' letter to incoming Prime Minister John Major in 1990, congratulating him on his new job and arguing for the importance of dialogue between the British government and Irish republicanism to find a way out of violence. While this did not indicate anything approaching a policy shift within militant Irish republicanism, it sent a more subliminal message to the effect that Sinn Fein was interested in jaw-jaw as well as, or *possibly* instead of, war-war. This was cast in retrospect by Gerry Adams as connecting his movement with other international revolutionary struggles for national independence, but can also be read as an attempt to get beyond the 'mutually hurting stalemate' that existed in Northern Ireland in 1990. 'It struck me, something I just read somewhere, that Ho Chi Minh or someone like that had, through all the decades for the liberation of Vietnam, continuously written to the colonial power. It just struck me that here we were, and we'd never made any attempt to proactively engage the British prime minister.'[15] From this point forwards, while little changed publicly and the armed conflict in Northern Ireland continued unabated (and at times intensified), a back-channel was constructed between the

British government and republican paramilitaries that discussed the possibilities for an end to the violence within the
context of an inclusive negotiated settlement. This back-
channel, referred to by those involved as 'the link',[16] was vital in
terms of preparing Irish republicans and the British government for the direct dialogue that was to come later during
formal negotiations in 1997. Despite a Provisional IRA mortar
attack on the British Cabinet in Downing Street in 1990, the
secret back-channel provided a fact-finding function between
the British government and Sinn Fein to determine whether
formal negotiations could be attempted, and a form of sema-
phore evolved where both sides would send each other their
speeches in advance with sentences underlined to emphasize
their meaning and significance. While the back-channel was to
break down in mutual recriminations when the secret talks
were made public in November 1993, John Major concludes
that it was an important building block on the road to peace
in Northern Ireland. 'The messages we received from the
Provisionals . . . and our substantive replies . . . helped to pave
the way for the cessation of violence by spelling out clearly what
was, and what was not, on offer. . . . I regretted the loss of the
back-channel. It gave us some difficult moments but it played
its part. Making peace is a tricky business.'[17]

A secret back-channel to negotiations was also integral to
the 1993 Oslo agreement between the Israeli Labour government and the PLO and was a central feature of the efforts to
find a peaceful settlement in the Middle East. Mahmoud
Abbas, the PLO's leading delegate in these secret communications, has commented on how these contacts helped to resolve
issues in advance of more formal agreements being made.

> The secret meetings and contacts had clarified many issues
> that had been submerged by the bloody conflict that had
> gripped the region. . . . the Palestinians made their aim clear,
> and the Israelis understood it. There was no choice but that

the protagonists should deal directly with one another, and this realisation finally led to the negotiating table and to the signing of the Declaration of Principles and the recognition of the Palestine Liberation Organisation.[18]

There may be a complex array of facilitators and mediators at both civil society and international levels. In the case of the Middle East, the US has attempted to act as a mediator, with varying degrees of success, its high point being the Camp David Agreement in September 1978 between Egypt and Israel. More recently, President Bill Clinton stage-managed a money-shot on the White House lawn in September 1993 to publicly unveil the Oslo agreement with the famous hand-shake between Yitzhak Rabin and Yasser Arafat. While the US has always attempted to facilitate/mediate and even coerce the parties in the Israel/Palestine conflict, the Norwegian government together with a Norwegian NGO, FAFO, played the key mediating role within the Oslo process. Representatives of the Norwegian government have also been directly involved as facilitators in talks to end the armed conflict in Sri Lanka since 1998. The Norwegians acted as a conduit for information to flow between the main Tamil separatist group, the LTTE, and the Sri Lankan government at a time when the governing party was unwilling to negotiate directly with what it deemed to be a terrorist organization.

The case of Sri Lanka brings us back to the point that negotiations designed to bring armed conflict to an end carry personal and political risks for all of those involved. After India attempted to intervene to mediate the war between the Tamils and the government of Sri Lanka during the late 1980s, the LTTE assassinated the Indian President in 1991. 'Rajiv Gandhi's assassination by the LTTE was the direct result of the failure of India's role as mediator in Sri Lanka's ethnic conflict which had begun under his mother's government as a calculated political response to the anti-Tamil riots of July

1983 in Sri Lanka.'[19] Gandhi's assassination was precipitated by the Indo-Sri Lanka Peace Agreement (ISPA) of 1987, which the LTTE believed to fall short of its separatist objectives. Under this agreement, India sent a 3,000-strong peace-keeping force to Sri Lanka to protect the Tamils from attack by the government, which was to be accompanied by an LTTE cease-fire and a gradual demilitarization on all sides. This initiative failed because it was negotiated between the political elites within the Sri Lankan and Indian governments and had little support within grass-roots communities on either side of the conflict. It also failed due to its unrealistic demands on the LTTE, requiring it to 'surrender' its weapons to Sri Lankan authorities within seventy-two hours. Irrespective of the problematic binary notion of legitimacy/illegitimacy between Tamils and the government, this was hopelessly ambitious in purely practical terms, as Sumantra Bose has illustrated in his excellent review of the failure of the ISPA to end the violence in Sri Lanka.[20] Within a matter of weeks the LTTE had directly attacked the Indian peace-keeping force and fighting between the peace-keepers and local Tamils resulted in a significant loss of life. As one analyst of the Sri Lankan conflict has remarked: 'Rarely in the history of inter-state mediation has the mediator been attacked by one of the parties to a negotiation.'[21]

The calamity of the ISPA illustrates the point that the success or failure of negotiations is often linked to their design, and if the direct actors in the violence are excluded from the process (as was the case with the ISPA), it may lose credibility in the eyes of the wider community. The exclusion from negotiations of radical belligerent groups also runs the risk that key issues and grievances that underpin the violent conflict are not discussed within the talks, which once again damages their credibility and the chances of any negotiated agreement being implemented successfully.

When the Talking Begins: Political Negotiations

After a sustained period of pre-negotiations where the modalities of who will talk to whom, when, where and about what are resolved, it may be possible for the direct actors to move into formal negotiations with one another. The typical pattern is that following a series of confidence-building measures (e.g. paramilitary cease-fires, recognition of 'terrorist' groups by governing parties or the release of prisoners), the parties enter a structured dialogue aimed at cementing tentative cessations of violence through a negotiated political settlement. Models of negotiation do, of course, vary widely, from the directed and coercive discussions of the Dayton agreement (which was little more than an American-driven 'Hobson's choice' for those involved) aimed at bringing an end to the Bosnian war in 1995, to the more consensus-based dialogue of the Northern Ireland negotiations during 1996–8.

While the techniques of the negotiation process will vary from case to case, a number of fundamental elements are required if these discussions are going to be capable of bringing an end to armed conflict in the region concerned. Negotiations have to be sufficiently inclusive of the diverse parties to the conflict in order to be viewed as being representative and legitimate across the divided community. They will have to have a structure which is loose enough to take account of the range of objections and demands made by the various conflict parties, but which retains sufficient coherence to proceed in a positive direction. The parties involved must be committed to engaging with one another (however obliquely) in pursuit of a settlement, rather than for more cynical motives connected to ethnic outbidding or avoiding blame for a collapse they have deliberately precipitated. External third parties must be capable of building some level of trust in the process if not in themselves, let alone between the direct actors. The pre-negotiation phase should have provided an agreed set of rules of engagement within which the talks will proceed. These might involve a combination of the following elements:

- a series of timeframes and deadlines;
- an accepted code of conduct for the negotiators, normally relating to the use of non-violence or confidentiality;
- agreement over the role of third-party mediators;
- agreement over the physical location; and
- agreement over the sequencing of issues for discussion.

In one of the more bizarre examples, negotiations over the ending of violence in South Vietnam in the early 1970s went as far as arguments over the shape of the negotiating table.[22] In the Northern Ireland case, it was agreed to hold the talks in three separate areas (Belfast, London and Dublin) to reflect the contested sovereignty claims of the parties involved. In the context of South Africa, Pierre du Toit has outlined how the choice of the venue for negotiations between the government and the ANC in 1991 (the World Trade Centre at Kempton Park in Johannesburg) provided a neutral – if architecturally challenged – space which was acceptable to both parties. '[T]his nondescript, ugly, semi-industrial area was also of no historical significance to any party and held no special emotional or symbolic meaning to anyone. This made it the perfectly neutral negotiating arena as nobody could, or wanted to, claim home-ground advantage.'[23] Finally, outside the negotiations themselves, other events (most obviously the recurrence of political violence) must not destabilize the discussions to the point where they collapse amidst mutual recriminations.

Bargaining, Brinkmanship and Trade-Offs

In most cases of political dialogue within protracted violent conflicts, the negotiations follow a very adversarial model and are characterized by negativity, suspicion and mistrust of the other actors. While hostile personal relationships are to be expected in these fraught circumstances, this creates a destabilizing dynamic in the process where any potentially constructive words and deeds of political opponents are dismissed as being part of some malign hidden agenda due to the antagonistic human relationships that exist in the negotiating chamber and beyond. Getting to the bottom line of the conflict parties in these circumstances and developing positions in ways that could produce positive-sum scenarios or bargained trade-offs often proves immensely difficult to achieve. This is an area where credible third parties can provide a useful mediation function and maintain a structured process which contains the mutual antagonisms and insecurities of the negotiating parties.

Within the context of Israel/Palestine, two sets of negotiations were conducted in parallel during the early 1990s, one public, the other secret, with two different sets of negotiators and two different third parties, American and Norwegian. While the Madrid conference (which took place between 1991 and 1993 and was mediated by the US government) produced little substantive progress, it sowed the seeds for the Oslo agreement that followed. Although these negotiations were fatally undermined by structural inadequacies in the wider peace process (notably the avoidance of key issues for the Palestinian community), they were based on a bargained trade-off commonly referred to as 'land for peace' based on a two-state solution. The secret back-channel negotiations between the PLO and representatives of the government of Israel resulted in the Declaration of Principles (DOP), signed amidst much pomp on the White House lawn in September 1993. The essence of the bargain here was that the PLO would maintain an end to the Palestinian *intifada* and deliver greater security for the Israeli community, in return for a set of timetabled negotiations between the PLO and Israel. The DOP stipulated that within four months of its signing, Israel would withdraw from Gaza and Jericho, and Palestinian autonomy would be created by the inauguration of a new Palestinian-controlled police force. In political terms, limited Palestinian autonomy was to be granted over education, health and a range of other social policy matters, though, crucially, Israel was to retain control over external security and foreign affairs. The DOP set out a series of timetables, including the scheduling of elections within nine months to a new Palestinian Authority and the scheduling of final-status negotiations which were to be started within two years and completed within five.

The negotiations that led to the DOP were enabled by the combination of three fundamental factors. Firstly, there was a mutually hurting stalemate between the Palestinians and the Israeli government and the realization on all sides that neither side could prevail militarily and that political dialogue would be required to produce political change and improve security. Secondly, the election victory of Yitzhak Rabin's Labour Party in 1992 ended fifteen years of Likud rule and produced a political mandate for dialogue with the PLO on the basis of the land for peace model. Thirdly, the lack of success of the Palestinian *intifada* in changing the policies of the Israeli government, the aftermath of the first Gulf War in 1991, which helped separate the PLO from more general Arab–West relations, and the general weakening of Yasser Arafat's internal position made him anxious – if not desperate – for some form of negotiated settlement which he could claim as a victory. All of these elements combined to produce a 'ripe moment' for negotiations to proceed.

The relative success of the Oslo negotiations in producing the DOP was, however, predicated on something of a deceit, namely that the fundamental grievances underlying the conflict were avoided under the guise of 'final-status issues', rather than addressed and resolved in the negotiations themselves. Thus both parties failed to bite the bullet over possible Palestinian statehood, the final borders of Israeli/Palestinian territories, the return of Palestinian refugees and the position of Jerusalem. All of these matters were pushed down the pipe, as not to have done so would have destabilized the negotiations, led to a breakdown of the Oslo process and the absence of any agreement whatsoever. In this context, the negotiating parties felt that limited agreement was better than none at all. The avoidance of these final-status issues in the negotiations themselves provided both sides with an opportunity to hold separate perceptions about the content of the DOP and its implications for the future. Consequently, it was sold to the Arab world by Yasser Arafat and its other advocates as a stepping stone to Palestinian statehood and as providing the foundations for Palestinian national self-determination. It was sold by Yitzhak Rabin, meanwhile, as limited autonomy and nothing more. These positions were far apart, if not incompatible, and explain why the DOP was beset by so many implementation problems after it was negotiated. Despite its flaws, though, some would hold out the DOP as an example of successful limited negotiations which improved communications between the PLO and the state of Israel and provided mechanisms for final-status issues to be negotiated subsequently in a more positive environment. Others, however, would contend that the avoidance of the main issues in the conflict was a fundamental failure in the negotiations that led to unrealistic expectations within the Palestinian community and frustration on all sides that led to multiple failures at the implementation stage. With the benefit of hindsight, the latter position seems the more convincing today.

The political negotiations in Northern Ireland illustrate the brinkmanship and bargaining that is endemic to this form of dialogue. Following a prolonged period of pre-negotiations, formal multi-party talks began in June 1996, though these excluded Sinn Fein due to the breakdown of the Provisional IRA cease-fire the previous January. When the IRA cease-fire was restored in July 1997 following the general election victory of Tony Blair, Sinn Fein was finally allowed to join the negotiations in September, though this in turn led to Ian Paisley's Democratic Unionist Party walking out of the talks in protest. The political negotiations in Northern Ireland were separated into three strands which would be tackled concurrently by the participants aided by a number of third parties. These three strands reflected the contested national identity claims of the main parties and it was a point of some debate (and eventual agreement) that strand one (internal relations within Northern Ireland), strand two (relations between Northern Ireland and the Irish Republic) and strand three (relations between the island of Ireland and the United Kingdom) would all be addressed at the same time, rather than sequentially. This, of course, relates back to the issue of trust (and the lack of it) in negotiations between political adversaries. One phrase that came to dominate the negotiations in Northern Ireland was that 'nothing is agreed until everything is agreed'. This was intended to free the participants from the fear that any concessions on their part would be pocketed and not reciprocated by their opponents. The hope here was that the security of mutual vetoes over final agreements would loosen up existing positions and allow a degree of horse-trading to take place across the three-stranded process. This procedural agreement over the interlocking nature of the multi-party talks was a vital element of the negotiations and one of the key foundations upon which their success was built. Former US Senator George Mitchell had been appointed as Chair of the negotiations and acted as the chief third-party mediator, while the Prime Ministers of Ireland and the UK (Bertie Ahern and Tony Blair) were also heavily involved as third parties during the course of the negotiations. Unlike the secrecy surrounding the Oslo back-channel, the Northern Ireland negotiations were conducted publicly in terms of the process, though the day-to-day details remained largely private. While the formal negotiations in Northern Ireland were often marked by personal vitriol and abuse between the main participants, some trust in the political process began to emerge through the slow progress that was made and due to the absence of any credible political alternative to dialogue.

Mitchell's mediating role, together with the third-party involvement of Blair and Ahern, was to prove vital to the negotiating process as party positions were teased out, issues were refined and concessions on all sides were sequenced to produce the basis for political agreement. In an effort to produce a catalyst within the process and probe the bottom line of the protagonists, Mitchell introduced a deadline for the talks of 9 April 1998. He did this following a long consultation with all the parties involved, but the purpose was to bring the negotiations to some denouement, prevent further destabilizations caused by violent events outside the talks and provide the final spur for the parties to indicate their bottom-line positions. The deadline mechanism worked in the sense of producing a pressure-cooker atmosphere in the negotiations and a series of knife-edge judgement calls from the main actors, most notably the decision by Ulster Unionist leader David Trimble to accept the terms of the deal without any guarantees (other than from Tony Blair himself) over IRA weapons decommissioning. Whether this produced a good settlement is another matter, however, as the Good Friday Agreement split the Ulster Unionist Party, weakened David Trimble's leadership of it and emboldened spoiler groups outside the negotiations. This political fall-out produced implementation problems that were very similar to those caused by the DOP in the Israel/Palestine context.

The fundamental bargain at the heart of the negotiations between Israel and the PLO was the granting of limited autonomy to the Palestinians in return for the recognition of the 'facts on the ground', namely the existence of the State of Israel and the ending of politically motivated violence. The central bargain of the multi-party negotiations that led to the Good Friday Agreement in Northern Ireland on 10 April 1998 was that unionists would accept and operate power-sharing with an Irish dimension together with Irish nationalists. This was granted in return for the renunciation of political violence by Irish republicans and their acceptance that Northern Ireland would remain part of the United Kingdom based on the consent of the people who lived there. In both of these cases, the bargained trade-offs at the centre of the negotiations produced what has been referred to as a 'constructive ambiguity', which allowed all sides to interpret the negotiated settlement in the way they wanted, as a means of reducing the risk of ethnic outbidding. In a speech at Cambridge University in September 2005, Mitchell Reiss, the US Special Envoy to Northern Ireland, commented on the potential of constructive ambiguity in the context of negotiations in Northern Ireland.

> Once the negotiations come out of the shadows, 'constructive ambiguity' may be a valuable tool for embedding the peace process even while violence continues. It allows the terrorist group to tell its supporters that it has not compromised its objectives, but is instead exploring the possibility of achieving them through political as well as military means. Clever moderates in terrorist groups can use constructive ambiguity to enhance their legitimacy and widen their appeal. . . . For the government and other parties, constructive ambiguity allows the authorities to take a gesture by the terrorists – such as a cease-fire declaration – and use it as grounds for publicly dealing with former political untouchables.[24]

While this sort of constructive ambiguity can provide space for negotiations to move forward towards agreement, it contains the potential for the negotiators to construct alternative narratives about what has been agreed. Thus, Rabin in Israel and Trimble in Northern Ireland were able to claim that the political status quo had been strengthened, while Arafat and Adams claimed that their negotiations had produced a stepping stone to future national self-determination for the Palestinians and Irish nationalists, respectively. These differences can come back to haunt the negotiators at a later stage in the peace process, as, of course, happened in the two cases discussed here. As Robert Rothstein has explained in the context of the Oslo agreement: '[I]f the leaders arrive at a settlement, it may be inherently unstable because one or both leaders may have to oversell what has been achieved, promise that ultimate goals have not been sacrificed, and read too much between the lines, thus guaranteeing disappointed expectations and escalating frustrations.'[25] While the examples of Arafat and Rabin indicate the proneness of political leaders to unstitch negotiated agreements as soon as they are reached, the example of Gerry Adams and Ian Paisley, given at the beginning of this chapter, indicates the important role that political leaders can play in the process of negotiating a settlement.

The Importance of Leadership in Negotiations

While political negotiations are unlikely to bring an end to armed conflict if structural factors are not present that create conducive circumstances, we should not ignore the fact that acts of human agency may also be vital on the part of political leaders, in the decision both to negotiate and to sign up to an agreed settlement. It is reasonable to conclude that in the three cases that have been discussed in this chapter, negotiated agreements would not have been reached without significant

commitments from the respective political leaders and important leadership changes that helped to reframe the central
issues at the heart of those armed conflicts. In several of these
cases, matters of structure and agency were separate but inter-
connected. While the replacement of P.W. Botha as leader of
the National Party and President of South Africa by F.W. de
Klerk in 1989 was connected to the rise in violence, rapid economic disinvestment and thus panic on the part of the white
elite, de Klerk took personal risks for peace and drove the negotiations forward in a way that Botha would have been unable to
do had he remained in office. One analyst of the South African
conflict puts the case for leadership starkly, though perhaps
underplays the structural imperatives for negotiations to take
place. 'Had P.W Botha not fallen ill in 1989 and been succeeded by de Klerk, the apartheid system may have continued
for at least another decade. The main success of political leadership has been with the cultivation of relationships between
some key players which led to the new constitutional arrangements.'[26] Nelson Mandela epitomizes for many the importance of leadership in bringing armed conflict to an end.
Commenting on the destabilizing effects of violence in the
context of the negotiations between the ANC and the National
Party, Mandela illustrated that this can also act to bind interlocutors together through fear of the alternative.

> Whenever things threatened to fall apart during our negotia-
> tions – and they did on many occasions – we would stand
> back and remind ourselves that if negotiations broke down
> the outcome would be a blood bath of unimaginable propor-
> tions and that after the blood bath we would have to sit down
> again and negotiate with one another. The thought always
> sobered us up, and we persisted, despite many setbacks.[27]

In the context of Northern Ireland, the leadership of Gerry
Adams was obviously crucial to the move by militant republicanism to pursue a negotiated settlement with unionists and

the British government. However, this was connected to a wider structural recalibration, where involvement by the Irish government and the Clinton White House would help overcome unionist/British 'securocrat' resistance to political change. Similarly, the replacement of Margaret Thatcher (Irish republicanism's *bête noire*) by John Major as British Prime Minister in 1990 paved the way for secret dialogue to begin between the Provisional IRA and the British government. The election victory of Tony Blair as British Prime Minister in 1997 moved the negotiations on a further stage and led directly to the restoration of the IRA cease-fire in July 1997, which paved the way for direct negotiations to begin between Sinn Fein and the Ulster Unionist Party. In her examination of the role of leadership during the Northern Ireland negotiations, Cathy Gormley-Heenan recognizes the connection between matters of structure and agency and describes a more organic form of 'chameleonic leadership' characterized by its inconsistency. 'The dichotomies of heroes and villains, foxes and lions, positive and negative leaders, power wielders and power seekers, ignores the likely difficulties in assigning villainy in matters of politics. . . . Chameleonic leadership is grounded in the reality of politics, which is much more complex and nuanced.'[28]

It is certainly true that political leadership is necessary for negotiations to succeed in ending violence, but this is itself inextricably linked to changes of structure and context within the conflict itself. During a particularly tense period in the negotiations in January 1998, when Protestant loyalist support for the process had begun to wane, British Secretary of State Mo Mowlam took the unprecedented political risk of visiting paramilitary prisoners in the Maze jail in an effort to maintain the loyalist cease-fire and their interest in political dialogue. This visit resulted in the loyalist prisoners accepting the explanations that were given by the Secretary of State and buying more time for the negotiations to progress. This has been widely seen as Mo Mowlam's biggest political risk during her period in Northern Ireland, but equally as a critical turning point for the negotiations that eventually led to the Good Friday Agreement in April 1998. Mowlam's recollection of the incident illustrates the importance of third-party actors in having a sophisticated understanding of the tensions that often surround these types of negotiations between warring factions.

> This meeting was very important to all of us, a point that was not brought out by the media. These men knew the peace process was fundamental to their futures and the future of their country. They took what they were doing very seriously indeed, and that was why it had been crucial to go and see them. By the very act of visiting these men they knew that I was taking them seriously. It was really of very little importance what was said – it was the act itself that held the meaning for them.[29]

Crucial leadership roles were also played by the other main protagonists in the Northern Ireland negotiations. David Trimble, leader of the Ulster Unionist Party, took a substantial political risk by agreeing to the final details of the Good Friday Agreement without prior weapons decommissioning. This resulted, as noted, in a major split in his party and his eventual resignation as its leader. Tony Blair and Bertie Ahern, meanwhile, the Prime Ministers of the UK and Ireland, respectively, demonstrated their leadership skills and commitment throughout the negotiations. This was especially necessary in the run-up to the deadline of 9 April, when they cleared their diaries to attend the negotiations and become directly involved in the discussions between the parties. Bertie Ahern left the talks to attend his mother's funeral and returned the following day to resume his involvement. Mo Mowlam recalls: 'The loss he felt was evident, but he kept his emotions under control and kept focused on the talks. His commitment to try and find a solution at a difficult time for him personally showed a great deal of courage. The other party leaders recognized it too.'[30] George Mitchell, the Chair and central mediator of the talks, is in no doubt about the importance of Blair's leadership role to the outcome.

> Blair possesses the elements of effective leadership in our era. He is intelligent, articulate, decisive, and photogenic. He knows the issues of Northern Ireland very well and has the courage to use his enormous political popularity to take risks for peace. His coming to Northern Ireland was a big gamble. There was no assurance of success, and most political consultants would have told him to stay away. But Blair came, and he had an immediate impact.[31]

In recognition of the UK Prime Minister's leadership role, the Irish government made a £5 million endowment to a Tony Blair Chair in Irish Studies at the University of Liverpool in 2007. Bertie Ahern commented on Blair's role in the peace process when he announced the initiative. 'It is a fitting way to mark Tony Blair's immense and historic contribution in helping bring peace to Ireland. It is a contribution that will be remembered by Irish people all over the world for as long as the history of our country is read and written.'[32]

In the case of the Oslo process that led to agreement between the PLO and the government of Israel, the leadership of Prime Minister Rabin and his Foreign Minister, Shimon Peres, together with that of Arafat and his senior colleagues, was clearly vital to the success of the initiative, despite the inherent flaws that were contained within it. Rabin sought to progress what his predecessor Yitzhak Shamir later admitted he was attempting to stall. 'I would have conducted negotiations on autonomy for ten years, and in the meantime we would have reached half a million people in Judea and Samaria.'[33] In other words, Shamir would have given the appearance of wanting to negotiate in order deliberately to undermine the talks and ensure that they would not bring about political change. Shamir rejected the 'land for peace' basis of the Madrid negotiations but Rabin endorsed this approach as it was being actively pushed by the US administration and was favoured by the electorate in Israel at the time. To this extent, therefore, Rabin's significant leadership role was in tune with wider changes in the structural context of the political conflict in the Middle East. Nevertheless, Rabin undertook what Shamir had set his face against and the risks he took in pursuit of a negotiated settlement with the PLO would ultimately cost him his life in 1995. Rabin was assassinated by an Israeli radical, Yigal Amir, who sought to use violence to precipitate a crisis in the negotiated agreement reached through the Oslo process and to reverse the policy being pursued by the Rabin government. Despite the wave of internal sympathy for Rabin and international condemnation of the assassination, the subsequent election was won by Likud's Benjamin Netanyahu, who defeated Rabin's successor, Shimon Peres, the chief Israeli architect of the Oslo negotiations. Peres declared at Rabin's funeral that his assassination would not derail the peace process. 'I see our people with tears in their eyes, but we know that the bullet that killed you cannot kill the idea you started. You did not leave a last will and testament, but you left a road upon which we will march with faith and determination.'[34] A few months later, of course, that faith had evaporated and the march on the road to peace had slowed considerably, as the new government (and the new Prime Minister) were opposed to the fundamental architecture of the 'land for peace' deal that had been negotiated with the PLO.

Political negotiations and subsequent agreements reached to end intra-state conflict are often derailed by those outside the process who believe that it undermines their interests, and it is to these 'spoiler' groups that we must now turn our attention.

CHAPTER FOUR

Resistance to the Peace

Wars begin when you will, but they do not end when you please.

Machiavelli[1]

Clearly, the road to ending war is a long and arduous journey, and even in relatively successful cases where negotiations result in political agreement, the whole process of moving out of violence can be destabilized by those with a reason and the capacity to resist change. This chapter examines the motivations and impact of those who resist peace agreements and the efforts to bring armed conflicts to an end. These individuals and groups are often referred to by social scientists as 'spoilers' and by the media as 'wreckers', 'insurgents' or, at the very least, 'radicals'.

This chapter will examine who resists peace agreements and why they do so, using case studies that include Bosnia, South Africa, Israel/Palestine and Northern Ireland, where powerful local actors have attempted to undermine political initiatives to bring armed conflict to an end. The chapter attempts to refine the concept of 'spoiler' groups,[2] arguing that not everyone who tries to resist a peace process is trying to wreck the chances of bringing political violence to an end. With this health warning in mind, it is nonetheless inevitable that for some of those who played no part in constructing a political settlement, or who see little personal or group advantage in its terms, resistance will follow. This is important in the context of this book's focus on ending wars, because violence often intensifies after the failure of political initiatives aimed at securing negotiated settlements. In some cases, therefore, where resistance to the terms of a settlement has led to the breakdown of negotiations, efforts to bring political conflict to an end really can be worse than useless. The clearest example of this is presented by the Rwandan genocide in 1994, which was triggered – though not caused by – the failure of the 1992 Arusha peace agreement. Similarly, violence rose in Sri Lanka and Angola following failed efforts to negotiate peace settlements. Those who seek to resist political accommodations to end violence are clearly a vital consideration for anyone involved in constructing attempts to bring such violence to an end.

Groups who may have a self-interest in violent conflict continuing, or who disagree with the political terms under which the war is being ended, may try to destabilize efforts to bring the war to a close. This is particularly relevant within intrastate warfare where some actors have political and economic interests in its continuation and may lose out if the conflict is brought to an end. Paul Collier popularized this resistance with the phrase 'greed or grievance' in his econometric study of the resistances to ending violence within civil wars. For Collier and his co-author Anke Hoeffler, those seeking a continuation of violence within civil war contexts are motivated more by greed than by grievance.[3] While Collier came up with a useful phrase, his analysis of the reasons why some groups choose violence over peace has come in for some sustained criticism over the last several years, not least because it tends to under-emphasize the role of the state in the continuation of violent conflict and is worryingly rebel-centric. As Karen Ballentine and Heiko Nitzschke have commented, the greed and grievance theory interprets the political significance of statistics without a sufficiently nuanced understanding of the complex conflicts concerned, the motivations of those within them or indeed how such regions have changed over time.

> While some may participate in war economies to 'do well out of war', others may do so out of the sheer need to survive, while still others may be coerced for their labour and land. Furthermore, individual motivations may change over time as conflicts mutate. Conflicts that begin as predominantly 'grievance'-based may over time be complemented and, for some, even surpassed by pecuniary motives. In fact, such mutation can be witnessed in the protracted conflicts of Colombia and Angola. Determining just which motivations matter where and when requires more careful categorisation of different behaviours and empirical validation.[4]

In other words, the reasons why some people try to resist peace settlements and maintain campaigns of violence are varied, complex and often context-specific. This chapter, therefore, explores the ways in which certain factions have tried to undermine efforts to end wars. Who are the 'spoilers'? How do their motives and strategies differ from one another, and are these people necessarily 'extremists' in favour of a continuance of violence? As Edward Newman and Oliver Richmond have noted, for example, '[W]e cannot necessarily assume that all peace processes are equitable or fair to all parties. Thus, the act of labelling a particular group as a "spoiler" may reflect a political agenda which is an extension of the conflict itself, or the interests of third parties.'[5] The reasons for resistance of a negotiated peace settlement can be complex, the strategies can be diverse and the impacts can be varied. The motives behind such resistance can be ideological or pragmatic; the strategies need not necessarily be violent and might, for example, include outward acceptance. The effects of such resistance can range from the negligible to the seismic, depending on the skill of the resisters, the support they can muster and the context within which they are operating.

Why Resist the Ending of War?

Many of the direct actors and some indirect actors in war may have a vested economic or political interest in the maintenance of armed conflict and may seek to destabilize any cease-fires or negotiations that emerge. To put it in simple terms, there is profit to be made from violence and 'war economies' often grow up around a conflict, providing an economic rationale for its continuation as local actors fight turf wars for resources and control. The Democratic Republic of Congo provides a textbook example of the way in which wars are frequently accompanied by the destruction of the civil economy (agriculture, cattle farming, internal trade and commerce) and the emergence of sporadic profiteering from governing factions or military forces. These groups have used the cover of war to exploit rich mineral deposits in the DRC such as coltan, diamonds, gold and tropical hardwoods, aided and abetted by regional governments such as Zimbabwe and multinational companies eager to share in the spoils.[6] Charles Taylor's role as President of Liberia during the 1990s epitomized this trend, as he used the coercive agencies of the state to cartel the diamond trade, build his own personal fortune and pay off local militias in return for their loyalty.[7]

While often regarded as an internal phenomenon, there is plenty of profit to be made from war outside of the conflict zone as well. The international arms industry has substantial financial and therefore political power and there is a correlation between developed counties that are the producers of arms and developing nations that are the unfortunate consumers of these weapons. As David Keen has pointed out,

> [I]t is worth noting that at the international level, the military industrial complexes dating from the Cold War era can be argued to have a vested interest in the continuation of conflicts of some kind. . . . The five permanent members of

the UN Security Council (the US, Russia, China, France and Britain), although charged with the primary responsibility of preserving global peace and security, are still responsible for 85 per cent of global arms sales.[8]

This view is corroborated by the human rights NGOs Oxfam and Amnesty International in their 2006 report *Arms without Borders*. 'In 2005, the traditional big five arms-exporting countries – Russia, the USA, France, Germany and the UK – still dominated global sales of major conventional weapons, with an estimated 82 per cent of the market.'[9] Despite public moralizing on the iniquities of warfare, Western countries have pushed their way to the front of the queue when it comes to providing the weapons of war through the multi-billion dollar arms industry. It will not surprise many readers of this book to learn that the largest players in the international arms trade (USA, Russia, France, Germany and the United Kingdom) overlap almost completely with the permanent members of the UN Security Council.

While it would be unfair to accuse either the United States or the United Kingdom of consciously trying to undermine peace negotiations and prolong violence in its foreign policies, these countries certainly do have an economic and political interest in maintaining (and expanding) their arms industries and, indirectly at least, facilitating the continuance of violent conflicts around the world. The point here is not that countries such as the US, UK and China are directly 'spoiling' peace processes that might end wars, but that their leading role in the manufacture and sale of weapons inevitably affects perceptions of victory amongst the direct actors in those conflicts. The provision of weapons (especially small arms) to countries such as Sierra Leone provides the tools for war to continue and bolsters the belief among some of the protagonists that they have the capacity to sustain the violence. This in turn damages the development of a mutually hurting stalemate or a ripe moment within which dialogue might make progress. Seen from this perspective, Western states (and the United States in particular) act as *invisible spoilers* to the ending of violence.

It is certainly the case that sustaining an armed conflict can produce its own political economy, fuelling the arms industry, increasing internal resources allocated to the security services and facilitating the black economy with smuggling and extortion opportunities. Armies have to be paid and military leaders like to expand their physical size, their economic resources relative to other segments of society and their political clout. As an example, the 2006 *BBC Richard Dimbleby Lecture*, given by General Sir Mike Jackson, was entitled 'Defence of the Realm in the 21st Century'. In a forthright address, the UK's former Chief of the General Staff made the link between the role of the UK's armed forces and the resources available to them, arguing that the army was over-stretched, under-resourced and under-valued.

> Let me now focus more sharply on the Armed Forces themselves as indispensable tools to achieve the country's objectives. Where are we? Have we got it right? Do we have what we need? Well, no, I don't think we have – certainly not entirely. . . . The defence budget at some 32bn pounds is just over two per cent of our gross national product, having been at the end of the Cold War double or more that figure. It's some five-and-a-half per cent only of the 550bn pounds which is today's Government spending. . . . When thinking about those percentages you might care to reflect as to whether they represent the importance, the proportionate importance, of what the Armed Forces do for this country and what they may have to do in the future. . . . The inescapable deduction therefore is that the funding allocated on the basis of assumptions is inadequate, because the virtual world defined by those assumptions has been overtaken by the real world. There is therefore a mismatch between what we do and the resources we are given with which to do it.[10]

Ending wars often has implications for the size, shape and function of these security services and may result in a demilitarization of the region and a reduced role for military forces. In the context of the Northern Ireland peace process, some have alleged that 'securocrats' have deliberately tried to undermine negotiated agreements because of the impact this would have on the power and resources of the security services. These allegations were fuelled in October 2002 following a police raid on the Sinn Fein office at Stormont and the arrest of a leading Sinn Fein administrator, Denis Donaldson, on a charge of spying for the Provisional IRA. The structures of the Good Friday Agreement were suspended shortly afterwards and the peace process was to remain in limbo from that point until March 2007. It subsequently emerged in 2005 that Donaldson was actually a *British* rather than an IRA spy and had been working for the British intelligence services periodically over a twenty-year period. In this case, the 'securocrats' in Northern Ireland were accused of arresting their own spy and, by doing so, precipitating a crisis in the peace process in an effort to protect their own interests and political power base.[11] Similar allegations were made by the ANC about the covert agenda of the security services in South Africa during the run-up to political negotiations with the National Party in the early 1990s. Stephen Ellis has written about the existence and activities of the so-called 'Third Force' in South Africa and its campaign of politically motivated violence in this period. 'At times, ANC leaders suggested that the government was perhaps not in full control of its security forces, and that these were intent on sabotaging negotiations completely or even creating conditions for a military coup.'[12]

Some of those involved may rely on the existence of war for status within their ethnic group and feel little incentive to move towards some form of civilian obscurity. Others may actually use warfare as a protective cloak and feel that their personal security or liberty would be threatened if a negotiated settlement was reached and old scores were quietly settled during the peace. This was the fate that befell the Serbian militia leader Željko Ražnatović, more familiarly known as Arkan, in the wake of the wars in former Yugoslavia and Kosovo during the 1990s. Arkan was indicted by the International Criminal Tribunal on Yugoslavia for acts of genocide and crimes against humanity, but was assassinated in 2000 while relaxing at a street café following an argument between criminal gangs. Once the infrastructure of warfare is removed, therefore, military leaders can become more vulnerable to physical attack, which may reduce their appetite for entering or supporting negotiations to end the conflict.

What is a Spoiler?

The greatest source of risk comes from spoilers – leaders and parties who believe that peace emerging from negotiations threatens their power, worldview, and interests, and use violence to undermine attempts to achieve it. . . . When spoilers succeed, as they did in Angola in 1992 and Rwanda in 1994, the results are catastrophic. In both cases, the casualties of failed peace were infinitely higher than the casualties of war. When Jonas Savimbi refused to accept the outcome of UN-monitored elections in 1992 and plunged Angola back into civil war, approximately 300,000 people died. When Hutu extremists in Rwanda rejected the Arusha Peace Accords in 1994 and launched a campaign of genocide, over 1 million Rwandans died in less than three months.

Stephen Stedman[13]

The term 'spoiler' has emerged in recent years as a short-hand for academic and policy analysts to categorize those opposed to a negotiated political settlement within war-torn societies. The term itself was coined in the late 1990s by Stephen Stedman to give form to the range of actors within civil wars who sought to resist and undermine negotiated settlements. It is an unfortunate term in the context of the complex and multi-faceted conflicts that are the subject of this book as it risks overly reductionist simplifications. Rather like the terms 'realist' and 'idealist' that so blighted discussions of international relations until relatively recently, to determine who 'spoilers' are and who they are not is to set up something of a self-serving binary discourse which does little to reflect the complexity of motivations within real-world cases. To be categorized as a 'spoiler' is to be labelled (implicitly at least) as an extremist who prefers violence to peace. More worryingly in the context of the post-9/11 global war on terror, will governments and transnational bodies such as the UN or the World Bank 'be tempted to label "spoilers" as "terrorists", with all the implications which would follow from this'?[14] At its most basic, to be a spoiler equates to being a problem in the wider political context. Thomas Weiss has referred to these groups as 'war entrepreneurs', which suggests a healthy degree of pragmatism.[15]

In some circumstances, of course, the dividing line between healthy debate and disagreement intended to hold political actors to account, on the one hand, and outright opposition to *any* form of peace settlement, on the other, can be difficult to define. Rejection of the *process* might not be the same as rejection of the *peace*, and it seems unwise to lump all of these motivations into the spoiler category *en masse*. While Stephen Stedman seeks to differentiate between various categories, such as 'limited spoilers', 'total spoilers' and 'greedy spoilers', this chapter argues that such labelling too easily collapses supposed spoiler activity with support for (or actual perpetration of) continued violence. Some of those who resist political efforts aimed at ending violent warfare or managing conflict may do so because they feel that these political processes are so seriously flawed that they will lead to the re-emergence of violence, or that they seek to end war by imposing unjust political and economic arrangements on one or more of the conflict parties. John Darby attempts to refine the spoiler typology by differentiating between 'dealers', 'mavericks', 'opportunists' and 'zealots'.[16] Peter Wallensteen discusses the potential of spoilers 'to undermine or slow down a peace process'[17] due to their ability to exert intra-communal muscle; this, in too easy a fashion, equates spoilers with opponents of peace and identifies the 'peace process' itself as being equivalent to moderation.

Edward Said was a critic of the 1993 Oslo Agreement between the PLO and Israeli government, and was certainly a spoiler in his opposition to that agreement and the subsequent US-inspired 'road map for peace' during the latter 1990s. In his searing critique of Oslo, *Peace and Its Discontents*, Said declared: 'When it was announced, I considered the Oslo Declaration to be an instrument of capitulation and when I was invited by President Clinton's office to attend the White House ceremony I refused, saying that for all Palestinians September 13th ought to be a day of mourning.'[18] However, Said's resistance to the 1993 Oslo Agreement does not mean that he advocated a return to the Palestinian *intifada*, or that he sought to destabilize the agreement for political or economic advantage.

The usage of Stedman's spoiler typology tends to focus on individuals and groups beyond the state level and shares certain rebel-centric characteristics with Collier's greed and grievance theory. Thus, rather than focusing on the structure of a political conflict and on the subtle indirect obstacles in the way of ending violence, the spoiler debate looks instead at agency and at the individuals and small groups that take advantage of structural failures within the political process. As an example, few analysts have cast the government of the United States or the United Nations as spoilers in the Israel/Palestine conflict. There are, of course, radical Palestinian groups who, in tandem with the government of Israel, have ratcheted up the level of violence in the area and made peace more difficult to achieve. However, it could be argued that this is a symptom of a wider spoiler presence, namely that of the international community, whose third-party failures have increased the space within which opponents to the peace process have prospered. One example of this will suffice. The decision of the United States and others, including the European Union, not to recognize Hamas as the democratically elected government of the Palestinian Legislative Council (PLC) following their defeat of the Fatah party in January 2006 arguably destabilized the region, imposed needless suffering on innocent people and further damaged Palestinian trust in finding a political route out of violence. Hamas secured a mandate in the election (albeit a narrow one), winning seventy-four seats in the council to Fatah's forty-five in a democratic contest, but were accused of destabilizing the region as a result. The Acting Israeli Prime Minister, Ehud Olmert, announced immediately after the result that Israel would not recognize the mandate of Hamas, or their right to form a government.

> It is clear that in light of the Hamas majority in the PLC and the instructions to form a new government that were given to the head of Hamas, the PA [Palestinian Authority] is – in practice – becoming a terrorist authority. The State of Israel will not agree to this. . . . Israel will not hold contacts with the administration in which Hamas plays any part – small, large, or permanent.[19]

The United States and the European Union reacted by freezing aid to the Palestinian Authority until Hamas recognized the state of Israel, renounced the use of violence and accepted previous agreements made between Palestinians and Israel. This was a severe financial penalty for the PA and for ordinary Palestinians in the region, as it amounted to approximately $600 million a year from the EU and around $400 million from the US.

Who are the spoilers here? Hamas for standing for office and obtaining a democratic mandate, or the international community for demonstrating that Palestinians can have a Hobson's choice, i.e. any democratic result approved of by Israel and the United States? The answers to these questions will, of course, depend on one's political view of the causes of political violence in the Middle East. Many will see the provision of aid being made conditional on the renunciation of violence by Hamas as entirely proper and a sensible incentive to encourage Palestinian militants to adopt exclusively peaceful methods. Others (including this author) believe that it is important to point out the double-standards at the root of this decision, namely that the government of Israel does not recognize Hamas, engages in violence against Palestinians on a daily basis and suffers no financial or political penalties from either the US or the EU for doing so.

The point here is that our definition of spoilers in peace processes often lies in the eye of the beholder and reflects pre-existing analyses of the dynamics of specific conflicts rather than meeting objectively definable criteria which can be de-contextualized from the region concerned. Thus, in the context of the Middle East at least, the spoilers of the author may not be those of the reader! Separating individuals and groups into spoilers and non-spoilers, wheat and chaff, good and bad, does little to encompass the complex and mobile patterns of behaviour that surround negotiations and settlements of violently divided societies. As Edward Newman and Oliver Richmond explain in their book on the subject: 'There is a capacity for spoiling in most actors at different phases of the process. Indeed, in some ways spoiling is part of peace processes, as much as conflict is a function of social and political change.'[20]

The preference here is to speak about *resisters* of negotiated peace settlements. The term 'resister' is less pejorative than spoiler and allows us to examine the range of motivations and strategies used by those who seek to resist the political settlement of violent conflicts.

Violent Resisters

The purpose here is not to argue that everyone is contaminated by resistance to peace settlements to some degree and that we are all therefore equally culpable in the perpetuation of violence. The aim, rather, is to broaden the perspective somewhat when we start allocating blame for human suffering and death as a consequence of war. It involves combinations of structure as well as agency, external as well as internal actors, and requires the physical resources to kill, in addition to the intent to do so.

Nevertheless, some opponents of peace processes clearly set out to destabilize cease-fires, negotiations or political agreements through the use of violence. It is not untypical for violence to increase as warring factions move down the road from pre-negotiation to settlement. This violence is rarely 'mindless', to use a popular media description, but is nearly always rational, targeted and media-aware. Groups who have been excluded from the political process, or who have broken away as a result of the compromises inherent in such dialogue, may use violent tactics in a pragmatic and cynical manner to destabilize the parties involved and undermine the political process. Stephen Stedman suggests that the likelihood of violent resistance within civil wars will increase if it involves more than two warring parties; if at least one of these parties is pursuing a secessionist claim; if coercion has played a significant role in producing a peace settlement; if the conflict involves in excess of 50,000 combatants; if neighbouring states oppose the settlement; and if valuable resources such as diamonds or minerals can be extracted from the region.[21] Those who engage in this form of violence will have a sophisticated understanding of the political dynamics within the region and how the tensions between opposing groups within political negotiations can be magnified and heightened. Thus, attempts may be made to shock public opinion by killing civilians or staging bombing 'spectaculars' to make it impossible for negotiations to continue or settlements to be implemented. In such circumstances, a rising level of violence can undermine what little trust there is amongst those involved in fragile negotiations, which might subsequently collapse amidst mutual recriminations and blame for the violence that has taken place.

On the other hand, violent resistance to negotiations can have the opposite effect, forcing reluctant delegates back to the table for fear of the alternative to a negotiated settlement, and even establishing internal solidarity within political talks due to the external hostility demonstrated by the perpetrators of violence. This was precisely what happened in the political process in South Africa during the early 1990s. While talks between the National Party government and the ANC had broken down twice due to rising levels of violence, the looming catastrophe of violent destabilization led to the establishment of the National Peace Accord between the ANC and the National Party government in September 1991, which was a precursor to the eventual Record of Understanding and the democratic transition that followed in 1994. Commenting on the role of violence in the context of the South African case, Tim Sisk points out that: 'Violence tends to polarise and impede negotiation when a single party is clearly culpable, but when parties are deemed by observers – especially by the international community – equally culpable, incidents of violence reinforce pressures to negotiate.'[22] The case of South Africa illustrates once again that violence was not simply a spoiling tactic, but was part of a much more complicated pattern of behaviour where some of those responsible for violence used it not to wreck peace talks, but to weaken opponents and produce a more favourable outcome in the negotiations. In this sense, resistance to the ending of armed conflict, even in its violent form, is malleable and can be seen as being an integral part of bringing political violence to an end.

Violent resistance can, of course, lack such perverse irony and may simply be aimed at wrecking a political process and maintaining an armed conflict. The assassination of Yitzhak Rabin by a Jewish radical in 1995 is an obvious example of an attempt to destabilize the Oslo process and policy of the Israeli government. At his trial, Yigal Amir stated that 'a Palestinian State is starting to be established. . . . Rabin wants to give our country to the Arabs.'[23] Amir's act of violence succeeded in its objective – in conjunction with other factors – notably the subsequent election victory of Likud leader Benjamin Netanyahu, who was a sworn opponent of the Oslo Agreement.

Violent resistance was also a feature of the peace process in Northern Ireland, before, during, and after the agreed settlement was reached in April 1998, but it evolved in terms of its sources and forms. Paramilitary violence rose prior to the declaration of cease-fires in 1994 in an effort to maximize the leverage of groups who wanted to emphasize their strength to both supporters and opponents. Forms of violence mutated, so that paramilitary groups who had committed themselves to cease-fires (or, more accurately in the case of the IRA in 1994, a 'complete cessation of military operations') could continue to conduct their affairs by beating people with baseball bats, hurling sticks and other 'non-weapons' such as concrete slabs. This pragmatic attitude to non-violence allowed republicans and loyalists to continue using coercion while maintaining publicly that their cease-fires were still intact. When Sinn Fein was excluded from the multi-party negotiations following the breakdown of the IRA cease-fire in 1996, violence was used as a 'sword of Damocles' against the British government and the other actors engaged in the talks, to indicate the violent potential of the organization if the peace process did not produce significant political change. This was backed up in practice with a curious form of proxy violence: bombs that failed to detonate; bomb-scares on the London underground; mortar bombs at Heathrow airport that failed to explode; and other similar incidents. The intention here was to demonstrate the violent *potential* of the republican movement, create disruption, annoyance, publicity and economic damage, without producing a death toll that would make it difficult for the British government or the internal parties in Northern Ireland to re-engage with Sinn Fein at a subsequent point in the process.

Once the IRA and loyalist parties were included in the negotiations, splinter groups emerged who tried to use violence to destabilize the Good Friday Agreement. The most obvious example of this was the emergence of the Real IRA, which was responsible for the Omagh bombing of 15 August 1998. This bomb attack killed twenty-nine people (plus two unborn children), which represented the largest single death toll of the Northern Ireland conflict. It was designed to destabilize the Agreement and make it difficult for the political parties to move forward in partnership with one another.

While we have been accustomed in recent years to the media and politicians equating political violence with 'terror', it would be a mistake to assume that this is an end in itself. Violent resistance to the ending of armed conflict is better viewed as a means to an end and as a strategy linked to a wider series of vested interests. As Kristine Hoglund has remarked in the context of violence in the Sri Lankan peace process, '[D]uring a negotiation process, violent acts can be committed by actors that are involved as well as those who are not involved in the peace talks. The purpose behind the violence will also differ, ranging from those actors who resort to violent behaviour for tactical gains, to those whose aim is to wreck the peace process altogether.'[24]

Peaceful Resisters

Those who seek to resist by violent means may frustrate or destabilize peace negotiations, but at least they are likely to be visible and articulate their demands/grievances towards the political process. Those who resist negotiated political settlements through non-violent means present a different set of problems and can be more damaging in the longer term to the prospects of armed conflict being brought to an end. Those actors who appear to be supporting an end to armed conflict may sometimes take part in negotiations in order to undermine them from within.

The example given in the previous chapter of Yitzhak Shamir, former Prime Minister of Israel, and his opposition to the 'land for peace' deal with the PLO is a case in point. Shamir's self-professed strategy was to participate in dialogue with Palestinians to placate international opinion, ensure that negotiations stalled and, in the meantime, strengthen the critical mass of the Israeli settler community to a point that it could not be reversed through negotiations.[25] While individuals such as Shamir may express their desire for an end to war and proclaim their opposition to violence, some may be more concerned with protecting their perceived vested interests or strengthening their political positions than they are with constructing or implementing a negotiated settlement. Others may declare military cease-fires or participate publicly in political dialogue as a means of avoiding international censure, delaying impending political change or, more cynically, wrecking a peace process from within, while maintaining the outward semblance of having a commitment to peaceful change. This type of behaviour rarely falls under the banner of spoiler activity but can be just as detrimental to the prospects for bringing warfare to an end.

To take another example, US Secretary of State Condoleezza Rice arguably played this role during the war in Lebanon in July 2006 by claiming that the conflict was one of the 'birth pangs' of a new Middle East. Rice openly opposed an early cease-fire in the war, alluding to the importance of the war *not* ending before Israel and Lebanon were sure that Hezbollah forces had been routed in a manner that would allow the region to be reshaped in a more stable fashion.

> A ceasefire would be a false promise if it simply returns us to the status quo, allowing terrorists to launch attacks at the time and terms of their choosing and to threaten innocent people, Arab and Israeli, throughout the region. That would be a guarantee of future violence. Instead we must be more effective and more ambitious than that. . . . What we're seeing here, in a sense, is the growing – the birth pangs of a new Middle East and whatever we do we have to be certain that we're pushing forward to the new Middle East not going back to the old one.[26]

As part of this effort, the US government fast-tracked the delivery of precision-guided bombs to Israel in July 2006 – at the same time as it spoke of the importance of humanitarian assistance for the people of Lebanon – and declared that Israel's response to Hezbollah was both an act of self-defence and a part of the global war on terror. Both the US and the UK governments gave the green light to Israel, not only to continue with their bombing of Lebanon, but also to go the extra mile in pursuit of what Rice argued was a more stable Middle East. An article in *Time* magazine at the end of July hinted at the impact of Rice's remarks on the region and pointed out the apparent ambivalence of the US government towards ending the war. 'It was revolutionaries like Lenin and Mao, after all, who rationalized violence and suffering as the wages of progress, in the way a doctor might rationalize surgery — painful, bloody, even risking the life of the patient, but ultimately necessary. Social engi-

neering is not surgery, however, and its victims find little comfort in the homilies of its authors.'[27] We can, of course, select
our own pet examples of this form of resistance to the ending
of wars as befits our own political prejudices. Nonetheless, it
illustrates that resistance to the ending of armed conflict comes
in many forms, is not limited to 'terrorist' groups and is an integral element of the wider political environment within which
that violence takes place.

One of the most notorious examples of non-violent resistance that led to more intensive warfare was presented by the
Arusha peace agreement in Rwanda in 1993 prior to the
genocide that took place in the following year. This negotiated
settlement was made between the Hutu-led government of
President Habyarimana and the Tutsi-dominated Rwandan
Patriotic Front (RPF). Unfortunately, this attempt to end the
civil war that had been underway since 1990 was never anything more than a paper tiger which failed to get adequate
internal or external support. It was signed due to pressure
from international actors and had little internal credibility
amongst either the Hutu or Tutsi communities. In 1990,
Habyarimana pledged himself to seeking a negotiated dialogue, under Organization of African Unity (OAU) auspices,
to bring the violence to an end. However, this commitment
was dependent upon both Tanzania and Uganda persuading
the RPF to declare a cease-fire and return to Uganda, which
everyone knew was highly unlikely. Habyarimana was in the
unenviable position of trying to manage external international pressure for reform while containing extremist Hutu
elements within his own party. While the Arusha negotiations eventually resulted in 'agreement', Habyarimana's
commitment did not extend far beyond the bland rhetoric of
working to 'eradicate the deep-seated causes' of violence.
In reality, Habyarimana was forced into it due to political
divisions within the Rwandan government, together with

pressure from regional African powers and the OAU. As Gilbert Khadiagala has illustrated in his analysis of the Arusha agreement, the threat of financial sanctions had also focused the mind of the Rwandan President on the negotiations during their final stages in 1993. 'Having suspended all but humanitarian assistance since early 1993, donor nations threatened to halt all funds if Habyarimana continued to procrastinate. . . . Despite the pattern of defiance and denial, military and economic pressure had delivered Habyarimana to the table and kept him there.'[28] While Habyarimana paid lip service to Arusha, extreme elements within his own party were at the very same time organizing and inciting the Hutu militia, the *Interahamwe*, to begin an organized campaign of assassination, 'a final solution' against Tutsis and moderate Hutus. These elements eventually assassinated Habyarimana, blamed it on the Tutsi community and used it to begin the slaughter, which commenced within an hour of his plane crash. With the benefit of hindsight, it is clear that the government of Rwanda resisted the end of armed conflict by both violent and non-violent means, with techniques of resistance that ranged from tactical diplomatic compliance, to the planning of genocide. Khadiagala's judgement of this violent episode seems reasonable. 'While [Habyarimana] could sustain the two-track strategy [of moderation and extremism] in the negotiations due to internal and external pressures, this strategy was untenable during the implementation and consequently cost him his life.'[29] Although tactical passive resistance gave way to active genocide, this, too, was rational and a cynical attempted power-grab by the Hutu elite against the Tutsis and those Hutu moderates who were pressing for a political accommodation. Gerard Prunier emphasizes that we should see the Rwandan genocide not as 'mindless' violence but as calculated, organized and rational activity.

It was anything but mindless. It was extremely carefully planned and well executed violence, because if you use mostly machetes to kill a million people, which is roughly the estimate, in the space of two and a half months, [that] is admirable. It requires extreme organization, extreme care, and extreme perseverance. . . . 90% of the people were killed with blunt instruments and with machetes, which means that day after day after day, crews of peasants including women were marshalled and taken to the fields exactly as if they had been reaping a crop and were killing people. . . . The political reason is once more extremely simple – it was the total elimination of the Tutsi as well, as a race, as the Hutu militants would say, as a group as we could say in a more neutral way.[30]

Christopher Clapham has noted that the Rwandan case demonstrated the capacity of the *conflict resolution process itself* to act as a spoiler to peaceful outcomes within a divided society. 'The process of international mediation is not merely an attempt to resolve a conflict at some point in the future; it is also a political intervention which carries important implications for the balance of advantage in that conflict in the present.'[31] As Marie-Joelle Zahar has illustrated in her work on the concept of spoilers in peace processes, the likelihood of internal parties seeking to resist negotiated settlements is often connected to the commitment of external parties to the agreement. This could certainly be said to be true of the Arusha agreement as it was clear to all and sundry that the international community had little political will and less staying power to see the agreement implemented effectively. 'Third party commitment to a given peace process can shape the opportunity structure of would-be spoilers. When third parties offer credible guarantees to the factions, they increase the costs of spoiling and thus decrease its likelihood.'[32] While this analysis may overplay the cost–benefit analysis of conflict actors, some of whom may simply be motivated by a desire for revenge, it seems reasonable to assume that those who resist peace agreements designed to bring armed conflict to an end have (from their perspective) good reasons for doing so.

The question to be asked, therefore, is not are some groups resisting the end of armed conflict, but rather why are these groups doing so and are any strategies available to transform such resistance?

There are, of course, those who enjoy the act of killing itself and warfare can be a convenient cover providing an opportunity structure for psychopaths and others who might be reluctant to give up violence. However, for the vast majority of those who resist peace processes either passively or actively, their opposition will be based on a rejection of the political process and, as such, their behaviour will be subject to modification as the context, issues and actors evolve over time. If this rational actor model is true, then those cast above as 'spoilers' have the potential to alter their positions to the point that they support the political process and advocate an end to violent conflict.

In the Northern Ireland context, both Ian Paisley and Gerry Adams have moved (at different times) from positions of resistance, to a point where they are both now advocates of the political process and peaceful co-existence. These positions did not change because of Road to Damascus conversions, but evolved over time as part of the wider context within which the peace process emerged. For Adams, the belief that unionists had a veto on political change and that the British government had a vested interest in the occupation of Ireland and could only be removed through an armed struggle gave way to the belief that participation in the democratic political process, as mediated by the Good Friday Agreement, would advance the goals of Irish republicanism in a way that violence could not. For Ian Paisley, the belief that the Irish state, the British government and nationalists within Northern Ireland were bent on undermining the constitutional position of Northern

Ireland within the United Kingdom, and that the Provisional IRA was committed to using violence for this purpose, has shifted. Paisley and the majority of his colleagues in the Democratic Unionist Party seem to have accepted – to the astonishment of outside observers – that Irish republicans have ended their war and that the Good Friday Agreement has the capacity to satisfy their vested interests and their British identity.

In the case of South Africa, armed conflict between the ANC and the white minority drew to a close when those who were engaging in the violence came to the conclusion that a political route was both desirable and achievable. Within the framework of the peace process itself, one of the main resisters, the Inkatha Freedom Party (IFP), was partly motivated by the belief that its interests would be damaged by an ANC-dominated government and black majority rule. At a more pragmatic level, its resistance to the Record of Understanding in the early 1990s was based on its exclusion from the process and the clear bilateral negotiations taking place between the ANC and the government. While some have cast the violence that took place between the IFP and the ANC during this period as 'tribal' in nature, it is more accurately viewed as being strategic and targeted, as well as being precipitated by those 'securocrats' who wished to foment violence as a means of dividing the non-white community.

The obvious question is this: why did the positions of these erstwhile resisters in Northern Ireland and South Africa change so dramatically? The most credible answer is because their resistance was related to the conflict itself and woven into the peace process that surrounded efforts to end the violence over a number of years. In other words, their resistance transformed in response to the changing context of the political process. In both cases, the direct actors came to the view that their goals and interests could not be achieved through the violent status quo and slowly came to accept both the need for and the possibility of a negotiated settlement. The argument here is that the vast majority of those who resist the end of armed conflict have the potential to be converted to advocates of peace settlements if they believe that their grievances and perceived vested interests can be satisfied.

To reiterate a central theme from earlier in this book, those who engage in war do so (in the main) for political reasons. These are usually complex and varied and may depend on the regional context involved. Nonetheless, such groups will usually view warfare as a tactic for the pursuit of political objectives that they believe cannot be attained by other means. If we accept this, then it follows that we may all exist along the axis of the 'spoiler' curve, depending on the degree to which a peace process deals effectively with our grievances, interests and identities. This was certainly true in the case of Edward Said's opposition to the Oslo process in the Middle East and suggests that we will all resist at some point if we believe that our core interests or values are being bypassed by the political process. Said's rejection of the Oslo Agreement illustrated his resistance to the poltical *process* and to elite accommodation between the PLO leadership and the government of Israel, rather than to the ending of armed conflict *per se* between Palestinians and Israelis. 'Always disunited and dithering, the Arabs have simply lost the will to resist. They now hope to gain acceptance from the United States and Israel by negotiations begun through an act of abjection that betrayed both the cause of liberation and those people – Arabs, Jews and others – who sacrificed their lives on its behalf.'[33]

Those who resist the ending of political violence rarely do so lightly, usually adopt this position for rational reasons and are themselves a product of the wider political environment within which their resistance is carried out. When this environment changes in a positive way, the pattern of resistance has the potential to evolve in a more peaceful manner. However, as the next chapter will illustrate, when the political environment takes a more negative turn, active and passive resistance to the ending of war can become extremely difficult to overcome.

CHAPTER FIVE

Ending the Global War on Terror

So far this book has focused mainly on the dynamics of intra-state wars and how this form of violence can be brought to an end through processes of political dialogue and negotiation. This chapter examines the aftermath of what has often been cast as a paradigm-shifting event, namely the September 11, 2001 attacks on the United States and the subsequent 'global war on terror' (GWOT).

In terms of the central theme of this book, the relevant question to ask is: can the global war on terror be brought to an end, and if so, how? To consider this we first must understand the dimensions and dynamics of the GWOT. The underlying argument of this chapter intersects with a central theme expressed elsewhere in the book, namely that the GWOT is the product of a destructive set of human relations and structural conditions and is not an inevitable force of nature. This war *can* be ended but is actually being prolonged and self-generated by those who advocate and prosecute the GWOT. The arguments that 9/11 and subsequent terrorist actions are part of a non-negotiable religious war, or that these acts were unconnected to the foreign policies of the US and its allies, are unconvincing. This is a war conducted by rational beings in pursuit of political goals. Fanatics Al-Qaeda may be, extremists, certainly – but they are not without rational aims and objectives. When these actors perceive violence to be an obstacle to, rather than a catalyst for, the attainment of these objectives, a political resolution may be possible.

Within that dwindling group sometimes referred to as the 'coalition of the willing', the GWOT is an unwinnable war fought against a disembodied enemy with (at best) hazy aims and objectives. This is a war of values fought against networks such as the Taliban and Al-Qaeda, and against states who harbour them. Yet there is a logical disconnect at both conceptual and operational levels. Waging a war in pursuit of values makes it difficult to maintain the separation between perpetrator and victim, not to mention the gap between protectors of freedom and the 'evildoers'. More immediately there is a noticeable gap between the identified enemies (the Taliban and Al-Qaeda) and the subsequent invasion of Iraq and occupation of the country. As David Keen has remarked: 'In many ways, we are witnessing a return to magical thinking – the belief and hope that we can re-order the world to our liking by mere force of will or by actions that have no logical connection to the problem we are addressing.'[1] One of Keen's central themes is that the pursuit of the GWOT and the *perception* that this is a just war which is being won are more important to the US and its allies than actually winning it. From this standpoint, the GWOT operates in the US rather like the Cold War functioned in the 1950s and 1960s, where the identification of an external threat maintained internal cohesion, provided political credibility for the regime and sustained the capitalist system. The GWOT is seen from this angle not as a destination, but as a never-ending journey, where the thirst for the goals of victory and security can never ultimately be quenched.

The GWOT cannot be won militarily as it is based on a fundamental paradox – the more it is violently pursued, the stronger its opponents become and the more spurious are the values that ostensibly underpin it. Like other violent conflagrations examined in this book, a mutually hurting stalemate is forming which might eventually contain the seeds for a ripe moment to emerge. In the context of Afghanistan, it seems clear that a mutually hurting stalemate has already been reached, in military terms at least, a fact recognized by a 2008 report issued by the Atlantic Council of the United States entitled *Saving Afghanistan.*

> Make no mistake, NATO is not winning in Afghanistan. . . . On the security side, a stalemate of sorts has taken hold. NATO and Afghan forces cannot be beaten by the insurgency or by the Taliban. Neither can our forces eliminate the Taliban by military means as long as they have sanctuary in Pakistan. Hence, the future of Afghanistan will be determined by progress or failure in the civil sector.[2]

Understanding the Global War on Terror

To discuss ending the GWOT, we must first understand it. The attacks on New York and Washington on September 11, 2001 killed approximately 3,000 people and changed the focus of international politics. From this point forwards, the emphasis of powerful Western countries, and the United States in particular, moved in two directions. Regionally the spotlight was trained more consistently on the Middle East with a more direct link made between the region and perceptions of national security in the developed West. In operational terms, this shifted the locus of interventionism to a strategic pragmatism, where resources, alliances and coercive diplomacy revolved around the ultimate goal of winning the war on terror. Conceptually the focus moved from ethnic violence to the scourge of international terrorism. Politically, meanwhile, the developed world, which was used to observing warfare at several removes or through media reportage, found itself directly involved in armed conflict and implicated in violence that was either directed at it, or undertaken in its name. As Roland Dannrauther has suggested, the end of the Cold War in the early 1990s allowed people in the developed West to breathe a

collective sigh of relief, and apart from those caught up in
ethnic violence, the threat of war for most seemed to be contained within a few regional hotspots in less developed areas
such as sub-Saharan Africa or less stable locations such as the
Balkans. 'Violence and war was . . . something that happened
to "them" and not to "us". The principal impact of 9/11 was
radically to subvert this confidence and self-assurance, demonstrating that violence and death could be inflicted on the
richest and seemingly most secure parts of the North.'[3] It
punctured the self-assurance and confidence of Western countries – the US in particular – that they were secure and it
changed the early Bush Presidency's isolationist perspective,
temporarily at least. As Ivo Daalder and James Lindsay, who
both worked in the Clinton administration, have pointed out,
9/11 introduced the US 'to the threats that most other countries faced on a daily basis, and showed the perils of trying to
go it alone in a dangerous world'.[4] Michael Cox points out that
the attacks shocked the US and forced it to question its sense
of power and security. 'Almost in an instant, Americans were
forced to confront the fact that no amount of power could
bring them either the security they sought or the security they
thought they had already acquired.'[5]

The 9/11 attacks were understandably condemned as being a
heinous act against defenceless civilians, and while the location
was the United States, the victims came from around the world.
The headline in the French newspaper *Le Monde* – 'We are all
Americans' – encapsulated the immediate reaction to what for
many observers seemed to be an unprovoked terrorist attack on
innocent people.[6] The reaction of the United States was to
shape the Presidency of George W. Bush and reorient the institutions of government as well as the foreign policy of the US
and its allies. In his agenda-setting address to a joint session of
the US Congress on 20 September 2001, President Bush
claimed that the attack opened up a new departure in conflict.

> This is the world's fight. This is civilization's fight. This is the
> fight of all who believe in progress and pluralism, tolerance
> and freedom. . . . Freedom and fear are at war. . . . The
> course of this conflict is not known, yet its outcome is certain.
> Freedom and fear, justice and cruelty, have always been at
> war, and we know that God is not neutral between them.[7]

This was not a fight in which it was going to be easy to abstain
or articulate a nuanced political position, as the undertone of
the GWOT was that it was a war between fundamental values
which could not be mediated by pragmatism or compromise.
This concept of the GWOT favoured by Bush, Blair and the
neo-conservative cheerleaders within the US administration,
that of a war between mutually exclusive *values* rather than
a war over *interests*, made ending the conflict an extremely
remote possibility. While rival political interests can be com-
promised through bargaining-style negotiation, the values
held to be at the heart of the GWOT were non-negotiable. In an
effort to generate the 'coalition of the willing', President Bush
himself declared on 20 September 2001 that there was no neutral space in the war on terror and that those who were not
behind his response to the attacks would be deemed an ally of
those who had carried them out. 'Every nation, in every region,
now has a decision to make. Either you are with us, or you are
with the terrorists. From this day forward, any nation that continues to harbor or support terrorism will be regarded by the
United States as a hostile regime.'[8]

Leaving aside for the moment the operational dilemmas
associated with the GWOT, there were several fundamental
problems related to defining its boundaries. Aside from Al-
Qaeda, it was unclear *who* the enemy was to be targeted, apart
from terrorists broadly defined, and a number of regimes considered as 'rogue states' such as Afghanistan and Iraq. This
unseen enemy added to the perception of terror and to the
political imperative of dealing with it urgently. At one level the

threat was seen to come from terrorist networks such as Al-Qaeda and other cells around the world that used violence for political ends. This was almost immediately linked to sovereign states such as Afghanistan, Iraq, North Korea and Iran, who were seen as havens for such cells and who were believed to be bent on the development of weapons of mass destruction.

It was also difficult to determine how this war would be fought, how much it would cost and how long it would last. This was a striking departure for US policy since the disaster of the Vietnam war a generation earlier. Since that point, and in the context of the changing nature of warfare and rise of intra-state conflicts in the modern era, the United States military and the politicians they advised had shied away from open-ended military interventions. The lesson many had drawn from the Vietnam war was to avoid being sucked into a quagmire where the military got bogged down and the political goals of the war became confused and unachievable due to a lack of public support. Ivo Daalder makes this point when explaining why the first Gulf War in 1991 was so attractive to US military strategists. 'The Gulf War was the type of war the U.S. military wanted to fight: decisive force was employed in support of a clear objective and applied in overwhelming fashion, in order to minimize casualties and allow for a quick exit of U.S. forces.'9 This logic was turned on its head by the GWOT, which sought to fight a proactive open-ended war at a huge financial cost, against an enemy that was difficult to define beyond the 'terrorist' label and even harder to find.

The GWOT certainly represents a new paradigm in warfare symptomatic of the age of globalization where the enemy was primarily represented by terrorist networks that transcended geo-political borders and the traditional state system. Mary Kaldor delineated a new form of 'network war' in her book *Global Civil Society*, characterized by loose coalitions of sub-state actors with an organic cell structure and broad strategy of paramilitary action that did not differentiate between military and civilian targets.[10] This geographical evolution, where war had moved beneath and beyond the state, was connected to technology, as digital communications such as mobile phones, e-mail and the internet could be used by these cells to subvert surveillance and connect these disparate groupings beyond the ability of individual states to police them. This Network-Centric War (NCW) required a revolution in how states such as the US, UK and others who sought to fight the GWOT organized their military and intelligence communities.[11]

This has been associated with the strategic shift in the US military from firepower and size to information and mobility, known by the acronym RMA (Revolution in Military Affairs). RMA was a strategy which sought to adapt to the decentralization of warfare and the declining importance of the nation-state in armed conflict. This moved the emphasis from large, relatively centralized and heavily armed forces typical of the Cold War era, to dispersed mobile forces where the emphasis was placed on intelligence-gathering activities, information-sharing and communication across departments and across states using satellite technology. NCW required large-scale monitoring, data-gathering and analysis of communications within civilian populations and the ability to detect (and, it is hoped, stop) terrorist activities of the sort that resulted in the 9/11 attacks. In practical terms this relates to increasing the surveillance of people entering and leaving the country (through biometric passports, fingerprinting at airports, etc.), monitoring communications between people within the country on an ongoing basis, using coercive questioning of suspects (aka torture) to extract information likely to be of use in the GWOT, and introducing a raft of new legislation to facilitate all of the above on the grounds of national security.

While there has been much discussion about how 9/11 presented a new form of terrorism and re-formulated the response to it within the US military as well as internationally, some fundamental points of continuity can be observed with the violent conflicts that preceded it. The events of 9/11 and subsequent attacks such as the Madrid train bombings in March 2004 and the London attacks of July 2005 were similar in nature (though larger in scale) to guerrilla warfare tactics of previous conflicts. These groups used terror against civilian populations to exert political pressure and leverage upon national governments and transnational organizations. While often opaque, these networks had a rational set of political grievances and objectives which they pursued through violent means. They sought to achieve these aims through the use of force, surprise, no-warning attacks, and by skilfully using the media to create an impact beyond the physical attacks themselves. In structural terms, networks such as Al-Qaeda were mobile and adaptable, organized in a decentralized manner, with a cell structure that protected them from infiltration by intelligence agencies or informers. The 9/11 attacks were 'spectaculars', similar in nature to high-profile terrorist attacks of other groups unconnected to Al-Qaeda, but underpinned by the same logic. These terrorist spectaculars are designed to capture public and policy-making attention, due to either the level of casualties or the audacious nature of the attacks themselves, or both. The Beslan school kidnappings in September 2004 and Moscow theatre hostage crisis in October 2002 carried out by Chechen separatists are examples of similar activity, both of which had no connection to the supposed paradigm shift in terrorism since 9/11.

In many ways the response to 9/11 was very familiar and fits into classic counter-insurgency strategies practised by security services and national governments for a number of decades, which sought to deal with guerrilla armies that were militarily small but politically versatile. The GWOT was based on traditional techniques which combined the primacy of surveillance and military intelligence with a broader strategy linked to the importance of sapping the 'soft power' of such groups and 'winning the battle of hearts and minds' within public opinion. A major element of this strategy involves demonizing and criminalizing the enemy, emphasizing the illegitimacy of the terrorist act and the extent to which this conflicts with the core values of the civilian population. The parallel with President Bush's speech to Congress quoted earlier in this chapter hardly needs to be made.

The central distinction between the tactics inherent in the GWOT and the counter-insurgency strategies of the past lies not in repressive legislation which curtails civil liberties, the extension of surveillance techniques or even torture in custody as represented by the policy of 'extraordinary renditions', the events at Guantánamo Bay detention centre or those at Abu Ghraib jail. The difference is represented by the fact that these corner-stones of counter-insurgency affected *different people* after 9/11. Put more starkly, these techniques began to impinge on the lives of middle-class white people living in Western countries in ostensible democracies, rather than the relatively voiceless people of sub-Saharan Africa or the Middle East. By way of an example, it emerged in February 2008 that conversations between Sadiq Khan, a British Member of Parliament, and one of his constituents whom he had visited in jail were secretly recorded by British counter-terrorism officers in the UK during 2005 and 2006. This surveillance had been carried out on a member of the British government on the basis that his constituent had been suspected of operating websites supporting Taliban and Chechen militants (though he faced no charges in the UK) and was in jail awaiting extradition to the US.[12]

Despite the questionable success of the wars in Afghanistan and Iraq, the central problem with the GWOT was that its advocates misunderstood the capacity of military power. While this was capable of toppling regimes such as the Taliban or Saddam Hussein, it was much less effective in dealing with dispersed adversaries such as Al-Qaeda and the other terrorist networks it was seeking to eradicate. It could be claimed that the GWOT articulated an ideological commitment to defeating terrorism but in doing so confused the ends with the means. Terrorism is a methodology, not an ideology. As Roland Dannrauther puts it, 'As a method of political violence it is ideologically neutral.'[13] The GWOT was focused, therefore, on the *symptom* rather than the *cause* of the security problem. That particular elephant in the room was represented by the ongoing political conflict in the Middle East between Israel and the Palestinian community, itself an emblem of tensions between Arab states and developed Western nations. This connection is not the preserve of commentators on the left of the political spectrum and was made by President Bush himself during the war in Lebanon in 2006. 'As we work to resolve this current crisis, we must recognize that Lebanon is the latest flashpoint in a broader struggle between freedom and terror that is unfolding across the region. . . . The experience of September the 11th made it clear that we could no longer tolerate the status quo in the Middle East.'[14]

The policy stance of the US and its allies towards the conflict between Israel and the Palestinians became emblematic for many of the hypocrisy at the core of the war on terror. Violence escalated in the region with increasing numbers of Palestinian suicide bombings, on the one hand, and harsh Israeli government repression of the Palestinian community, on the other. Ariel Sharon's Likud government used the GWOT to convince President Bush to allow him free rein in the region on the basis that he was fighting the war on terror at a regional level. To add insult to injury from the Palestinian (and wider Arab) perspective, Sharon was doing so with US-supplied aircraft and munitions. The fact that US soldiers do not even bother counting the death toll among Iraqi civilians feeds the critique of the GWOT, namely that 'Operation Iraqi Freedom' was (or has become) a war of occupation rather than a war of liberation. There are, of course, nuances of opinion within Iraq itself over the US–UK liberation/occupation, with Kurds taking the former view, the Sunni Arab minority the latter and the Shi'a Arab majority hedging their bets between the two. It seems reasonable to suggest, however, that local enthusiasm for 'Operation Iraqi Freedom' has waned somewhat as the region has descended into civil war. Quantitative evidence would tend to corroborate this view, as reported by the Global Policy Forum.

> Polls have consistently shown that a substantial majority believe that the presence of US troops has increased violence in Iraq. . . . A common theory heard in the streets of Baghdad is that the US military is deliberately creating a civil war in Iraq to have an excuse to stay. In addition, a very large majority believes that the US will remain in the country, even if the Iraqi government asks it to withdraw, and that the US government plans to maintain permanent bases in the country – a view shared by all ethnic groups in Iraq.[15]

While the US administration realized that fighting the GWOT would be made easier by a de-escalation of Israeli–Palestinian violence, this was always seen primarily in security rather than in political terms. The Sharon government was to be encouraged (on rare occasions cajoled) to show restraint in its treatment of the Palestinian community. While periodic efforts were made to revive the dog-eared 'road map for peace', these lacked credibility and at no time was a fundamental reassessment of US policy towards the region seriously considered. This is illustrated not just by political rhetoric, which painted Palestinian suicide bombings as *heinous* and the Israeli Defence Force actions as *heavy-handed*, but also by material resources. Paul Rogers, writing in 2004, illustrates

how US commitment to the Sharon government was demonstrated by the provision of weapons and money. 'The [US]
administration remains firmly committed to Israel and even to
the Sharon government's hard-line policies. Israel remains the
largest recipient of US aid, the 2002 programme including
$2.4 billion in military aid and $730 million in other support,
close to one fifth of the entire US aid budget.'[16] Viewed
through a non-Western lens, therefore, the advocates of the
GWOT were speaking out of both sides of their mouths, facilitating and endorsing a terror regime in the occupied territories
while at the same time claiming to be campaigning against
repressive regimes who sought to develop and use weapons of
mass destruction.

Finally, the GWOT risked reducing a rich and diverse global
Islamic community to the belief systems – if not methodologies – of the Taliban and Al-Qaeda, and, through crass if not
brutal stewardship of the GWOT, producing the very thing it
was ostensibly trying to eradicate. While hindsight is the won-
derful luxury of those who write books rather than design and
implement policies, it is clear that the reaction to the 9/11
attacks on the US failed adequately to understand what the
cause of the security problem was, and pursued policies which
could only make it worse. This was wrapped up in emotional
and moralistic rhetoric which suggested that the GWOT was a
battle between freedom and servitude, civilization and fear,
good and evil. While this might have helped motivate people to
fight the war, it did not equip them to understand its causes or
possible remedies. This fact has been recognized by none
other than Zbigniew Brzezinski, former National Security
Adviser to President Jimmy Carter and not a figure associated
with leftist critiques of US foreign policy.

> The 'war on terror' has created a culture of fear in America.
> The Bush administration's elevation of these three words into
> a national mantra since the horrific events of 9/11 has had a

pernicious impact on American democracy, on America's psyche and on U.S. standing in the world. Using this phrase has actually undermined our ability to effectively confront the real challenges we face from fanatics who may use terrorism against us.[17]

President Bush declared the end of formal combat operations in Iraq from the USS *Abraham Lincoln* in May 2003, while Saddam Hussein was captured in December of the same year. While this amounted in all but name to a victory lap, it proved premature in the extreme, and while strategists of the GWOT thought they were winning, they were actually losing. Although estimates of casualties vary alarmingly (caused in part because the US military does not catalogue Iraqi deaths), most surveys agree that more people have been killed since 2003 than died during the formal military campaign. Over 4,000 US troops have been killed and over 30,000 wounded, while the body count among the Iraqi population since the invasion has been estimated to be as high as 655,000, taking account of non-battle-related fatalities such as disease. As often happens in war, the length of time it was taking to bring the violence to an end, together with the rising death toll among US and allied troops, damaged public support for the conflict within the US and elsewhere. The removal of Saddam Hussein and imposition of the ironically titled 'Government of National Unity' within the context of US occupation of a Middle East state which was presiding over a *de facto* civil war was nothing less than a recruiting sergeant for Al-Qaeda and other paramilitary groups who had framed the GWOT as an attack on Islam.

Can the Global War on Terror be Ended?

It is hardly earth-shattering to conclude that the global war on terror has failed to achieve its objectives. Moreover, it is reasonable to assume from the course of events since 2003 that it will continue to fail for as long as the policy of the US and its allies remains the same. To understand this fact is not to condone terrorism, despite Bush's 'you're either with us or against us' rhetoric at the beginning of his doomed campaign. There are several important corner-stones that could conceivably contain and eventually bring the GWOT to a close.

The first is a philosophical rather than an operational change, namely an admission that the war on terror has failed either to rid the world of terrorism, or to make those nations that advocate it more secure than they were before September 11, 2001. The second starting point for an end to the GWOT is an acceptance that it has actually facilitated and emboldened Al-Qaeda and other terrorist networks and made them stronger rather than weaker. This point has been conceded by none other than the US National Intelligence Council in its report *The Terrorist Threat to the US Homeland* in July 2007. It was admitted here that the US was actually in greater danger from an Al-Qaeda attack than it had been before the GWOT was initiated.[18]

While it will not be easy for the US and its allies to convince the Arab world that they are a benign global presence, they must at least return to diplomatic rather than military means of engagement and proper multilateral action through the United Nations, within the context of building new relationships in the Middle East. In his thoughtful book *Liberalism and War*, Andrew Williams provides a useful historical context within which to assess the post-9/11 world. In his careful analysis, Williams makes some judicious and convincing observations about the reasons why liberal interventionism went so badly wrong following the 9/11 attacks on the US. In comparing the successful multilateral intervention that accompanied the first Gulf War in 1990–1 with the war in Iraq of 2003 onwards, Williams points to the fact that liberal

consensus within the West was fatally undermined by US uni-
lateralism, and by its failure to engage with and consult the
United Nations. As a consequence, the 2003 war lacked legitimacy, popular support and anything amounting to a recog-
nizable international intervention. His conclusion pulls no
punches.

> Practically the two cases are no different. Ideologically they
> differ enormously, and the fault lies with those who were too
> impatient or too arrogant to understand the need of liberal
> world leaders to carefully nourish and promote a global coali-
> tion of like-minded democratic states. In that sense Blair and
> Bush are to blame for the deaths of many young Muslims in
> Iraq who have taken on the practically invincible American
> army equipped with their own courage and a few sticks of
> explosive, as well as for the deaths of the equally blameless
> young American and British soldiers who have paid the price
> of neo-con hubris.[19]

'Terrorism' of the type witnessed on 9/11 comes from long-
term grievances linked to 'experiences of sustained exclusion'[20] and not from opportunist acts of demagogues or
psychopaths. Whether or not this explains the mind of Osama
Bin Laden or his colleagues in Al-Qaeda, the fact is that the
GWOT has widened the space within which they can operate
and helped to justify their actions within the Arab world.
Rather than defeating terrorism, the GWOT has facilitated and
worsened it, presenting a remedy for an illness that risks
killing the patient it was designed to cure. US internment of
suspects at Guantánamo Bay, together with the torture of prisoners by American soldiers at Abu Ghraib prison, has acted as
a recruiting sergeant for Al-Qaeda and its allies. From this perspective, while the advocates of the GWOT preach to others
about good and evil, freedom and barbarism, they are guilty of
the very sins they accuse Al-Qaeda of committing. The argument that the world is a more dangerous place today than it

was on September 11, 2001 is not a difficult one to make, a 'no-brainer' in the American vernacular. However, the strategists behind the GWOT are largely the authors of their own misfortune. Ending the GWOT will only take place when the US understands that its homeland security is inextricably linked with its foreign policy and that efforts to 'root out the terrorists' will only succeed in creating new ones. This will present a paradox of Catch-22 proportions for Western policy-makers, where security measures must be at a level which matches the terrorist threat, yet each increase in security ratchets up that very threat.

In essence, however, the problem is a familiar one that has been covered in previous chapters of this book. Armed conflict is (in the main) a rational act pursued by those who believe it will further their vital interests/objectives. This form of terrorism is not apolitical behaviour carried out by psychopaths, though it undoubtedly attracts and harbours its share of such people. A recognition that Al-Qaeda is a product of a particular political environment and that it has a rational political agenda (however repugnant that agenda is) would be a useful starting point from which to proceed. While the war in Iraq and the GWOT are separate entities, they are conceptually linked, and ending the former is clearly a prerequisite to ending the latter.

Ending the War in Iraq

In operational terms the first item on the agenda needs to be US–UK military disengagement from Iraq followed by a series of political de-escalation measures, as set out in the 2005 Institute for Policy Studies report *Ending the US War in Iraq*.

> The continuing presence of the U.S. troops has strengthened, not weakened, the resistance. Resistance attacks are killing far more Iraqi civilians than U.S. troops, but the target of almost all the attacks remains institutions and individuals

associated with – and thus viewed as collaborating with – the U.S. occupation forces. . . . As with any guerrilla war, the Iraqi resistance is unlikely to be defeated by military means. Political and diplomatic solutions must be the key components to change the terrible situation Iraqis are in today.[21]

It is clear that support in the US for the war in Iraq has dropped significantly since 2003 as the US body count has increased, human rights abuses such as 'extraordinary renditions' and torture in Abu Ghraib prison have come to world attention, and as the conflict has dragged on with no end point in sight.[22] As has been argued throughout this book, this sense of stalemate and the recognition that a military victory is unlikely are often a prerequisite for more pragmatic policies to emerge. If the US and UK administrations do not *admit* that a military solution to Iraq's problems is impossible, they may nonetheless *accept* it. When this happens, a more positive range of political options becomes a more realistic aspiration. The changing climate in the US is reflected by the fact that both Senator Barack Obama and Senator Hillary Clinton in their campaigns to win the Presidential nomination of the Democratic Party advocated a US troop withdrawal in the short term. Clinton's website contained the following mission statement on Iraq which she clearly believed to be in tune with American public opinion.

> Our message to the president is clear. It is time to begin ending this war – not next year, not next month – but today.
> We have heard for years now that as the Iraqis stand up, our troops will stand down. Every year, we hear about how next year they may start coming home. Now we are hearing a new version of that yet again from the president as he has more troops in Iraq than ever and the Iraqi government is more fractured and ineffective than ever.
> Well, the right strategy before the surge and post-escalation is the same: start bringing home America's troops now. [23]

Commentators such as Richard Falk have already proposed a plan for ending the war which is based on military disengagement, the development of proper multilateral political dialogue with the Iraqi people involving the UN as well as regional actors such as Turkey and Iran, and a re-orientation of US policy towards the Middle East which recognizes the rights of the Palestinian people.[24]

It seems reasonable to believe that a military victory in Iraq is not possible and that a political route must replace military action in the region. Combined with the economic costs of the war to the US economy and fear of an imminent recession, this begins to resemble a mutually hurting stalemate. This could conceivably contribute to the end of armed conflict in the region if it was linked to a long-term political strategy that was based on US withdrawal from the area combined with local-level capacity-building sustained over a period of time. However, even in the best scenario, it is unlikely that this is a war that will end quickly. Any peace process in Iraq, like the others explored elsewhere in this book, is likely to be characterized by breakdowns in cease-fires that are eventually declared, mistrust at the local level and wrangling over any subsequent political or economic institutions that are proposed for the region. However, laying the foundations for peace in Iraq is far from impossible and can be done in the context of a re-evaluation of US foreign policy and within the broader framework of the GWOT. The 2006 report of the Iraq Study Group chaired by former US Secretary of State James Baker pointed out some harsh realities to the Bush administration in its assessment of US policy and the ongoing problems in the region.

> There is no magic formula to solve the problems of Iraq. However, there are actions that can be taken to improve the situation and protect American interests.
> Many Americans are dissatisfied, not just with the situation in Iraq but with the state of our political debate regarding

Iraq. Our political leaders must build a bipartisan approach to bring a responsible conclusion to what is now a lengthy and costly war. Our country deserves a debate that prizes substance over rhetoric, and a policy that is adequately funded and sustainable.[25]

President Bush thanked the Iraq Study Group for their efforts and promptly ignored most of their recommendations. As the next chapter will argue, the Bush administration's attempt at post-war reconstruction in Iraq merely built on foundations of sand. The political and civil institutions established post-Saddam have little internal or external credibility, have stimulated greater internal violence, and are likely to collapse the moment American and British troops withdraw from the country.

Ending the Global War on Terror

Conceptually, ending the GWOT presents some difficulties as it is a relatively open-ended conflict against a very loosely defined enemy, for at best vague (at worst spurious) objectives. Nonetheless, the GWOT can be brought to an end when its perpetrators – the US and its allies, on the one side, and Al-Qaeda and similar paramilitary networks, on the other – come to the conclusion (a) that they have reached a military stalemate and (b) that a political route is possible. As with other violent conflicts that have wound down, it seems reasonable to suggest that on the US side, at least, the ideological war is waning. For its part, Al-Qaeda has a series of political goals linked to rolling back Western occupation of Islamic countries and diminishing what it regards as the global subjugation of Muslims around the world. While this may be regarded as being a reprehensible agenda by some, it is nevertheless one capable of being open to dialogue and negotiation. More importantly, while cloaked in the rhetoric of fundamentalist

Islam, this is primarily a political project not a theological one. Al-Qaeda and its allies do not attack their targets for theological reasons so much as they do for political purposes, even though this is dressed up in the clothes of Jihad.

Andrew Williams points out an obvious dilemma here in that, in its present form, Al-Qaeda appears to be an impossible political interlocutor, committed as it is to the promotion of a worldwide Islamic Caliphate through violent means. 'An organization like Al-Qaeda which is prepared to wage war not only on "infidels" without mercy or quarter for civilians or military forces alike, or even on Muslims if they are considered "apostate" by the extreme standards set by Al-Qaeda, can have nothing to talk about to liberal democracies. They are quite simply incompatible.'[26] However, all organizations have varieties of opinion within them, ideologues as well as pragmatists (though admittedly perhaps more of the former than the latter in this case). As Al-Qaeda is a loose coalition rather than a formal organization, it is likely that here, too, there are zealots driving it forward and others who have been attracted to it out of a range of motives such as the actions of the West in pursuit of the GWOT. In another context, it was once said that the Provisional IRA was beyond the pale in Northern Ireland as it consisted of terrorists bent on human destruction who would not settle for anything less than its goal of a thirty-two-county socialist republic. While a hardcore remains within Irish republicanism which is committed to violent means, it has become marginalized as the energy that fuelled the 'armed struggle' burnt out. The point here is that while Al-Qaeda seems to be beyond political dialogue *today*, this might not always be the case, and stemming the flow of recruits into its ranks is something that can be addressed within the context of the foreign policy behaviour of Western countries. This does not mean conducting a policy of appeasement or turning a blind eye to murderous acts of sub-state demagogues, but a

useful starting point might be to desist from actions that but-
tress their ideology, underpin their methodology and swell
their support bases. It should also be remembered that the
'rogues gallery' of Saddam Hussein, Osama Bin Laden and
their cohorts were supported and sustained in the past by
Western governments and did not emerge from nowhere.

Beyond the starting point of recognizing that the GWOT has
increased the threat of the very thing it was supposed to eradicate, it is possible to conceive of this violent conflict being
brought to an end in the context of 'regime change' in the US
over forthcoming years. There is at least a *possibility* that the
new US administration will assess the benefits of the GWOT
and conclude the obvious, namely that the existing policy is
damaging rather than assisting the goal of national security. To
successfully begin the process of ending the GWOT, America
and its allies will need to embark on a root-and-branch re-
evaluation of domestic and foreign policies in a way that shifts
the emphasis from a zero-sum 'us and them' mentality to a
sense of inter-dependence between security and prosperity in
the West and in the Middle East. This may require action
around some or all of the following principles:

- There should be an acceptance that the perception of
  America and its allies by many in the developing world is of
  being over-bearing at best, imperialist at worst, and that
  this negative view is directly connected to (rather than separated from) the homeland security of developed Western
  states.
- There should be a serious engagement with the violent
  armed conflict in Israel/Palestine linked to credible third-
  party intervention and use of the considerable American
  financial leverage on the Israeli government to grant further
  autonomy to the Palestinian community, up to and including statehood. The connection between the GWOT and the

crisis in the Middle East was recognized by Tony Blair himself when addressing the US Congress in 2003.

> I want to be very plain: this terrorism will not be defeated without peace in the Middle East between Israel and Palestine. Here it is that the poison is incubated. Here it is that the extremist is able to confuse in the mind of a frighteningly large number of people the case for a Palestinian state and the destruction of Israel, and to translate this moreover into a battle between East and West, Muslim, Jew and Christian.[27]

- There should be a rolling back of the operational infrastructure of the GWOT and, in particular, repressive detention, including the use of 'extraordinary renditions' (torture) and the release of those prisoners at Guantánamo Bay who have not been found guilty of crimes against America or its allies.
- There should be a reversal of the policy of pre-emption announced by the Bush administration after the 9/11 attacks and recognition that US military power cannot ensure homeland security in the absence of wider external credibility for foreign policy issues.
- There should be a renewed emphasis on proper multilateralism through a strengthened, reformed and properly financed United Nations and a downgrading of US unilateral action. While this is not a panacea on its own, it is an important element in combination with other reforms.
- There needs to be a realization that the rebuilding of relations with Arab communities is vital, as well as a public articulation that the GWOT cannot be won by military means but must be pursued though the building of 'soft power' relations between the West and the Middle East.
- It must be recognized that terrorist acts will always take place in pursuit of some political agenda but that the best way of reducing these to a minimum is through building consensus-based relations with other states, reducing the

political and economic grievances that might produce such attacks and minimizing the wider support framework which terrorists require in order to operate.

Conclusion

The truism that there is nothing to fear but fear itself is not to trivialize the security problems faced by America, its allies in the GWOT and all of the rest of us. However, this is not a war that can be won by keeping the enemy from the gate, not least because no one is entirely sure who or where that enemy is. No amount of surveillance will be enough to apprehend those committed to carrying out attacks like the ones witnessed on September 11, 2001. No credible legislation can be enacted to protect us from such threats unless we are content to live in a police state or precisely the sorts of totalitarian regimes that the GWOT has itself critiqued. Robert Jackson and Philip Towle make this point with an historical analogy.

> Walls never keep out enemies for long, as the history of Hadrian's Wall and the Great Wall of China attest. Rather than building security walls, America and its allies would be better off to invest funds, energy and diplomacy to build bridges, reaching out and improving other people's lives and futures. . . . There can never be a permanent victory in the war on terrorism, nor perfect homeland security. America and its allies will need to learn to live with the risks of terrorism just as they do with some diseases and traffic accidents.[28]

This is surely wise counsel, and it is difficult to escape the logic that the underlying goals behind the GWOT can only be achieved by de-escalation rather than a further ratcheting up of police powers and curbing of civil liberties in the name of national security. By demonstrating that the West is not a malign imperial presence in Muslim countries; that it does not seek to occupy and control the oil supply in the Middle East;

that it will use its political and economic clout to make Israel observe its own obligations to the international community and to the Palestinian community in the occupied territories; and that it is sincere in its belief that *national* security is connected to *international* security issues, the US and its allies will substantially reduce the space within which terrorist networks thrive. This case is persuasively made in *Beyond Terror* by the Oxford Research Group, which advocates a policy of 'sustainable security' that looks beyond the concept of terror to the root causes of conflict within the international system.[29] 'The current approach to security is deeply flawed and is distancing the world's political elites from developing realistic and sustainable solutions to the non-traditional threats facing the world, among which terrorism is by no means the greatest or most serious.'[30]

This policy (or series of policies), rather than a litany of doomed military adventures, threats to sovereign states deemed to be rogue regimes and reductionist rhetoric about good and evil, presents the means to end the war on terror in a way that can provide better security for all of us.

CHAPTER SIX

Reconciliation and Rebuilding[1]

> Most of the excuses not to remember say that we should not re-open the wounds of the past, but denying the past will never lead to the closing of wounds. People have to remember because they have not forgotten. The [wounds] are there, fresh and painful. The society must do something to heal them. 'Forgive and forget' is always a tempting option (often called for by those who had a role to play in the war), but sooner or later it will prove to be useless.
>
> Roberto Cabrera[2]

The majority of this book has looked at the immediate environment that surrounds war and at the difficulties and opportunities associated with transforming these armed conflicts into more peaceful human relationships and political structures. Ending war, of course, is rarely a quick-fix operation. While cease-fires can be declared, negotiations can be completed and new political structures can be established, wars only truly end when the underlying issues and grievances that led to violence are satisfactorily addressed and human relationships within the conflict zone are transformed. This distinction between *terminating the act* of war and *ending the desire* for war often requires the development of reconstruction and reconciliation strategies to ensuring that armed conflict does not re-emerge.

Two separate arguments run through this chapter. The first is that reconciliation is a long-term process which can be encouraged through a range of initiatives that are sensitive to the dynamics of the conflict. While reconciliation is required by a society to deal with the past and move forward into a post-conflict environment, it involves rebuilding relationships between individuals and communities and cannot simply be applied onto victims of violence from the outside. Reconciliation may evolve organically and at variable speeds, as the survivors of war deal with issues such as grief, anger, hatred, fear, mistrust and a range of physical or psychological injuries. These are not issues that can easily be tackled, and in some cases it may be impossible for any meaningful reconciliation to take place in the short term.

The second argument that runs through this chapter is that while the process of rebuilding and reconstruction after war is essential for reconciliation to occur, this is frequently infused by a liberal ethos which, since the end of the Cold War in particular, has narrowed the distinction between the *fighting* of the war and the effort to *rebuild* afterwards. This section of the chapter looks at how the concept of reconstruction has evolved since the end of the Cold War. More specifically, it details the way in which multinational peace-enforcement operations, together with the more recent wars in Afghanistan and Iraq, have politicized reconstruction and narrowed the gap between the waging of war and the process of rebuilding after it. This reflects back on the discussion of the ethics of war in chapter 1 and, in particular, on the concept of *jus post bellum* (justice after war). As the boundaries between the ethics and nature of war in the contemporary world have become more opaque, so too have the borders of reconstruction in the post-violence phase of armed conflict. While the Marshall Plan, which focused on rebuilding post-war Europe, represents a traditional case, the new post-Cold War interventionism, not to mention the GWOT, has blurred the boundaries between waging war and waging peace. Some of the key questions here reflect back on previous chapters of the book in terms of the changing nature of contemporary warfare and third-party intervention that has combined humanitarian aid with coercive political and economic force. When does economic reconstruction become part of a political project linked to the *modus operandi* of war itself? When does development policy, or the provision of aid, or the re-ordering of a state's institutions along democratic lines stop being the rebuilding of a war-torn region and start becoming the construction of a more sinister project? In this scenario, reconciliation and reconstruction can sit uneasily beside nation-building enterprises, political occupation and imperial domination. This chapter connects with the previous one by arguing that Afghanistan and Iraq have reduced the space for external parties to participate in rebuilding programmes without appearing to be pursuing the war aims of the US and its allies in the region. This potentially implicates aid workers, engineers and peace-keepers in the war itself, if they are implementing a reconstruction agenda designed by the political/military forces of occupation. This point has been made in trenchant terms by François Calas and Pierre Salignon in the context of the relationship between humanitarian aid organizations that were trying to operate in Afghanistan during 'Operation Enduring Freedom' in 2001.

> From the beginning, operation 'Enduring Freedom' introduced a pernicious confusion between the exercise of the United States' right to legitimate self-defence and the independent and impartial humanitarian action of aid organizations. The first American bombardments were accompanied by high-altitude drops of individual food rations accompanied by leaflets offering a reward to anyone who made possible the capture of Bin Laden. . . . Furthermore, the humanitarian organizations were called on to abandon all neutrality and join with the Western forces to form what the British Prime Minister called 'a military-humanitarian coalition'. The American Secretary of State was equally explicit, asking humanitarian NGOs to convey a message about

American values to the rest of the world and considering them to be a 'force multiplier for us, such an important part of our combat team'.[3]

Within a context such as this, differentiating between pre-war objectives, the conduct of a war and post-war reconstruction is a tricky business and the boundaries can be difficult to see, especially on the ground. Andrew Williams captures this dilemma in his book *Liberalism and War* with his observation that what is meant by the term 'reconstruction' today has evolved from the way in which it was understood in the post-1945 period.

> Many in the Middle East see reconstruction as an ideology of Western invention, even imperialism. And one of the main objections that Islamic (but also nationalist) militants in these areas have is to what is perceived as an over-emphasis on individuals and on capitalist practices. In short the bearers of reconstruction are seen not only as Infidels but also as interlopers.[4]

At a wider level, ending war relates not just to the physical violence, but to the underlying grievances and perceived injustices that led to the outbreak of violence in the first place. Consequently, post-war reconstruction and reconciliation are vital elements in the effort to ensure that violence ends in a way that is durable and sustainable over the longer term.

Rebuilding through Reconciliation[5]

> Reconciliation matters and if it mattered enough to enough of us in Northern Ireland then we would have it.
>
> Norman Porter[6]

One of the best known figures within the 'reconciliation industry', Archbishop Desmond Tutu, captures the essence of the need for reconciliation and how such processes are connected to armed conflicts themselves. Writing the foreword to the International IDEA Handbook *Reconciliation after Violent Conflict*, he said, 'Creating trust and understanding between former enemies is a supremely difficult challenge. It is, however, an essential one to address in the process of building a lasting peace. Examining the painful past, acknowledging it and understanding it, and above all transcending it together, is the best way to guarantee that it does not – and cannot – happen again.'[7] How to achieve these ambitious aims is less certain and involves a complex combination of new political institutions and personal transformations which aim to provide 'justice' for the 'victims' of conflict and some form of new beginning for those living within the conflict zone.

More cynically perhaps, it could be argued that the terms of reconciliation and the institutions developed to encourage it are designed by the victors rather than the vanquished, which inevitably colours/taints the exercise. Thus, the terms of reference of war crimes tribunals are typically established by Western liberal states while the remits of truth and reconciliation commissions are usually determined by those who have overcome the *ancien régime*. In this sense, reconciliation, like history, tends to be determined by the victor, or at least by those who are in political control after the violence is brought to a close.

The Institutional Response

When wars end physically, attention often turns quickly to how the state can foster reconciliation through new political institutions or economic initiatives. These may be linked to the pursuit of justice or the commemoration of the victims of violence, and may also be infused with political sensitivities linked to the armed conflict itself. What sort of new institutions are appropriate and who is worthy of being commemorated, punished or reconciled are only a few of the sticky issues that face any attempt to promote public policy initiatives and new institutions in the post-violence phase of an armed conflict. While cease-fires may have been underwritten and peace treaties endorsed, dissipating the grief and anger felt by civilian populations is a slow process and new initiatives designed to promote reconciliation between warring factions are likely to be scrutinized for evidence of bias towards or even appeasement of former enemies. In the immediate aftermath of war, the line between justice and revenge can be a very fine one and is likely to be caught up in the contested narrative of the conflict itself. This was summed up by Eva Hoffman in her introduction to Martin Meredith's study of the South African Truth and Reconciliation Commission.

> Landscapes after battle are often strewn with the detritus of partisan vengeance and personal vendettas. It is partly to contain those impulses that the first and most urgent need in societies that have been subjected to or riven by violence is to formally recognize the wrongs that have been committed and to invert the perverse order of atrocity. . . . Whatever the specific criteria of judgement or punishment, the first task is to name wrongs *as* wrongs.[8]

In some cases where a long process of political negotiation is involved, these institutions may well form part of the *process* of pre-settlement dialogue. While it seems sensible to ensure that post-settlement institutional mechanisms aimed at building reconciliation can claim some level of consensus and mandate, this illustrates the connection between the violent phases of an armed conflict and the post-settlement period. In the case of the Northern Ireland conflict, the terms of new initiatives surrounding reconciliation were written into the text of the Good Friday Agreement in 1998 and at the same time fudged by the negotiators, who agreed only to establish an independent Victims' Commission. It was the commission's job to assess the public mood and recommend what options were available that could credibly promote the process of reconciliation. The text of the agreement illustrates that the devil was very much in the detail and that the Victims' Commission had been given a difficult political job to do. 'The participants believe that it is essential to acknowledge and address the suffering of the victims of violence as a necessary element of reconciliation. They look forward to the results of the Northern Ireland Victims Commission.'[9] The question left hanging in the air here was *who exactly were* the victims of violence within the context of the Northern Ireland conflict? The terms of reference given to the Victims' Commission referred to 'those who have become victims in the last thirty years as a consequence of events in Northern Ireland', which did little to narrow the issue down.[10]

The pursuit of reconciliation may connect into difficult issues relating to the legitimacy/criminality of a conflict and even questions of morality, which can have the potential to re-open barely healed wounds during the fragile peace phase of a political conflict. While it may be pragmatic to recalibrate those previously defined as terrorist criminals as now being victims of war, there are likely to be some who regard this as a moral ambivalence which fails to distinguish between the perpetrators of premeditated murder, on the one hand, and innocent victims of violence, on the other. In such circumstances, any meaningful reconciliation will be extremely unlikely to take place. Before reconciliation can be considered, therefore, the first issue to be addressed is who the victims are and how they might be helped to deal with their pain and suffering. Are the victims of an armed conflict limited to civilian casualties, or should the term 'victim' be applied to those who have carried out acts of violence themselves and are suffering for the consequences of that? Within the context of protracted conflicts such as those in Northern Ireland and the Middle

East, the issue of whether the mother of a bomber or a para-military qualified to be viewed as a victim or not was directly related to wider questions of legitimacy. While it is under-standable that those who have suffered from political violence may attempt to establish a hierarchy of victims, this carries the risk that the reconciliation process will simply lead to more bit-terness and division.

These are not just theoretical distinctions, as our determi-nation of who the victims are in a war will have a direct effect on the type of policies we recommend in the post-settlement reconciliation phase of a conflict. If we limit victims to specific categories (e.g. civilians, innocent bystanders, members of the legal security forces), then we can exclude certain groups (e.g. 'the terrorists') from memorials, compensation, grief coun-selling, re-integration into the community, and so on. If we define the victims more widely, then we may advocate prisoner release schemes, counselling, compensation and economic aid for those who were responsible for kidnapping, armed rob-bery and even murder. The political and emotional dimen-sions to this are not difficult to see, especially in the context of the rise of intra-state wars and the involvement of civilian pop-ulations that have characterized the pattern of warfare since the end of the Cold War.

The problem inherent in defining victims in modern warfare relates to another concept that underlies post-war attempts at reconciliation. This concerns the connection between reconciliation and the imperative of obtaining 'jus-tice'. Many victims will understandably demand that the process of reconciliation delivers justice for their suffering in one form or another, often through some judicial process or institution. As Andrew Rigby has pointed out: '[T]he capacity of people to relinquish the desire for revenge fed by feelings of bitterness towards former perpetrators is enhanced to the extent that they feel genuine efforts have been made to "make things right".'[11] This process lies at the heart of *jus post bellum*, or justice after war, which, theoretically at least, connects the morality of going to war with the effort to provide justice in its aftermath. Two basic institutional models of justice have been evident within the rebuilding and reconciliation phases of violent conflicts, which are commonly referred to as retributive justice, on the one hand, and restorative justice, on the other. Put another way, justice is understood as either seeking retribution for crimes that have been committed and punishing those deemed to have been responsible, or, alternatively, restoring relationships between the victim and the aggressor as a way of rebuilding personal and group respect. Both of these models have attempted to institutionalize *jus post bellum* principles and are at the centre of the debate on how justice can be pursued after the physical phase of war has ended.

Retributive Justice

Advocates of the retributive justice model see retribution not as an alternative to reconciliation, but as a prerequisite for it to occur. Retributive justice is envisaged as being not an arbitrary or emotional punishment, but, rather, a measured and controlled response, administered objectively. Examples of retributive justice are epitomized by war crimes tribunals (WCTs), such as the Nuremberg trials which followed World War II and convicted and punished those Nazis held responsible for war crimes. More recently, the war in the former Yugoslavia led to the International Criminal Tribunal for the Former Yugoslavia (ICTY) and a tribunal also followed the genocide in Rwanda. The logic of these institutional approaches to justice is that the perpetrators of war crimes, including genocide and torture, will be made accountable for their actions and that this will contribute to the healing process and reconciliation within the community. The rationale

behind WCTs revolves around 'bringing wrongdoers to justice'. This was also the logic behind demands for the extradition of former Chilean dictator Augusto Pinochet from Britain
to Spain in 1998, to bring him to justice for his actions in Chile
during his period as President. As Thomas Weiss has suggested in *Humanitarian Intervention*, the establishment of
WCTs during the 1990s was connected to the shifting balance
after the end of the Cold War between state sovereignty and
human rights within international law. '[This] signalled that
atrocities committed against human beings by their own governments – including war crimes, crimes against humanity,
and genocide – trumped claims of state sovereignty.'[12]

Those who promote retributive justice as a component of the
reconciliation process argue that such institutions will make
progress in several interrelated areas. Firstly, they will establish
the facts surrounding allegations of war crimes and investigate
specific allegations of wrongdoing. Secondly, they will find and
try those suspected of war crimes and punish the guilty, thus
easing the pain of the victims and giving them the feeling that
justice has been done. Thirdly, by doing this they will act as
a deterrent on others and dissuade them from engaging in similar acts of aggression in the future. The ICTY's own website
illustrates this argument by listing what it claims to be its
core achievements: 'Spearheading the shift from impunity to
accountability, establishing the facts, bringing justice to
thousands of victims and giving them a voice, . . .strengthening
the *Rule of Law*.'[13] Andrew Williams locates the notion of retributive justice within an historical analysis, suggesting that
such institutions 'form a conceptual bridge with both the realist
idea of reparation and at the same time with the liberal ideal
of reconciliation'.[14] Fundamentally these institutions are based
on the assumption that war is a rational act carried out by
those who use violence for political ends, and thus can be held
accountable for their actions. Supporters of retributive justice

mechanisms see them as a potential means to deliver justice to victims after the direct physical violence has de-escalated. These are legal institutions that will establish the facts about who did what to whom, determine blame for such activities and apportion punishment, usually in the form of prison sentences or execution. Advocates of such institutions argue that this provides an official, legal due process that allows victims to pass on their demand or need for retribution to the state, thus reducing the desire for personalized revenge or reprisal and the continuation of the cycle of violence through tit-for-tat murders or retaliation. James Gow has gone further in his assessment of the ICTY, claiming that the tribunal was 'the invisible hand that made progress in Bosnia possible'[15] after the 1995 Dayton agreement. He argues that the ICTY had a political as well as a legal role and was a crucial element in the carrot-and-stick diplomacy that surrounded the Dayton process.

> Without enforcement of the war crimes issue, it is highly conceivable that agreement would not have been reached at Dayton, with figures such as Karadžić and Mladić in a position to hinder success. It is also quite probable that indictees would not have been excluded from running for, or holding, public office in Bosnia, which would have left the country, even with agreement at Dayton, still completely in the hands of the authors of war and mass murder.[16]

Critics of these attempts at retributive justice, such as the two *ad hoc* WCTs established by the United Nations to examine alleged abuses in Rwanda and former Yugoslavia, claim that they have been ineffective. These WCTs usually rely on states giving up those accused of war crimes to the tribunals and are therefore dependent upon the co-operation of national governments. This is one reason why major figures such as Radovan Karadžić and General Mladić have not been held accountable for their actions in Bosnia in the 1990s, though Slobodan Milošević was handed over and stood trial in the Hague before his death in 2006. This dents one of the main criticisms of WCTs, namely that they can only catch the small fry rather than the big fish. We have also seen Saddam Hussein tried in an Iraqi court and executed at the end of 2006 for human rights abuses in Iraq, though some have argued that this was a rigged kangaroo court which owed more to the settling of old scores in Iraq than to the proper exercise of retributive justice.

The case of the *ad hoc* tribunal in Rwanda highlights other practical problems facing WCTs as mechanisms of retributive justice. In a conflict that involves large sections of a population rather than a few ring-leaders at the head of a government, it is simply impossible to arrest and try everyone who was involved in genocidal acts or torture. The tribunal in Rwanda has been beset with problems over the resources available, the quality of the legal teams involved and disagreements between the Rwandan government and the UN about the number of possible defendants who might be put on trial. Andrew Williams offers the following stern judgement on this example of retributive justice. 'Although there is in existence an official WCT to deal with the aftermath of the 1994 massacres in Rwanda, it has been largely discredited and has had little effect.'[17]

Despite their failings, many people believe that the establishment of these mechanisms to investigate war crimes could, with sufficient political backing, become an effective deterrent in the future for those contemplating similar acts. Their critics would allege that they are a token gesture which powerful states will successfully evade and a political façade of justice of little real use to those victims trying to pick up the pieces of their lives and move on.

Restorative Justice

The Commission was not required to muster a definitive and comprehensive history of the last three decades nor was it

> expected to conjure up instant reconciliation . . . yet we are
> confident that it has contributed to the work in progress of
> laying the foundation of the edifice of reconciliation. The fur-
> ther construction of that house of peace needs my hand. It
> needs your hand.
>
> Nelson Mandela[18]

The alternative model for institutionalizing justice during the
post-war phase of a violent conflict is generally referred to as
'restorative justice'. Unlike retributive justice, which seeks to
isolate the offender from society and inflict punishment,
restorative justice focuses on the future rather than the past,
and on reconciliation rather than blame and punishment.
Restorative justice also expands the idea beyond the personal,
to the group level, including the concept not simply of recon-
ciling the individual victim with the aggressor, but of reconcil-
ing the society as a whole with the past in order to move into a
new era of peaceful coexistence.

The South African Truth and Reconciliation Commission
(TRC), which was set up in 1995 to investigate torture and
unlawful killings during the apartheid era, was an institution
that focused on restorative rather than retributive justice. The
emphasis here was on using the past to move forward, rather
than analysing the past to attribute blame and impose punishment. The South African TRC saw it as important that the
story of human rights abuses was told publicly through tele-
vised public hearings and that this would be a healthy experience for both the individuals and the society. Archbishop
Desmond Tutu, who chaired the South African TRC, provided
a perfect definition of the connection between restorative justice and reconciliation when he spoke subsequently about the
rationale behind the initiative.

> To pursue the path of healing for our nation, we need to
> remember what we have endured. But we must not simply
> pass on the violence of that experience through the pursuit of

punishment. We seek to do justice to the suffering without perpetuating the hatred aroused. We think of this as restorative justice. We recognize that the past can't be remade through punishment. . . . There is no point exacting vengeance now, knowing that it will be the cause for future vengeance by the offspring of those we punish. Vengeance leads only to revenge. . . . Denial doesn't work. It can never lead to forgiveness and reconciliation. Amnesia is no solution. If a nation is going to be healed, it has to come to grips with the past. . . . We aim to remember, to forgive and to go on, with full recognition of how fragile the threads of community are.[19]

South Africa's was not an isolated case. TRCs are quite in vogue as political institutions for publicly addressing human rights abuses that accompany violent conflicts. While South Africa's is the most famous, there were also Truth Commissions in El Salvador and East Timor, with rather less admirable attempts to establish one in Guatemala in the 1980s and 1990s. In the Guatemalan case, much of the pressure came in the mid-1980s from the Catholic Church and an NGO formed by relatives of the disappeared. Owing to public pressure, the government set up a commission to look into the disappearances that had taken place. This was composed of a conservative Catholic Bishop, a member of the military and a member of the justice department. After a few months of inactivity, which involved no interviews with any witnesses or victims' families, it dissolved itself, making no formal report. Despite opposition from the military, another commission was set up in 1994. This was grandly entitled the 'Commission for the Historical Clarification of the Violations of Human Rights and Acts of Violence which have caused Suffering to the Guatemalan Population'. Despite the impressive name, this was another paper tiger weakened by three aspects of its remit. Firstly, it was only allowed to investigate abuses 'linked to the armed conflict'. This meant that the killing and torture of civilians and the disappearance of hundreds of non-combatants within Guatemala were outside the remit or jurisdiction of the Commission. Secondly, the Commission was only supposed to exist for six months yet it was tasked to investigate abuses over a thirty-six-year period from the beginning of the civil war in 1960 to its formal end in December 1996. This was an impossibly short timeframe. Thirdly, the Guatemalan Truth Commission had very limited legal powers. Unlike the South African TRC, the Guatemalan version had no powers of search, seizure or subpoena. This knocked a few more of its teeth out and made serious investigations impossible. It is clear from the Guatemalan example that TRCs are only as good as the political will behind them, the remits that are provided and the powers they are given to conduct their investigations.

One way of looking at TRCs is as legal institutions that dispassionately record and document the grim facts of armed conflict, compiling information about who killed whom, where, when, how and why. Alternatively, they function as emotional institutions, facilitating an outpouring of grief from victims and (it is hoped) remorse from perpetrators who are participating voluntarily in the process. TRCs can claim to be part of the reconciliation process by providing some level of public acknowledgement to the victims of the suffering they have gone through. Albie Sachs, the former ANC activist who became a leading member of the government after 1994, commented that the TRC allowed South Africa to move 'from knowledge to acknowledgement'[20] of the crimes of the apartheid era. It involves a public recognition of individuals' suffering and a public acceptance of who has been responsible for the crimes that have been committed. However, while the emphasis is often on the individuals – whether they are victims or perpetrators of violence – TRCs are also aimed at providing an institutional mechanism that will reconcile the

society in the post-war era. This presents a possible disjunc-
ture, as what the society and individual victims need might not
neatly coincide. Thus, while the state needs a process, leading
to an acknowledgement that this has produced justice, leading
to community stability, the individual victim might need time
to reflect or might be unable to forgive, at least within the timeframe set out within the TRC itself. Donna Pankhurst has suggested that this is a problem which is encountered when the
individual and collective aspects of the reconciliation process
collide.

> When the linguistic meanings of reconciliation are trans-
> posed onto a political situation, there is thus a shift in focus
> from an individual to some type of collective process, . . . what
> is required psychologically for an individual to recover from
> trauma and be reconciled with the past . . . need bear no
> resemblance to what might be required for a society to do so.[21]

The logic of the South African TRC was that those who
testified before it and admitted their guilt would demonstrate
remorse and seek forgiveness for what they had done.
However, in reality most of the contrition and remorse came
from Archbishop Desmond Tutu and his other commission-
ers, rather than from those who testified before them. The
record of the TRC in South Africa is rather mixed. It did, on the
one hand, give many people their day in court and allowed
many to discover the gruesome facts about the circumstances
surrounding the death of their relatives and friends. It also
indicated through the national and international media coverage and the state commitment to the process that South Africa
itself was recognizing the suffering and grief of victims in a
way that might provide them with a new beginning and an
enhanced capacity to forgive. The extent to which this experience provided for reconciliation to emerge between victims
and perpetrators or more broadly between the black and white
communities in South Africa is more difficult to determine.

Opinion polls suggested that the TRC was failing to achieve further reconciliation in any measurable way, and was actually making race relations worse, though, given the history of South Africa, an improvement in race relations was never going to be achieved quickly.

> In a survey carried out in July 1998, some 72 percent of whites felt that the TRC had made race relations worse; almost 70 percent felt that the TRC would not help South Africans to live together more harmoniously in the future; and some 83 percent of Afrikaners and 71 percent of English-speaking whites believed the TRC to be biased.[22]

The much-invoked 'rainbow nation' is just as much of an illusion as its meteorological namesake, and – to stretch the metaphor – there is no pot of gold at the end of it. It would be too glib, however, to write off the South African TRC as a cack-handed institutional attempt to promote reconciliation. Mary Burton has written of the positive impact it had on individuals who took part in it and on the society more widely.

> What have been the effects of this search for the truth? Sometimes, we can say with honesty and humility, the generosity of forgiveness has astonished us all. Sometimes, at least, speaking out has provided a kind of catharsis, or perhaps a safe channel for long submerged anger. The right to be heard and acknowledged, with respect and empathy, did contribute to a process of healing in many cases. People have told us that being enabled to set out their own understanding of events has been a relief to them. For some, the exhumation of the bodies of their family members has brought much comfort. The opportunity to observe traditional burial ceremonies has brought a degree of closure to the mourning process.[23]

Ultimately these institutional approaches to promoting reconciliation after warfare can only provide a space within which new relationships might be developed, slowly and over time. Clichéd though it may sound, reconciliation cannot be done *to* communities that are coming out of violent conflict and must instead be done *by* them. Given this more realistic set of performance indicators, the record of TRCs and WCTs begins to look less futile and, given sufficient resources, time and political will, such institutions can create solid foundations on which the difficult process of healing can be built.

Rebuilding through Reconstruction

The process of rebuilding societies that are coming out of violent conflict may also involve post-war reconstruction. This has been a regular component of dealing with the aftermath of war, and, from a neutral perspective, amounts to picking up the pieces after violence has abated. At its most basic, reconstruction involves feeding the starving, housing the displaced, rebuilding infrastructure destroyed by war and providing the basic amenities of life in the short term until the region is capable of functioning again. Medium-term objectives often focus on reviving the economy, which will have been debilitated during the conflict, and overseeing a range of social reforms seen as vital to the region's stability. Typically, of course, post-war reconstruction has a political agenda and involves devising and implementing new political institutions, over-seeing and perhaps arranging democratic elections, and designing economic policies that will affect those living in the conflict zone. Much of this effort may be targeted at specific groups that were disproportionately damaged by the violence and will frequently be designed with a view to making the region less prone to violent conflict in the future.

Once again the terminology for this process lacks clarity and may be referred to as deep (or structural) conflict prevention, post-conflict peace-building or post-war reconstruction. The common denominator in all of this is that peace (or at least non-violence) is promoted in the hope that the conflict zone will become more stable in the future and capable of managing its internal and external relations in a way that obviates the need to resort to violence.

While this reconstruction was a feature of post-war environments during the twentieth century (with the Marshall Plan being one of the more notable examples), its political aspects have become more hotly contested since the end of the Cold War and the new interventionism of the 1990s as practised by transnational organizations such as the United Nations, the European Union and the World Bank. The notion of reconstruction after war emerged partly as a response to the mistakes following the end of World War I, when the reparations demanded of Germany within the terms of the Versailles Treaty caused political humiliation and economic distress that fuelled Hitler's rise to power in the 1930s. The shift from reparation to reconstruction mirrors, to some degree, the debate earlier in this chapter about retributive and restorative justice. After World War II, the emphasis was placed on ensuring that Germany and other European countries were rebuilt in a way that bound them together in a positive relationship through new political and economic structures. There was an obvious agenda to the post-1945 reconstruction programme based on the promotion of liberal ideals and capitalist economics. But the recipients of this reconstruction were in no position to argue about its terms. Reconstruction efforts that have taken place since the end of the Cold War have had to deal with more complex conflicts where questions about the motivation, content and impact of reconstruction efforts have been central to the study of international relations.

The starting point for reconstruction efforts has been a liberal one, predicated on the assumption that peace will be encouraged through the promotion of liberal-democratic political structures and market liberalization. The standard operating procedure for reconstruction efforts of transnational bodies such as the UN and World Bank focuses on drafting new constitutions enshrining civil rights, planning free and fair democratic elections and retraining the civil administration. Roland Paris encapsulates this model in his book *At War's End.*

> Although the fourteen peacebuilding operations launched between 1989 and 1999 varied in many respects, their most striking similarity is that they all sought to transform war-shattered states into 'liberal market democracies' as quickly as possible. . . . Peacebuilding, in this sense, was a specific kind of social engineering, based on a particular set of assumptions about how best to establish durable domestic peace.[24]

These assumptions were based on a liberal template and implemented by coalitions of (mostly) Western states on (mostly) non-liberal regions such as the former Yugoslavia, Iraq and Afghanistan. The central question that has hung over the post-war reconstruction efforts in these regions has been posed by a number of scholars in recent years. Andrew Williams has done so concisely: 'Can we therefore not see reconstruction attempts as a form of (perhaps enlightened) liberal imperialism?'[25]

Rebuilding Whose Peace?

The extent to which reconstruction is perceived as helping or hindering a region to rebuild shattered lives, economies and political structures after war may depend largely on our view of why these agencies are involved, the connection between the rebuilding phase and the conflict itself, and the impact such activity has on the people living in the area. While few would argue with the assumption that war-torn regions should be helped to rebuild political institutions and economies after a conflict has 'ended', there is a major difference of opinion about how the reconstruction *industry* has been doing this since the end of the Cold War. This debate intensified during the 1990s following the humanitarian interventions in regions such as the former Yugoslavia and Kosovo and reached its peak following the invasions of Afghanistan and Iraq. In essence, this debate revolves around the fact that in contemporary patterns of armed conflict, reconstruction is inherently political in nature (rather than a neutral or technical process) and can be seen as being organically connected to the war itself. Roger Mac Ginty makes this observation in his book *No War, No Peace*, when he points out that Western models of post-war reconstruction are inevitably political in nature. 'This peace-making model often depicts itself as a neutral, non-partisan and non-ideological intervention in civil wars. It often uses the language of "common sense" and humanitarianism, offering to intervene in a dispassionate manner. Yet, in a socially constructed world, all actors and actions are political, more so in the highly contested context of a deeply divided society.'[26] Consequently, while some observers, such as Mary Kaldor, see the advantages of international intervention developing 'zones of civility' for new institutions and human rights standards to develop, others, such as David Chandler, caution that this amounts to paternalistic nation-building which ultimately disempowers local communities. Chandler argues that in the Bosnian case at least, top-down efforts to link anti-corruption and good governance criteria with the promotion of new democratic structures had the unexpected consequence of benefiting nationalists rather than cross-ethnic interests. 'Despite the anti-corruption campaigning focus, funded and encouraged by international institutions at successive elections, up to the present time the main nationalist parties have continued to dominate the political scene and achieve much better showings than expected, while no genuine cross-ethnic political alternative has emerged.'[27]

Those wishing to extend these 'zones of civility' tend to focus on a Western liberal agenda, of course, and so the emphasis tends to be placed on democratization, economic liberalization, preparation for democratic elections, the revivification of civil society, and so on. Here, the project of post-war reconstruction is synonymous with preventing the region from relapsing into violence in the future and providing it with the economic, institutional, even philosophical capacity to move forward in a stable (if not entirely peaceful) manner. This view of post-war reconstruction is in essence the applied phase of democratic peace theory. Make the region less prone to war though fast-tracking its democratization, building internal liberal norms and controlling this through a complex web of political and economic controls. However, as Roland Paris has pointed out in the context of post-war reconstruction in Bosnia following the 1995 Dayton agreement,[28] the process of democratization had the opposite effect, fuelling the very divisions and grievances which caused the war to begin in the first place. 'Peacebuilders have sponsored elections in war-shattered states as a means of facilitating the peaceful management of societal conflicts through competition at the ballot box, rather than through combat on the battlefield. But elections do not always foster peaceful forms of competition . . . or for that matter, governments committed to preserving democracy.'[29] Bruce Baker, commenting on post-war reconstruction efforts in sub-Saharan Africa, underlines the point that while the central tenets of 'good governance' are uncontroversial in theory, the problems arise when they are translated into practice. 'The fundamental problem is that the principles of good governance, namely fairness, participation, transparency, effectiveness, openness, responsiveness, accountability, legitimacy, and rule of law are more normative than technical issues.'[30] The criticism, therefore, of much of the reconstruction effort in recent years has been that its one-size-fits-all model is excessively prescriptive and fails to appreciate the unintended consequences it produces. A more nuanced understanding is needed on the part of external policy-makers that they are not neutral technocrats in such 'post-war' societies and that their actions can materially affect finely balanced (and often tense) relationships between the conflict actors in the region. One of the supreme ironies in all of this is that while most reconstruction efforts champion democratization, its operation and impacts often fall short of its own standards. Thus, democracy has a top-down quality to it with new institutions being imposed on local communities, while the agents of reconstruction themselves are unelected officials, or aid agencies who cannot be removed by democratic means.

The example of post-war reconstruction efforts in Bosnia illustrates the point. Following the Dayton agreement of November 1995, the international focus fell primarily on the need for new democratic institutions and economic liberalization. The rather hopeful assumption behind this was that promoting economic inter-dependence between the warring factions would produce pragmatic capitalists rather than zero-sum nationalists within the Serb, Croat and Muslim populations and that this could be fostered following some short-term shock therapy from external third parties. Following Dayton, the UN led the post-war reconstruction effort and exercised temporary sovereignty over the region. Judith Large has illustrated both the scale of this enterprise and its limitations.

> For several years after the war, Bosnia operated with three different legal systems; three sets of license plates; three international telephone exchanges; three currencies; two alphabets; increasingly three languages; and three school systems. Such conditions contravened Dayton's specific guarantees that Bosnia's residents should have freedom of movement, could return voluntarily to their prewar homes,

have their basic human rights protected and have confidence in a future increasingly respectful of democratic participation.[31]

Andrew Williams is rather more optimistic, concluding that 'Bosnia still looks like the hardest liberal nut to crack open with the tools of reconstruction but it would be illiberal to say that this cannot yet happen.'[32] While anything is possible if we take a long enough perspective, the post-war reconstruction effort in Bosnia has been beset with structural and operational problems. Chief among these has been the failure fully to appreciate that rebuilding cannot be applied onto a region in a manner that is immune from the political dynamics that fuelled the conflict. Furthermore, it was not sufficiently realized (or admitted) that post-war reconstruction is not a neutral act but rather involves redistributing power and resources from one set of actors to another, all of whom will have been contesting these political and economic goods during the war itself. If the transitional authorities had been more aware that they were political players in a power-struggle over the spoils of war, rather than neutral agencies engaged in a technical exercise, their efforts may have been more attuned to the nuances, sensitivities and needs of the Bosnian communities. Notwithstanding the need for conflict sensitivity in post-war rebuilding efforts, the blunt fact is that any such post-war re-ordering will benefit some and penalize others. This in turn is likely to colour how such policies are accepted internally (and may, of course, create new grievances and conflicts).

The connection between the reconstruction phase and the armed conflict itself inevitably politicizes the rebuilding efforts that are made and potentially implicates aid agencies, human rights groups and others (architects, engineers, civil servants, etc.) in the war itself. This is magnified when powerful Western states and transnational agencies such as the UN or NATO supported the military intervention and are controlling the subsequent reconstruction. One of the most popularly cited examples of this critique was in the case of Iraq, with US Vice-President Dick Cheney's connections to the energy company Halliburton. Cheney was CEO of Halliburton in 1995, and while he claimed to have severed all links with them when he became US Vice-President, he reportedly retained stock options in the company. The fact that Halliburton was appointed as the main government contractor responsible for 'restoring' Iraq's oil industry in an open-ended contract which was awarded without competitive tendering was seen by many as being linked to Cheney's former involvement and as an attempt to benefit from the spoils of war. Unsurprisingly, Osama Bin Laden himself made the link between Halliburton and the war in Iraq in 2004. From this perspective, reconstruction might be cast as the pursuit of war through development and little different from the imperial exploitation of the past. However, as Roger Mac Ginty has suggested, it would be overly simplistic to argue that all post-war reconstruction programmes are devious plots by the developed West to exploit and re-order war-torn societies.

> It is important not to conceive of the liberal democratic peace as a vast Machiavellian plot foisted on societies emerging from civil war by a handful of scheming foreign ministries, IFIs [international financial institutions] and tame international organisations and NGOs in their pay. Nor should the liberal democratic peace be viewed as omnipresent and all-embracing; it has been implemented and advocated with varying degrees of intensity.[33]

As with the top-down nature of post-war reconstruction in Bosnia, the 'rebuilding' effort in Iraq is floundering, though this has to date been incapable of providing even the basic levels of stability that Dayton managed to offer. The American administration has an obvious legitimacy problem in Iraq, having intervened on the pretext of Saddam Hussein's weapons of mass destruction, not found any, removed the head of state and precipitated a civil war. It is understandable in these circumstances that American claims to be interested in the welfare of the Iraqi people are falling on deaf ears. The military involvement can hardly be described as being a peace-keeping force, while the new government is seen by its critics as being a stooge of the US administration. It seems reasonably clear that insufficient planning was put into the post-war reconstruction phase of the intervention, with the result that while the US won the war, they have lost the peace. The conclusions of the Iraq Study Group Report in 2006 do not over-state the issues. 'There is a substantial need for continued reconstruction in Iraq, but serious questions remain about the capacity of the U.S. and Iraqi governments. The coordination of assistance programs by the Defense Department, State Department, United States Agency for International Development, and other agencies has been ineffective. There are no clear lines establishing who is in charge of reconstruction.'[34] The Initial Benchmark Assessment Report produced by the White House itself on 12 July 2007 admitted that out of eighteen benchmarks set for the new government, satisfactory progress had been made on less than half of them, and most of these were military goals.

Whether we view post-war reconstruction as being malign or benign, the fact remains that its ideological and policy agenda is a liberal one which seeks to promote stability in war-torn regions though a particular set of norms and values. This is operationalized by transnational organizations such as the UN, EU, NATO, OSCE, IMF and the World Bank, as well as many powerful INGOs. In effect, therefore, buying into post-war reconstruction often means accepting the ideological and policy agenda that goes with it. Given the liberal bias of post-war reconstruction, its political role is obvious. The overlap between liberal states waging war on non-liberal regimes, then promoting post-war reconstruction based on liberal notions of 'good governance' inevitably leads to accusations of imperialism. It is difficult to avoid the conclusion that the post-war activities of the Bush administration in Afghanistan and Iraq have tarnished the image of reconstruction and implicated those involved in these rebuilding efforts in the violence that went before it. As Jean-Hervé Bradol remarked in the context of the post-2003 reconstruction effort in Iraq: 'The abusive employment of humanitarian aid can then offer the double advantage of justifying the war and suppressing the memory of its crimes.'[35] One consequence of this is that those engaged in the reconstruction process have at times been targeted by militant groups as 'legitimate targets' and have found it difficult to function effectively. Following attacks on its staff in 2005, the International Committee of the Red Cross (ICRC) announced that it was scaling back its services in Iraq. The ICRC representative for the Middle East and North Africa, Balthasar Staehlin, gave an interview to the *Al Hayat* newspaper outlining the reasons behind this decision.

> Regrettably, the ICRC, despite its purely non-political and humanitarian character, has suffered deliberate attacks against its offices and staff. This meant that while we decided not to withdraw from Iraq, we had to adopt a new way of working and reduce the services we provide to the population. This is very frustrating for us and we continuously look for ways to establish a dialogue with all parties to the conflict to convince them of our humanitarian work so that we may be able to increase this work in the future. . . . The parties to the conflict have to accept that the ICRC, as a neutral organization, must talk to everyone. This means that armed groups have to accept that we talk with the authorities and that the authorities have to accept that we talk to armed groups. We have always been very transparent with this goal and we need this dialogue. It is aimed at impressing upon all parties the

need to distinguish between combatants and civilians and to treat civilians with respect.[36]

While the ICRC and other aid agencies involved in post-war reconstruction and rebuilding efforts may be non-partisan, they are not non-political, as they are inevitably operating within an environment created by the combatants. As Roger Mac Ginty has pointed out, 'In many ways, the NGO sector (or elements within it) has become complicit in this marketisation of reconstruction and peace support. In most cases, this has been borne of necessity as they have reacted to a changing operating environment.'[37] From the humanitarian interventions of the early 1990s to the invasions of Afghanistan and Iraq, the neutral space within which NGOs such as the ICRC can operate has narrowed considerably. If post-war reconstruction becomes integrated into pre-war planning, as some have suggested, then the project of reconstruction becomes a *de facto* war aim and those at the operational end of that are likely to suffer the consequences. This is linked to the fact that post-war reconstruction efforts are designed with a very clear liberal bias, often articulated as 'values' by the leaders of liberal states before they have used military action against non-liberal regimes. This problem might be offset if powerful liberal states would put more effort into rebuilding shattered societies and were less responsible themselves for doing the actual shattering. In this sense, post-war reconstruction needs to be viewed not as a stand-alone phase in armed conflict but as being intimately connected to it and shaped by it.

The Need for Effective Reconstruction to End Wars

This chapter has focused on the need to rebuild shattered communities after an armed conflict, while at the same time pointing out that to do so is an inherently political act that will reorder the material fortunes (and perceptions of legitimacy) of internal communities in ways that will benefit some and disadvantage others. It is important at the end of this discussion to observe that while post-war reconstruction may well be a neo-liberal project designed and controlled by powerful Western interests, this will be of little concern to those at the receiving end of war, who are desperate for help. In the real world, those who are in need of assistance do not have the luxury of worrying about the motives or agenda of those agencies providing relief and are unlikely to be interested in a sermon on the evils of liberal hegemony in the twenty-first century. While some academics and activists might not like it, they have to face the fact that despite its liberal agenda and conservative bias for *order* over *justice*, post-war reconstruction programmes funded and operated by Western agencies have improved many people's lives. To assert that such victims are living under a false consciousness and are insufficiently aware of structure might be comforting to Marxist academics, but is of little use to people on the ground, especially those trying to put their lives back together following an armed conflict. In reality, it is only powerful Western capitalist states that possess the capacity to engage in reconstruction efforts of a sufficient scale to make a positive difference to the economies of war-torn regions such as those of Afghanistan and Iraq.

The problem here lies not in the fact that the providers of economic reconstruction are capitalist themselves, but rather that they seek to create others in their own economic and political image when reconstruction policies are devised and implemented. Thus, such policies are typically designed by external actors on the outside for the benefit of those living on the inside, within a pattern of top-down delivery. Leaving aside the fact that at the political level those in control of reconstruction efforts are often unelected officials, foreign soldiers and INGO

aid workers, at the economic level the benefits of reconstruction are sometimes difficult to discern. This disconnect
between the efforts put into reconstruction and the outputs
experienced by those at the receiving end was recognized in
the context of Afghanistan by the Atlantic Council of the
United States in January 2008.

> Little coordination exists among the many disparate inter-
> national organizations and agencies active in Afghanistan.
> Legal and judicial reform (including reducing corruption),
> and control of narcotics are interdependent efforts and must
> receive the highest priority. To add insult to injury, of every
> dollar of aid spent on Afghanistan, less than ten percent goes
> directly to Afghans, further compounding reform and recon-
> struction problems.[38]

Despite its flaws at the policy level, the reconstruction of
war-torn societies is an essential element of rebuilding that is
vital to ending these conflicts. Given that powerful capitalist
countries look likely to remain the only credible source of such
efforts, there are a number of ways in which the problems
highlighted above might be offset.

Firstly, to be credible, agencies of post-war reconstruction
must be able to distance themselves from those responsible
for the violent phase of the conflict. There is a fatal credibility
gap in reconstruction efforts where foreign military forces
attack you on a Monday and try to patch up your wounds on a
Tuesday. In the context of many of today's wars, of course,
where violence lingers long after the reconstruction efforts
have begun, the scenario is more akin to being attacked on a
Monday and helped by your attacker the same day. One example of this is enough to illustrate the point. NATO's attempts in
Afghanistan to reduce support for the Taliban and build a new
police force were not helped in February 2008 when it killed
seven civilians during an air-strike, two of whom were children. This attack that 'went wrong' was not a cruise missile

which developed a glitch, but a 1,000-kg laser-guided J-Dam bomb dropped from a plane which would have killed anyone within 50 yards of impact. The idea that you can be regarded by a local population as having their welfare in mind when you are indiscriminately killing the civilian population seems unsustainable.

Secondly, those engaged in the post-war reconstruction 'industry' must be capable of demonstrating an even-handed approach in the rebuilding efforts which does not favour one internal group over another and exacerbate the existing tensions and grievances within the society. This comes back to the issue that agents of reconstruction often bring significant economic resources with them and powers of patronage over public jobs and rebuilding contracts which are likely to be contested by the internal population. At the very least the distribution of this largesse will be scrutinized by local communities for evidence of bias and discrimination. Worse still, those engaged in delivering reconstruction schemes will lose legitimacy if the pragmatic desire to 'get things done' or to 'take the long view' results in close relationships with local paramilitary factions. Roger Mac Ginty illustrated this danger in the context of reconstruction efforts in Afghanistan. 'Media reports from Afghanistan have revealed how the United States and United Kingdom have paid cash bribes to warlords, many with appalling human rights records, in order to secure their support for the Karzai government.'[39]

Thirdly, reconstruction efforts need to proceed in partnership with local communities, where external agencies listen as well as tell, and adapt policy to the needs and wishes of those who will have to buy into such reforms over the long term. This returns us to the old chestnut that external interventions need to be tailored to local needs rather than conforming to off-the-shelf types of delivery. As Thomas Weiss reminds us: 'The off-the-rack humanitarian suit (neutrality, impartiality and consent) may fit some, but certainly not all, contemporary armed conflicts.'[40] The necessary caveat here is that this has to be done within a context where post-war sectarian and ethno-national tensions are managed successfully.

Fourthly, international agencies involved in the post-war reconstruction effort must not appear to be profiting from the policies they are designing or implementing. While there is certainly a role for the business sector in the economic revitalization of war-torn regions, the privatization of oil industries and granting of huge contracts to foreign companies without competitive tendering, as in the case of Iraq, begins to look like the lining of pockets rather than enlightened capitalism. Naomi Klein has referred to this with the phrase 'predatory disaster capitalism', and cites the role of the World Bank in Afghanistan as an ongoing example of the practice.

> It has already managed to privatize healthcare by refusing to give funds to the Ministry of Health to build hospitals. Instead it funnels money directly to NGOs, which are running their own private health clinics on three-year contracts. It has also mandated 'an increased role for the private sector' in the water system, telecommunications, oil, gas and mining and directed the government to 'withdraw' from the electricity sector and leave it to 'foreign private investors.' These profound transformations of Afghan society were never debated or reported on, because few outside the bank know they took place: The changes were buried deep in a 'technical annex' attached to a grant providing 'emergency' aid to Afghanistan's war-torn infrastructure – two years before the country had an elected government.[41]

Chris Alden has written about similar problems in the case of Mozambique, where the macro-economic structures imposed by structural adjustment programmes of the World Bank have resulted in private profiteering for corrupt local politicians and the opening up of markets for foreign companies. He cites the destruction of local cashew nut farming due to IMF-imposed

cuts in state subsidy as 'one egregious example of the undermining of local capacity, employment and entrepreneurship
through misguided policies . . . favouring international business concerns over that of local needs'.[42]

Finally, the reconstruction effort must have a long-term
strategic commitment which is co-ordinated, integrated, properly funded and accepted by internal constituencies in a
manner that represents a break with the past, rather than looking like an occupation by other means. If this approach is followed, post-war reconstruction efforts can play a major part in
the reconciliation process. It almost goes without saying that
the rebuilding initiatives discussed here require long-term
political commitment from outside agencies and internal parties (to be measured over decades rather than years), adequate
resources and a commitment to implement them effectively.
Unless steps are taken to deal with the physical and psychological scars of war, it cannot be said to have ended and the likelihood is that it will re-emerge at a later date.

Conclusion

The search for stability will be a transient one if this is not
accompanied by a sustainable peace, and in order for that to
occur, the process of reconciliation must commence. While
this is a difficult journey for most of us caught up in violent
conflict, it is not an impossible one. However, it requires
institutional structural reform as well as personal agency
transformation.

Provided that viable political institutions are developed
within a consensual framework and economic rejuvenation is
properly supported, bitterness can fade and wounds can heal.
But for reconstruction to blend into reconciliation, those who
have suffered from the violence have to *want* to rebuild relationships with their former enemies. As Norman Porter has

observed in the context of Northern Ireland, 'Reconciliation is worth fighting for (through non-violent words and deeds). And without fighting for it we will not get it.'[43] Staying with the same case study, the last word on reconciliation can be given to an unlikely source to illustrate the point. The Rev. Ian Paisley, regarded by many people over many decades as being an obstacle to community reconciliation in Northern Ireland, made the following comment on the occasion of the opening of the Northern Ireland Assembly in May 2007. When this book was being planned and during most of the time that it was being written, it was not envisaged that the chapter on rebuilding and reconciliation would end with a quotation from Ian Paisley. The fact that it does illustrates the potential that exists for reconciliation to eventually emerge out of violent conflict.

> From the depths of my heart I can say to you today that I believe Northern Ireland has come to a time of peace, a time when hate will no longer rule. How good it will be to be part of a wonderful healing in this province. Today we have begun the work of plenty and we will all look for the great and blessed harvest.[44]

Conclusion

This book has sought to examine the different ways in which modern wars end. Regardless of the scale of armed conflict, the focus here has been on the potential that exists for helping to precipitate peaceful change and the strategies that are followed by internal and external agencies to achieve cease-fires, negotiations, settlements and post-war reconstruction. While much of the discussion in the preceding pages has critiqued the international capacity to intervene effectively to bring these violent conflicts to an end and to reconstruct the societies involved, the overall argument of the book is one of hope and optimism for the future.

The premise that runs through the book is that violent conflict is, for the most part, a rational act carried out by those who believe that it will achieve what dialogue cannot. The way forward is to recognize the fact that violence is a tactic rather than a goal, a methodology rather than an ideology, and those who use it (from governments to sub-state paramilitary factions) will be prepared to stop doing so when they see a more viable political alternative. This does not mean that we have to appease those who use violence to achieve their political objectives, but instead it involves undermining the support-base of those who advocate violent means for political ends. The power to wage war in the modern world does not come out of the barrel of a gun so much as it does from the mind-sets that support such violence. Al-Qaeda's power (in terms of its perceived threat) comes not from any vast arsenal of weapons or military capability, but rather from a radicalized (and brutalized) Islamic community. Thomas Weiss has invoked the reported quip of former President of the DRC Laurent Kabila 'that all that was required in (then) Zaïre to have an army was $10,000 and a cell phone'.[1] In another context, the power to wage war in the United States does not rest fundamentally with the President, but lies in the acquiescence of sufficient numbers of the American public for the military activities that are pursued. The fact that the leading candidates in the US Presidential election race critiqued the war in Iraq is not disconnected from the fact that US public opinion is now vehemently against the war.

Operationally, of course, wars are started and ended by those with coercive ability, be they Presidents or paramilitaries. However, ultimately, the power to start and end wars lies with us, who vote for, harbour, finance or otherwise accept (even through fear) the use of violence in our names. Anyone who has read this book possesses this form of power over war to a greater or lesser extent, and when we collectively demand an end to war, it becomes extremely difficult to continue it. This is not arguing that the structural circumstances that led to armed conflict can automatically be overcome by personal transformation. The point is rather that we need to decouple acts of political violence (terrible though they are) from the us-and-them morality associated with the 'evildoers' of contemporary discourse on terrorism. Rather than condemning a whole country as 'the great Satan', an ideology linked to a nation-state as 'the evil empire' or the international political system as a 'clash of civilizations', we need to understand political violence for what it is, namely as a means to an end rather than an end in itself.

Wars are (in the main) started and maintained by rational actors in pursuit of their perceived interests and objectives and can be ended when these perceptions shift to the belief that violence is unsustainable and is unlikely to lead to their desired goals. Once this is accepted, it becomes possible for the direct actors in conflict to look for possible political alternatives. The emergence of such a 'ripe moment' is not, of course, a linear progression in the real world of modern political conflict. Many of the direct actors in war will come to accept their mutually hurting stalemate at different times and will prefer the short-term certainties of the conflict to the longer-term risks associated with dialogue and negotiation. Those who are milking a war economy within a conflict zone and beyond it will not easily give the cash-cow up, or take the long view. Any progress that is made in the journey from war to peace is likely to be slow, frustrating and accompanied by sporadic upsurges of violence.

Fundamentally, however, for wars to end, those engaged in the violence must, firstly, want to seek alternatives to it and, secondly, believe that a political route is possible. In these circumstances much can be done by the internal actors to prepare their constituencies for dialogue and by external third parties to help foster a ripe moment that seems to be emerging.

This book has made the case that wars can often be ended when a ripe moment for doing so emerges. This is not a manifesto for inaction where we must all sit around and wait for such a moment to appear. The task for those within a conflict zone and for external third parties beyond it is to help bring such a moment about, recognize it when it appears, and then act on it to build on the faltering steps that are being taken away from violence. This book has outlined the different ways in which these ripe moments were successfully nurtured in some cases and wasted in others by internal leaders, civil society activists and external third parties. The intention here has been to demonstrate that armed conflicts and political initiatives designed to bring them to an end are organic in nature and evolve in unique and complex ways in response to the

structural environments that surround them and the direct
and indirect actors who operate within them.

A key element in this account of how modern wars end has
been the fact that armed conflict has evolved dramatically over
the last fifty years in ways that have impacted on the possibilities for bringing a cessation of violence. On the one hand,
the end of the Cold War freed up the international system to
deliver on its rhetoric and facilitated multilateral peace-keeping
and conflict prevention operations by external states and
by transnational organizations such as the UN, the EU and
NATO. On the other hand, however, these international interventions have moved from peace-keeping to peace-enforcement activities, where powerful political and economic actors
are restructuring nation-states, advocating regime-change and
re-ordering the internal civic institutions of countries in the
name of peace and democracy. We are currently in an interesting period of flux within the international system between
those uneasy bed-fellows of state sovereignty and individual
human rights. Kofi Annan's above-cited remark in the
Economist in 1999 that '[h]umanity, after all, is indivisible'[2] has
not been borne out by events. In addition, such lofty rhetoric
was drowned out by the post-9/11 security environment and
subsequent global war on terror, which has tarnished the
image of external intervention as a means of ending armed
conflict. As argued in the previous chapter, the GWOT and
specifically the invasions of Afghanistan and Iraq have resulted
in greater violence rather than less, in increased support for the
Taliban and Al-Qaeda, and in the politicization of humanitarian agencies, many of whom now run the risk of being
regarded as the civilian face of enemy military forces. This book
has tried to illustrate the difficult balancing act faced by international agencies that intervene in armed conflict, between
stopping the violence, on the one hand, and creating new grievances and causes of violence, on the other. The argument here

has not been that we should return to the conservative certainties of the Cold War, value the integrity of state sovereignty above all else, and leave people to die at the hands of reprehensible political regimes. The plea from this book is that humanitarian intervention should not be used to disguise asset-stripping land-grabs or good old-fashioned invasions with scant regard to the consequences for the people who live there (as in the case of Afghanistan and Iraq). External intervention should at the very least abide by Mary Anderson's axiom and 'do no harm',[3] while providing as much non-military support, economic assistance and political will as possible, applied in a consistent manner.

Another element related to the changing nature of war is the fact that civilian populations are now much more connected to violent conflict than they were in the past. The rise of intra-state and decline of inter-state conflicts since the end of the Cold War has brought violence to the doorsteps of many of us, and the proximity of warfare and involvement of civilian populations in the fighting have changed how wars are fought and how they can be ended. At another level, we have seen the democratization of war, as decisions over starting and ending this type of violence have been decentralized from Presidents, parliaments and military leaders to paramilitary factions, militia units, diaspora activists and even loose networks such as Al-Qaeda. The more diffused picture of the actors in modern intra-state warfare has made ending violence through political dialogue a difficult and complex process. Within this type of armed conflict the pain of violence is felt more keenly by civilian communities and the cycle of tit-for-tat murder is often extremely difficult to stop. However, to return to a comment made by Peter Wallensteen in *Understanding Conflict Resolution* and quoted earlier in this book, 'A strong statement is that conflicts *are* solvable. This is not necessarily an idealistic or optimistic position . . . it is a realistic proposition.'[4]

This book has argued that we should be cautious about accepting the hubris from political and military leaders surrounding the necessity of war. This goes for those paramilitary leaders who claim that their cause is noble and their violence honourable, as well as it does for governments, Presidents and Popes. The insidious slippage between the notions of 'legitimate force' and 'terrorist violence' only works if you accept that the state and the international community are non-corrupt institutions dedicated to establishing peace with justice around the globe. Unfortunately, we live in a more cynical world where powerful Western countries export weapons to other states and then condemn the killing that subsequently takes place, while international institutions are largely controlled by those same Western states, which inevitably impacts on their strategic outlook and operational activities.

In the Western world, the use of violence is frequently sold to us as being an unfortunate necessity, a last resort for an overwhelmingly important cause. We can all pick our favourite examples of this in defence of numerous efforts by governments and transnational actors to justify going to war. A textbook case was provided by Lord Robertson (then George Robertson) when he was the UK Secretary of State for Defence in 1999 and trying to drum up British support for a NATO military campaign in Kosovo. In an interview given to the tabloid newspaper *News of the World*, Robertson made the connection between the 'serial ethnic cleanser' Slobodan Milošević and Hitler's Nazi Germany.

> For over a year Slobodan Milošević – the butcher of Belgrade – has been embarked on a path of ethnic cleansing. . . . With his murderous secret police and thugs in uniform, he has been killing men, women and children in Kosovo. . . . We must learn the lesson of the early days of Hitler. Had we stood up to his tyranny earlier, the course of history might have been very

> different. . . . And so we had to bring Milošević to heel, before
> the spark of violence erupted throughout the Balkans.[5]

The act of killing will be proportionate rather than indiscriminate and targeted against those who deserve it. Some leaders,
such as Robertson (above), go as far as arguing that not to
engage in such violence would be immoral and that they are
choosing the lesser of two evils. The reality of warfare is usually rather different. War is rarely a necessity, or a last resort,
and political dialogue frequently goes by the wayside as states
or paramilitary leaders prepare for battle. Iraq is the most obvious parallel here, but this is far from being an isolated case.
This point is not necessarily an advocacy of pacifism, nor is it
an exercise in hand-wringing utopianism. It is, instead, an
observation that in order to construct the case for war and generate public support for it, policy-makers are often premature
in closing down options that fall short of it. In order to sell the
case for war, it becomes necessary to accentuate the sense of
threat and fear within public opinion while presenting crude
and simplified binary choices of the 'you are either with us or
against us' variety.

While much of this book has been critical of British and
American foreign policy, especially in relation to their interventions in Afghanistan and Iraq, it is recognized that these
powerful Western states, together with the international
organizations which they dominate, such as the UN, NATO
and the World Bank, will remain vital in the struggle to bring
armed conflicts to an end for the foreseeable future. The argument in this book has not been that the UN or the US should
stay out of third-party interventions, but, rather, that they need
fundamentally to rethink the connection between the internal
security that they crave, the foreign policies they adopt and the
international peace and security which they claim to want. It
has been argued here that while the global war on terror can be

ended, this will only happen when those leading it recognize that it cannot be won through military means and must be replaced by a political process which reduces the critique of the 'terrorists' and marginalizes the most extreme elements in groups such as Al-Qaeda. The way forward here is not to try to build higher barriers, introduce new security laws and frighten people into acquiescence, but to deal with the causes of this conflict rather than its symptoms. While creating a climate of fear is very useful for enabling governments to exercise executive power, it ultimately undermines the very values that the advocates of the 'democratic peace' claim to protect. Eroding civil liberties in the name of national security will do little to keep people in the rich developed world safe from the threat of terrorism and will do nothing to combat the more serious security threat for the twenty-first century caused by environmental decay. There will, of course, continue to be wars that cannot be brought to an end at any given moment in time, but if we are more attuned to the causes and dynamics of armed conflict and the possibilities (and limitations) for bringing them to an end, the chances of jaw-jaw triumphing over war-war look more promising. This book has tried to make the case that wars can be ended though changes in the structural conditions of a conflict and by transformations of human agency. Wars are started and maintained by us and, given conducive conditions, they can be ended by us too. This book has attempted to contribute to the debate about how this can be achieved.

Notes

INTRODUCTION

1 In Walter Isaacson, *Benjamin Franklin: An American Life* (New York: Simon & Schuster, 2003), 392.
2 Peter Wallensteen, *Understanding Conflict Resolution: War, Peace and the Global System* (2nd edn; London: Sage, 2007), 12.
3 Oliver Ramsbotham, Tom Woodhouse and Hugh Miall, *Contemporary Conflict Resolution* (2nd edn; Cambridge: Polity Press, 2005), 61–2.
4 Peter Wallensteen and Margareta Sollenberg, 'The End of International War? Armed Conflict 1989–95', *Journal of Peace Research* 33 (3), Aug. 1996, 356.
5 Andrew Mack, *War and Peace in the 21st Century, Human Security Report 2005* (New York: Oxford University Press, 2005), 148.
6 William Reno, *Corruption and State Politics in Sierra Leone* (Cambridge: Cambridge University Press, 1995).
7 Roy Licklider, 'The Consequences of Negotiated Settlements in Civil Wars 1945–1993', *American Political Science Review* 89 (3), 1995, 681.
8 See Hugh Miall, Oliver Ramsbotham and Tom Woodhouse, *Contemporary Conflict Resolution* (Cambridge: Polity Press, 1999), 66.
9 I. William Zartman, 'Dynamics and Constraints in Negotiations in Internal Conflicts', in I. William Zartman (ed.), *Elusive Peace: Negotiating an End to Civil Wars* (Washington: Brookings Institution, 1995), 3.
10 Stephen John Stedman, 'Spoiler Problems in Peace Processes', *International Security* 22 (2), 1997, 5–53; see also Stephen John Stedman, Donald Rothchild and Elizabeth M. Cousens (eds), *Ending Civil Wars: The Implementation of Peace Agreements* (London: Lynne Rienner, 2002).

11 Stedman et al., 'Introduction', in Stedman et al. (eds), *Ending Civil Wars*, 12.

CHAPTER I THE CHANGING NATURE OF WAR

1 Joseph Nye, *Power in the Global Information Age* (London: Routledge, 2004), 35.
2 Robert Fisk, *The Great War for Civilisation: The Conquest of the Middle East* (London: Harper Perennial, 2006), xix.
3 Quincy Wright, *A Study of War* (Chicago: University of Chicago Press, 1966), 5–6. Quoted in Lawrence Freedman (ed.), *War* (Oxford: Oxford University Press, 1994), 70.
4 It is recognized, of course, that there are complexities surrounding this point, but the concern here is to emphasize that war is a matter of scale and not one of legitimacy.
5 Dennis Sandole, *Capturing the Complexity of Conflict: Dealing with Violent Ethnic Conflicts of the Post-Cold War Era* (London: Pinter, 1999), 6.
6 In their excellent overview of the conflict resolution field, Oliver Ramsbotham, Tom Woodhouse and Hugh Miall make the implications of this disparity clear. See their *Contemporary Conflict Resolution* (2nd edn; Cambridge: Polity Press, 2005), 57.
7 The definition by the Swedish-based Uppsala Conflict Data Program, headed by Peter Wallensteen, is that wars involve more than 1000 battle deaths per year (as opposed to intermediate armed conflicts or minor armed conflicts). Within the Uppsala study's methodology, intermediate armed conflicts were required to have over twenty-five but fewer than 1000 battle-related deaths per year and more than 1000 over the course of the conflict. Minor armed conflicts required more than twenty-five but fewer than 1000 for the year and over the course of the conflict. See Peter Wallensteen, *Understanding Conflict Resolution: War, Peace and the Global System* (2nd edn; London: Sage, 2007), 22.
8 Fred Halliday, *The World in 2000* (Basingstoke: Palgrave, 2001), 51.
9 Michael Doyle, 'Kant, Liberal Legacies and Foreign Affairs', *Philosophy & Public Affairs* 12 (3), 1983, 214. Quoted in Lawrence Freedman (ed.), *War* (Oxford: Oxford University Press, 1994), 106.

10 Todd Landman, *Democracy, Conflict and Human Security: Further Readings* (Stockholm: International IDEA, 2007), 20.

11 Andrew Mack, *War and Peace in the 21st Century, Human Security Report 2005* (New York: Oxford University Press, 2005), 3.

12 Roland Paris, *At War's End: Building Peace after Civil Conflict* (Cambridge: Cambridge University Press, 2004), 44.

13 David Keen, 'Liberalization and Conflict', *International Political Science Review* 26 (1), 2005, 73.

14 Roger Mac Ginty, *No War, No Peace* (Basingstoke: Palgrave, 2006), 44.

15 Thomas Friedman, *The Lexus and the Olive Tree* (New York: Farrar, Straus & Giroux, 1999).

16 Stephen Chan, *Out of Evil* (London: I.B. Tauris, 2005), 78.

17 The seven principles of Just War Theory are:
   - a war is just only if it is waged by a legitimate authority;
   - a war must have a just cause;
   - a just war can only be waged as a last resort; all non-violent options must be exhausted;
   - a war must have a reasonable prospect of success and must not inflict suffering for a hopeless cause;
   - the cause of a just war must be proportionate to the losses expected in the conflict;
   - the conduct of the war must discriminate between combatants and innocent civilians; and
   - innocent civilians must not be directly attacked. (from Hugh Miall, *The Peacemakers: Peaceful Settlement of Disputes since 1945*, London: Macmillan, 1992, 32)

18 Thomas Weiss, *Humanitarian Intervention: Ideas in Action* (Cambridge: Polity Press, 2007), 21.

19 Tony Blair, 'Doctrine of the International Community', Chicago, 24 April 1999, *http://www.number10.gov.uk/output/Page1297.asp* (last accessed 17 April 2008).

20 David Rieff, 'Kosovo: The End of an Era?' in Fabrice Wiessman (ed.), *In the Shadow of Just Wars: Violence, Politics and Humanitarian Action* (London: Hurst, 2004), 293.

21 David A. Welch, *Justice and the Genesis of War* (New York: Cambridge University Press, 1993), 19.

22 Halliday, *The World in 2000*, 57.

23 Gary Bass, '*Jus Post Bellum*', *Philosophy & Public Affairs* 32 (4), 2004, 384.

24 Brian Orend, 'Jus Post Bellum', Journal of Social Philosophy 31 (1), Spring 2000, 123.
25 Alex J. Bellamy, Just Wars: From Cicero to Iraq (Cambridge: Polity Press, 2006), 214.
26 'Bush: The First 100 Days', BBC News Online, 30 April 2001, http://news.bbc.co.uk/1/hi/world/americas/1302232.stm (accessed 17 April 2008). See also the preface in Paul Rogers' Losing Control: Global Security in the 21st Century (London: Pluto Press, 2000).
27 Mac Ginty, No War, No Peace.
28 International IDEA, Democracy, Conflict and Human Security: Pursuing Peace in the 21st Century (Stockholm: International IDEA, 2006), 36.
29 Hugh Miall, Oliver Ramsbotham and Tom Woodhouse, Contemporary Conflict Resolution (Cambridge: Polity Press, 1999), 153.
30 Sandole, Capturing the Complexity of Conflict, 3.
31 Peter Harris and Ben Reilly (eds), Democracy and Deep-Rooted Conflict: Options for Negotiators (Stockholm: International IDEA Handbook Series 3, 1998), v.
32 Lotta Harbom, Stina Hogbladh and Peter Wallensteen, 'Armed Conflicts and Peace Agreements', Journal of Peace Research 43 (5), 2006, 619.
33 International IDEA, Democracy, Conflict and Human Security, 26.
34 Ramsbotham et al., Contemporary Conflict Resolution (2nd edn), 81.
35 Mary Kaldor, New and Old Wars: Organized Violence in a Global Era (Cambridge: Polity Press, 2001).
36 Lewis Fry Richardson, Statistics of Deadly Quarrels (Pittsburgh: Boxwood Press, 1960).
37 Wright, A Study of War.
38 Vesna Bojicic-Dzelilovic and Mary Kaldor, 'The Political Economy of the War in Bosnia-Hercegovina', in Mary Kaldor and Basker Vashee (eds), New Wars: Restructuring the Global Military Sector (London: Pinter, 1997), 137.
39 Stephen Ellis, 'Interpreting Violence: Reflections on West African Wars', in Neil Whitehead (ed.), Violence (Oxford: James Currey, 2004), 107.
40 International IDEA, Democracy, Conflict and Human Security, 36.
41 Wallensteen, Understanding Conflict Resolution (2nd edn), 27.

42 Ramsbotham et al., *Contemporary Conflict Resolution* (2nd edn),
     161.
43 Dan Smith, 'Trends and Causes of Armed Conflict' (Berlin:
     Berghof Research Center for Constructive Conflict Management,
     2004), 4.
44 Wallensteen, *Understanding Conflict Resolution* (2nd edn), 28.
45 See Saadia Touval and I. William Zartman, 'Conclusion:
     Mediation in Theory and Practice I', in Saadia Touval and I.
     William Zartman (eds), *International Mediation in Theory and
     Practice* (Boulder, CO: Westview Press, 1985), 258–60; I. William
     Zartman, 'The Timing of Peace Initiatives: Hurting Stalemates
     and Ripe Moments', *The Global Review of Ethnopolitics* 1 (1),
     September 2001.
46 Zartman, 'The Timing of Peace Initiatives', 8.
47 I. William Zartman, 'Negotiating Internal Conflict: Incentives
     and Intractability', *International Negotiation* 6, 2001, 300–1.
48 Fen Hampson, *Nurturing Peace: Why Peace Settlements Succeed or
     Fail* (Washington: United States Institute of Peace, 1996), 210–14.
49 Ramsbotham et al., *Contemporary Conflict Resolution* (2nd edn),
     167.
50 Zartman, 'The Timing of Peace Initiatives', 9.

CHAPTER 2 THIRD-PARTY INTERVENTION

1 'Middle East Fears Broken Iraq', BBC News Online, 22 March
    2007, *http://news.bbc.co.uk/1/hi/world/middle_east/6476907.stm*
    (last accessed 21 April 2008).
2 I. William Zartman, 'The Unfinished Agenda: Negotiating
    Internal Conflicts', in Roy Licklider (ed.), *Stopping the Killing:
    How Civil Wars End* (New York: New York University Press,
    1993), 20–36.
3 Peter Harris and Ben Reilly (eds), *Democracy and Deep-Rooted
    Conflict: Options for Negotiators* (Stockholm: International IDEA
    Handbook Series 3, 1998), 164.
4 Eamonn Mallie and David McKittrick, *Endgame in Ireland*
    (London: Hodder & Stoughton, 2001), 70.
5 Ibid., 72.
6 CBI Northern Ireland, *Peace – A Challenging New Era* (Belfast:
    CBI, 1994), 4.

7 Jessica Banfield, Canan Gunduz and Nick Killick, 'The
   Confederation of British Industry and the Group of Seven: A
   Marathon Walk to Peace in Northern Ireland', in Jessica Banfield,
   Canan Gunduz and Nick Killick (eds), *Local Business, Local Peace:
   The Peacebuilding Potential of the Local Private Sector* (London:
   International Alert, 2006), 439.
8 Ibid.
9 John Paul Lederach, *Building Peace: Sustainable Reconciliation in
   Divided Societies* (Washington: United States Institute of Peace,
   1997), 83.
10 For an in-depth examination of the nature and impact of NGO
   activity in Northern Ireland, consult: Feargal Cochrane, 'Unsung
   Heroes? The Role of Peace and Conflict Resolution Organisations
   in the Northern Ireland Conflict', in John McGarry (ed.), *Northern
   Ireland and the Divided World* (Oxford: Oxford University Press,
   2001); Feargal Cochrane, 'Beyond the Political Elites: A
   Comparative Analysis of the Roles and Impacts of Community-
   based NGOs in Conflict Resolution Activity', *Civil Wars* 3 (2),
   Summer 2000, 1–22; Feargal Cochrane and Seamus Dunn,
   *People Power? The Role of the Voluntary and Community Sector in
   the Northern Ireland Conflict* (Cork: Cork University Press, 2002);
   Colin Knox and Padraic Quirk, *Peace Building in Northern Ireland,
   Israel and South Africa* (Basingstoke: Macmillan, 2000).
11 Frances McCandless, 'Funding and Sustaining the Sector', *Scope*,
   March 2003, 12.
12 Joseph Nye, *Soft Power: The Means to Success in World Politics* (New
   York: Public Affairs, 2004).
13 Rupert Taylor, 'South Africa: The Role of Peace and Conflict
   Resolution Organizations in the Struggle against Apartheid', in
   Benjamin Gidron, Stanley Katz and Yeheskel Hasenfeld (eds),
   Mobilizing for Peace (Oxford: Oxford University Press, 2002), 69.
14 André Fourie and Theuns Eloff, 'Exploring the Contributions of
   the Private Sector to the Social, Economic and Political
   Transformation Process in South Africa', in Banfield et al. (eds),
   Local Business, Local Peace, 508.
15 Knox and Quirk, *Peace Building in Northern Ireland, Israel and
   South Africa*, 167.
16 Taylor, 'South Africa', 84.
17 Angelika Rettberg, 'El Salvador: A Firm Grip on the Peace
   Process', in Banfield et al. (eds), *Local Business, Local Peace*.

18 For an excellent insight into micro interventions by civil society third parties in violent conflicts of all degrees of intensity, see Paul van Tongeren, Malin Brenk, Marte Hellema and Juliette Verhoeven (eds), *People Building Peace II: Successful Stories of Civil Society* (London: Lynne Rienner, 2007).

19 Oliver Ramsbotham, Tom Woodhouse and Hugh Miall, *Contemporary Conflict Resolution* (2nd edn; Cambridge: Polity Press, 2005), 168.

20 Peter Wallensteen, *Understanding Conflict Resolution* (2nd edn; London: Sage, 2007), 220.

21 See Thomas Weiss, *Humanitarian Intervention: Ideas in Action* (Cambridge: Polity Press, 2007), 123; Stephen Ryan, *The United Nations and International Politics* (London: Macmillan, 2000), 133–5.

22 Report of the International Commission on Intervention and State Sovereignty (ICISS), *The Responsibility to Protect* (Ottawa: International Development Research Centre, 2001), 1.

23 Ramsbotham et al., *Contemporary Conflict Resolution* (2nd edn), 170.

24 Weiss, *Humanitarian Intervention*, 1.

25 Karin Fierke, *Diplomatic Interventions: Conflict and Change in a Globalizing World* (Basingstoke: Palgrave Macmillan, 2005), 84.

26 Kofi Annan, 'Two Concepts of Sovereignty', *The Economist*, 18 September 1999, *http://www.un.org/News/ossg/sg/stories/articleFull.asp?TID=33&Type=Article* (last accessed 28 April 2008).

27 Gareth Evans, 'Foreword', in Weiss, *Humanitarian Intervention*, ix–x.

28 Kofi Annan, United Nations Press Release, 7 April 2004 (SG/SM/9197 AFR/893 HR/CN/1077).

29 'Report Condemns Sudan over Darfur', BBC News Online, 12 March 2007, *http://news.bbc.co.uk/1/hi/world/africa/6440719.stm* (last accessed 21 April 2008).

30 Weiss, *Humanitarian Intervention*, 57–8.

31 Roland Paris, 'International Peacebuilding and the "Mission Civilisatrice" ', *Review of International Studies* 28, 2002, 638.

32 Norrie McQueen, *Peacekeeping and the International System* (London: Routledge, 2006), 100.

33 Wallensteen, *Understanding Conflict Resolution* (2nd edn), 267.

34 Ibid., 220–1.

35 McQueen, *Peacekeeping and the International System*, 200.
36 Ramsbotham et al., *Contemporary Conflict Resolution* (2nd edn),
    129.
37 Annan, 'Two Concepts of Sovereignty'.
38 Weiss, *Humanitarian Intervention*, 1.
39 Svante Cornell, 'International Reactions to Massive Human
    Rights Violations: The Case of Chechnya', *Europe-Asia Studies*
    51 (1), 1999, 87–8.
40 Thornike Gordadze, 'Chechnya: Eradication of the Enemy Within',
    in Fabrice Weissman (ed.), *In the Shadow of 'Just Wars': Violence,
    Politics and Humanitarian Action* (London: Hurst, 2004), 202.
41 See McQueen, *Peacekeeping and the International System*, 1.
42 See *http://www.unicnairobi.org/display.asp?section_id=30&storynr=*
    100 (last accessed 21 April 2008).
43 *http://assembly.coe.int/Mainf.asp?link=http://assembly.coe.int/
    Documents/AdoptedText/ta04/ERES1403.htm* (last accessed 21
    April 2008).
44 'Dispatches from a Savage War', *Guardian*, 15 October 2004,
    http://www.guardian.co.uk/women/story/0,,1327791,00.html
    (last accessed 21 April 2008).
45 While responsibility for her death has never been claimed and no
    one has been charged, some believe that this was a contract
    killing. The day after her murder, the police seized her computer
    hard disk together with material she had gathered for an article
    on torture practices used by Russian security forces in Chechnya.
    Politkovskaya was due to file this story for publication on the day
    of her murder. Immediately following her murder, Alexander
    Litvinenko, himself murdered in London in November 2006,
    accused Vladimir Putin of being personally responsible for her
    assassination. Anna Politkovskaya was murdered on Putin's
    birthday.
46 Cornell, 'International Reactions to Massive Human Rights
    Violations', 96.
47 See note 37.

CHAPTER 3 NEGOTIATION OR VICTORY?

1 Statement by Rev. Ian Paisley, leader of the Democratic Unionist
  Party (DUP), at a joint DUP/Sinn Fein press conference on 26

March 2007 outlining an agreement between the two main
parties in Northern Ireland to restore the structures of the Good
Friday Agreement on 8 May 2007.

2 Statement by Gerry Adams, President of Sinn Fein, at the joint
press conference with the DUP on 26 March 2007 outlining the
terms of Sinn Fein's agreement with Ian Paisley and the DUP.

3 Peter Wallensteen, *Understanding Conflict Resolution: War, Peace
and the Global System* (2nd edn; London: Sage, 2007), 28–9.

4 Ibid., 29.

5 Stephen John Stedman, 'Negotiation and Mediation in Internal
Conflict', in Michael E. Brown (ed.), *The International Dimensions
of Internal Conflict* (Cambridge, MA: MIT Press, 1996), 342.

6 I. William Zartman, 'Negotiating Internal Conflict: Incentives
and Intractability', *International Negotiation* 6, 2001, 298.

7 Oliver Ramsbotham, Tom Woodhouse and Hugh Miall,
Contemporary Conflict Resolution (2nd edn; Cambridge: Polity
Press, 2005), 161.

8 See Chapter 1, p. 36.

9 Marina Ottaway, 'Eritrea and Ethiopia: Negotiations in a
Transitional Conflict', in I. William Zartman (ed.), *Elusive Peace:
Negotiating an End to Civil Wars* (Washington: Brookings
Institution), 103.

10 John Paul Lederach, 'Cultivating Peace: A Practitioner's View of
Deadly Conflict and Negotiation', in John Darby and Roger Mac
Ginty (eds), *Contemporary Peacemaking: Conflict, Violence and
Peace Processes* (Basingstoke: Palgrave, 2003), 33.

11 John Major, *House of Commons Hansard Debates*, 1 November
1993, Column 35, *http://www.publications.parliament.uk/pa/
cm199293/cmhansrd/1993-11-01/Debate-2.html* (last accessed 21
April 2008).

12 John Darby and Roger Mac Ginty, 'Introduction', in Darby and
Mac Ginty (eds), *Contemporary Peacemaking*, 7.

13 Pierre du Toit, *South Africa's Brittle Peace* (Basingstoke: Palgrave,
2001), 54.

14 Robert Slater, *Rabin of Israel: Warrior for Peace* (New York:
HarperCollins, 1996), 513–14.

15 Gerry Adams, quoted in Eamonn Mallie and David McKittrick,
Endgame in Ireland (London: Hodder & Stoughton, 2001), 73.

16 'The link' was a back-channel authorized by the British
government consisting of a British intelligence officer known as

'Fred' and a former Catholic priest in Derry, Dennis Bradley, who knew the Sinn Fein leader, Martin McGuiness. The discussions between Fred and Bradley were reported back to Sinn Fein and John Major, respectively.

17 John Major, *The Autobiography* (London: HarperCollins, 2000), 447.

18 Mahmoud Abbas, *Through Secret Channels* (Reading: Garnet Publishing, 1995), 217.

19 K.M. De Silva, 'Sri Lanka's Prolonged Ethnic Conflict: Negotiating a Settlement', *International Negotiation* 6, 2001, 454.

20 Sumantra Bose, 'Flawed Mediation, Chaotic Implementation: The 1987 Indo-Sri Lanka Peace Agreement', in Stephen John Stedman, Donald Rothchild and Elizabeth M. Cousens (eds), *Ending Civil Wars: The Implementation of Peace Agreements* (London: Lynne Rienner, 2002), 642.

21 Howard Wiggins, 'Sri Lanka: Negotiations in a Secessionist Conflict', in Zartman (ed.), *Elusive Peace*, 52.

22 Adrian Guelke, 'Negotiations and Peace Processes', in Darby and Mac Ginty (eds), *Contemporary Peacemaking*, 59.

23 Du Toit, *South Africa's Brittle Peace*, 61.

24 Mitchell Reiss, 'Lessons of the Northern Ireland Peace Process', 9 September 2005, Press Release, US Department of State, available from *http://www.state.gov/p/eur/rls/rm/54869.htm* (last accessed 22 April 2008).

25 Robert Rothstein, 'In Fear of Peace: Getting Past Maybe', in Robert Rothstein (ed.), *After the Peace: Resistance and Reconciliation* (London: Lynne Rienner, 1999), 9.

26 Cathy Gormley-Heenan, *From Protagonist to Pragmatist: Political Leadership in Societies in Transition* (Derry: INCORE, 2001), 69.

27 Nelson Mandela quoted in Padraig O'Malley, 'Northern Ireland and South Africa: "Hope and History at a Crossroads"', in John McGarry (ed.), *Northern Ireland and the Divided World* (Oxford: Oxford University Press, 2001), 276.

28 Cathy Gormley-Heenan, *Political Leadership and the Northern Ireland Peace Process* (Basingstoke: Palgrave, 2007), 155.

29 Mo Mowlam, *Momentum* (London: Hodder & Stoughton, 2002), 187.

30 Ibid., 214.

31 George Mitchell, *Making Peace* (London: William Heinemann, 1999), 169.
32 'Tony Blair Chair in Irish Studies for University of Liverpool', *http://www.liv.ac.uk/news/press_releases/2007/06/blair_chair.htm* (last accessed 22 April 2008).
33 Yitzhak Shamir, quoted in Slater, *Rabin of Israel*, 505.
34 Shimon Peres, quoted in ibid., 608.

CHAPTER 4 RESISTANCE TO THE PEACE

1 Niccolò Machiavelli, *The Florentine History* (New York: Harper & Row, 1960), 68.
2 See Stephen John Stedman, 'Spoiler Problems in Peace Processes', *International Security* 22 (2), 1997, 5–53; Peter Wallensteen, *Understanding Conflict Resolution: War, Peace and the Global System* (2nd edn; London: Sage, 2007), 48–9.
3 See Paul Collier and Anke Hoeffler, *Greed and Grievance in Civil Wars*, Policy Research Paper no. 2355 (Washington: The World Bank, 2000); Paul Collier, *Breaking the Conflict Trap: Civil War and Development Policy* (Washington: The World Bank, 2003).
4 Karen Ballentine and Heiko Nitzschke, *The Political Economy of Civil War and Conflict Transformation* (Bonn: Berghof Research Center, 2005), 4.
5 Edward Newman and Oliver Richmond, *Challenges to Peace Building: Managing Spoilers during Conflict Resolution* (New York: United Nations University Press, 2006), 3.
6 Stephen Jackson, *Fortunes of War: The Coltan Trade in the Kivus* (New York: Overseas Development Institute, 2003), 4.
7 Jean-Hervé Jezequel, 'Liberia: Orchestrated Chaos', in Fabrice Weissman (ed.), *In the Shadow of 'Just Wars': Violence, Politics and Humanitarian Action* (London: Hurst, 2004), 165.
8 David Keen, 'War and Peace: What's the Difference?', *International Peacekeeping* 7 (4), 2001, 5.
9 Amnesty International, the International Action Network on Small Arms, and Oxfam International, *Arms without Borders* (London, 2006), 2.
10 Full text available on Wanabehuman website: *http://wanabehuman.blogspot.com/2006/12/politics-richard-dimbleby-lecture-2006.html* (last accessed 24 April 2008).

11 Denis Donaldson was found shot dead on 6 April 2006 at a remote cottage in Donegal where he had apparently been living under the licence of the Provisional IRA. The IRA issued a statement denying responsibility, though few people in Northern Ireland were surprised by his demise.

12 Stephen Ellis, 'The Historical Significance of South Africa's Third Force', *Journal of Southern African Studies* 24 (2), 1998, 262.

13 Stedman, 'Spoiler Problems in Peace Processes', 5.

14 Newman and Richmond, *Challenges to Peace Building*, 9.

15 Thomas Weiss, *Humanitarian Intervention: Ideas in Action* (Cambridge: Polity, 2007), 137.

16 John Darby, *The Effect of Violence on Peace Processes* (Washington: United States Institute of Peace Press, 2001), 50.

17 Peter Wallensteen, *Understanding Conflict Resolution: War, Peace and the Global System* (London: Sage, 2002).

18 Edward Said, *Peace and Its Discontents* (London: Vintage, 1995), xxv.

19 'Israeli Cabinet Announces Measures in Reaction to Hamas Election Victory', 19 February 2006. From Jewish Virtual Library: *http://www.jewishvirtuallibrary.org/jsource/Peace/cabinet021906. html* (last accessed 24 April 2008).

20 Newman and Richmond, *Challenges to Peace Building*, 4.

21 Stephen John Stedman, 'Peace Processes and the Challenges of Violence', in John Darby and Roger Mac Ginty (eds), *Contemporary Peacemaking: Conflict, Violence and Peace Processes* (Basingstoke: Palgrave, 2003), 105.

22 Tim Sisk, *Democratisation in South Africa: The Elusive Social Contract* (Princeton: Princeton University Press, 1994), 219. Quoted in Colin Knox and Padraic Quirk, *Peace Building in Northern Ireland, Israel and South Africa* (Basingstoke: Macmillan, 2000), 157.

23 'Rabin's Alleged Killer Appears in Court', CNN.com 7 November 1995. See *http://www.cnn.com/WORLD/9511/rabin/amir/11-06/ index.html* (last accessed 24 April 2008).

24 Kristine Hoglund, 'Violence and the Peace Process in Sri Lanka', *Civil Wars* 7 (2), Summer 2005, 159.

25 See Chapter 3, pp. 99–100.

26 Speech by US Secretary of State Condoleezza Rice, 'Special Briefing on Travel to the Middle East and Europe', 21 July 2006.

See *http://www.state.gov/secretary/rm/2006/69331.htm* (last accessed 24 April 2008).

27 Tony Karon, 'Condi in Diplomatic Disneyland', *Time* (26 July 2006), see *http://www.time.com/time/world/article/0,8599,1219325,00.html* (last accessed 24 April 2008).

28 Gilbert Khadiagala, 'Implementing the Arusha Peace Agreement on Rwanda', in Stephen John Stedman, Donald Rothchild and Elizabeth M. Cousens (eds), *Ending Civil Wars: The Implementation of Peace Agreements* (London: Lynne Rienner, 2002), 475–6.

29 Ibid., 492.

30 Gerard Prunier, interview with Fergal Keane, at *http://www.pbs.org/wgbh/pages/frontline/shows/rwanda/etc/interview.html* (last accessed 24 April 2008). For Prunier's definitive analysis of the Rwandan genocide read: Gerard Prunier, *The Rwanda Crisis: History of a Genocide* (New York: Columbia University Press, 1995).

31 Christopher Clapham, 'Rwanda: The Perils of Peace-Making', *Journal of Peace Research* 35 (2), 1998, 204.

32 Marie-Joelle Zahar, 'Reframing the Spoiler Debate in Peace Processes', in John Darby and Roger Mac Ginty (eds), *Contemporary Peacemaking: Conflict, Violence and Peace Processes* (Basingstoke: Palgrave, 2003), 122.

33 Said, *Peace and Its Discontents*, xxi.

CHAPTER 5 ENDING THE GLOBAL WAR ON TERROR

1 David Keen, 'How to Sell an Endless War', *Counterpunch*, 21 July 2007. Available at *http://rmf.net/keen07212007.html* (last accessed 25 April 2008).

2 Atlantic Council of the United States, *Saving Afghanistan: An Appeal and Plan for Urgent Action* (Washington: International Security Program, 2008), 1.

3 Roland Dannrauther, *International Security: The Contemporary Agenda* (Cambridge: Polity, 2007), 165.

4 Ivo Daalder and James Lindsay, *America Unbound: The Bush Revolution in Foreign Policy* (Hoboken, NJ: Wiley, 2005), 77.

5 Michael Cox, 'American Power before and after 11 September: Dizzy with Success?' *International Affairs* 78 (2), 2002, 270.

6 Jean-Marie Colombani, *Le Monde*, Paris, France, 12 September 2001. Available at *http://www.worldpress.org/1101we_are_all_americans.htm* (last accessed 25 April 2008).

7 President George W. Bush, Address to Joint Session of Congress and the American People, 20 September 2001, *http://www.whitehouse.gov/news/releases/2001/09/20010920-8.html* (last accessed 25 April 2008).

8 Ibid.

9 Ivo Daalder, 'The United States and Military Intervention in Internal Conflict', in Michael E. Brown (ed.), *The International Dimensions of Internal Conflict* (Cambridge, MA: MIT Press, 1996), 464.

10 Mary Kaldor, *Global Civil Society* (Cambridge: Polity, 2003), 119.

11 See D.S. Alberts, J.J. Garstka and F.P. Stein, *Network Centric Warfare: Developing and Leveraging Information Superiority* (2nd edn; Washington: CCRP Publication Series, 1999).

12 See *http://news.bbc.co.uk/1/hi/uk_politics/7225556.stm* (last accessed 25 April 2008).

13 Dannrauther, *International Security*, 167.

14 President George Bush, 'President's Radio Address', White House Radio, 29 July 2006, *http://www.whitehouse.gov/news/releases/2006/07/20060729.html* (last accessed 25 April 2008).

15 Global Policy Forum, *War and Occupation in Iraq*, June 2007, Chapter 11, *http://www.globalpolicy.org/security/issues/iraq/occupation/report/110ther.htm#_ednref12* (last accessed 25 April 2008).

16 Paul Rogers, *A War on Terror: Afghanistan and After* (London: Pluto Press, 2004), 125.

17 Zbigniew Brzezinski, 'Terrorized by "War on Terror" ', *Washington Post*, 25 March 2005, B01, *http://www.washingtonpost.com/wp-dyn/content/article/2007/03/23/AR2007032301613.html* (last accessed 25 April 2008).

18 Tom A. Peter, 'National Intelligence Estimate: Al Qaeda Stronger and a Threat to US Homeland', *Christian Science Monitor*, 19 July 2007, *http://www.csmonitor.com/2007/0718/p99s01-duts.html* (last accessed 25 April 2008).

19 Andrew Williams, *Liberalism and War: The Victors and the Vanquished* (London: Routledge, 2006), 215.

20 John Paul Lederach 'The Challenge of Terror: A Travelling Essay', 16 September 2001, *http://www.nd.edu/~krocinst/sept11/ledtrav.shtml* (last accessed 25 April 2008).

21 Phyllis Bennis and Eric Lever, *Ending the US War in Iraq: How to Bring the Troops Home and Internationalize the Peace* (Washington: Institute for Policy Studies, 2005). Report available at *http://www.tni.org/achives/bennis/endingwar.pdf* (last accessed 25 April 2008).

22 For polling statistics on US public opinion on Iraq, see *http://www.pollingreport.com/iraq.htm* (last accessed 25 April 2008).

23 Senator Hillary Clinton, 'Ending the War in Iraq'. Available at *http://www.hillaryclinton.com/issues/iraq/* (last accessed 25 April 2008).

24 'I would propose several steps that together constitute a plan, or at least an approach, that moves toward hope for the future; in important respects what I am suggesting reinforces the Murtha resolution that is now before Congress:

- a clear statement by the US Government that it intends to withdraw completely from Iraq and renounces all plans to build permanent military bases;
- a timetable for withdrawal of US forces that calls for the complete phasing out of the American (and coalition) presence within one year;
- a defensive military posture adopted immediately; American forces in Iraq will only attack if attacked from now on;
- private and public encouragement of Iraqi forces to pursue a diplomacy of compromise and reconciliation as an alternative to prolonged civil war;
- diversify the effort at economic and social reconstruction to the extent possible, including seeking a new role for the United Nations acting with full independence of the American occupation;
- encourage regional initiatives that include Turkey, Iran, as well as Arab countries, that explore peacekeeping and political contributions to the post-occupation transition;
- affirm an American and British commitment to the unity of Iraq;

- exert greater pressure to end the Israeli occupation of Palestinian territories, and move toward a solution of the conflict that recognizes the legal rights of the Palestinian people and the necessity of peace based on equality and mutual respect.
  In the end, this approach has no chance of becoming operative without a major mobilization of anti-war opinion in the United States, reinforced by the expression of similar sentiments throughout the world, and on the part of regional leaders in the Middle East. Without a great heightening of anti-war activism, the war will drag on until a hasty terminal process is adopted in a spirit of desperation. What I am advocating is a comprehensive rethinking of American regional goals and behavior, with a fair chance that the results are likely to be more positive than can be realistically anticipated.' (Richard Falk, 'Ending the Iraq War', November 2005, *http://www.wagingpeace.org/articles/2005/11/00_falk_ ending-the-iraq-war.html*, last accessed 25 April 2008).
25 The Iraq Study Group Report (Washington: United States Institute of Peace, 2006), 4. See *http://www.usip.org/isg/iraq_ study_group_report/report/1206/iraq_study_group_report.pdf* (last accessed 25 April 2008).
26 Williams, *Liberalism and War*, 199.
27 Speech given to US Congress on 18 July 2003. Available from *http://www.guardian.co.uk/usa/story/0,,1000619,00.html* (last accessed 25 April 2008).
28 Robert J. Jackson and Philip Towle, *Temptations of Power: The United States in Global Politics after 9/11* (Basingstoke: Palgrave, 2006), 165.
29 Chris Abbot, Paul Rogers and John Sloboda, *Beyond Terror: The Truth about the Real Threats to Our World* (London: Rider, 2007), 6.
30 Ibid., 82.

CHAPTER 6 RECONCILIATION AND REBUILDING

1 A note on terminology may be useful at the outset here in that the definitional boundaries of reconciliation and rebuilding are far from concrete. What some call reconciliation, others refer to as

post-conflict peace-building, while reconstruction for one is deep conflict prevention for another. As definitive boundaries cannot be established for these terms and do not exist within the various literatures on the subject, this chapter adopts a pragmatic approach, conscious that these terms may flow into rather than being discrete from one another.

2 Roberto Cabrera, 'Should We Remember? Recovering Historical Memory in Guatemala', in Brandon Hamber (ed.), *Past Imperfect: Dealing with the Past in Northern Ireland and Societies in Transition* (Derry: INCORE, 1998), see *http://www.brandonhamber.com/publications/Chap%203%20-%20Guatemala%20Roberto%20 Cabrera.pdf* (last accessed 25 April 2008).

3 François Calas and Pierre Salignon, 'Afghanistan: From Militant Monks to Crusaders', in Fabrice Weissman (ed.), *In the Shadow of 'Just Wars': Violence, Politics and Humanitarian Action* (London: Hurst, 2004), 81–2.

4 Andrew Williams, *Liberalism and War: The Victors and the Vanquished* (London: Routledge, 2006), 128.

5 While it is important to point out that reconciliation activities can take place at many points in the cycle of an armed conflict, owing to contraints of space this chapter focuses in particular on the period following military cessations and political settlements.

6 Norman Porter, *The Elusive Quest: Reconciliation in Northern Ireland* (Belfast: Blackstaff Press, 2003), 1.

7 Archbishop Desmond Tutu, 'Foreword', in David Bloomfield, Teresa Barnes and Luc Huyse (eds), *Reconciliation after Violent Conflict: A Handbook* (Stockholm: International IDEA, 2003), 4.

8 Eva Hoffman, 'Introduction', in Martin Meredith, *Coming to Terms: South Africa's Search for Truth* (Oxford: Public Affairs, 1999), xi.

9 *The Agreement: Agreement Reached in the Multi-Party Negotiations* (Belfast: HMSO, 1998), 18.

10 Sir Kenneth Bloomfield, *We Will Remember Them* (Belfast: HMSO, 1998).

11 Andrew Rigby, 'Civil Society, Reconciliation and Conflict Transformation in Post-War Africa', in Oliver Furley and Roy May (eds), *Ending Africa's Wars* (Aldershot: Ashgate, 2006), 48.

12 Thomas Weiss, *Humanitarian Intervention: Ideas in Action* (Cambridge: Polity Press, 2007), 27.

13 The International Criminal Tribunal for the Former Yugoslavia, available at *http://www.un.org/icty/glance-e/index.htm* (last accessed 25 April 2008).

14 Williams, *Liberalism and War*, 154–5.

15 James Gow, 'The ICTY, War Crimes Enforcement and Dayton: The Ghost in the Machine', *Ethnopolitics* 5 (1), 2006, 50.

16 Ibid., 62.

17 Williams, *Liberalism and War*, 196.

18 Nelson Mandela, quoted in Meredith, *Coming to Terms*, 306.

19 Archbishop Desmond Tutu, quoted in Colin Greer, 'Without Memory, There Is No Healing. Without Forgiveness, There Is No Future', *Parade Magazine*, 11 January 1998, 4–6.

20 Albie Sachs quoted in Hoffman's 'Introduction' to Meredith, *Coming to Terms*, viii.

21 Donna Pankhurst, 'Issues of Justice and Reconciliation in Complex Political Emergencies: Conceptualizing Reconciliation, Justice and Peace', *Third World Quarterly* 20 (1), 1999, 240–1.

22 Meredith, *Coming to Terms*, 314–15.

23 Mary Burton, 'The South African Truth and Reconciliation Commission: Looking Back, Moving Forward – Revisiting Conflicts, Striving for Peace', in Brandon Hamber (ed.), *Past Imperfect: Dealing with the Past in Northern Ireland and Societies in Transition* (Derry: INCORE, 1998), see *http://www.brandonhamber. com/publications/Chap%202%20-%20TRC%20Mary%20Burton.pdf* (last accessed 25 April 2008).

24 Roland Paris, *At War's End: Building Peace after Civil Conflict* (Cambridge: Cambridge University Press, 2004), 5–6.

25 Williams, *Liberalism and War*, 125.

26 Roger Mac Ginty, *No War, No Peace* (Basingstoke: Palgrave, 2006), 178.

27 David Chandler, 'Building Trust in Public Institutions? Good Governance and Anti-corruption in Bosnia-Herzegovina', *Ethnopolitics* 5 (1), 2006, 92–3.

28 The Dayton agreement is more formally known as the General Framework Agreement for Peace in Bosnia and Herzegovina (GFAP). It was concluded at Dayton, Ohio, on 14 December 1995.

29 Paris, *At War's End*, 106 and 188.

30 Bruce Baker, 'Post-Settlement Governance Programmes: What Is Being Built in Africa?' in Furley and May (eds), *Ending Africa's Wars*, 42.

31 Judith Large, 'Global Governance and Resistance in Post-War Transition: The Case of Eastern Slavonia and Bosnia', in Feargal Cochrane, Rosaleen Duffy and Jan Selby (eds), *Global Governance, Conflict and Resistance* (Basingstoke: Palgrave, 2003), 108–9.
32 Williams, *Liberalism and War*, 135.
33 Mac Ginty, *No War, No Peace*, 179.
34 The Iraq Study Group Report (Washington: United States Institute of Peace, 2006), 23.
35 Jean-Hervé Bradol, 'The Sacrificial International Order and Humanitarian Action', in Weissman (ed.), *In the Shadow of 'Just Wars'*, 16.
36 'Iraq: The ICRC Carries on Scaled Back Activities'. Available on ICRC website: *http://www.icrc.org/Web/Eng/siteengo.nsf/html/ iraq-violence-200705* (last accessed 25 April 2008).
37 Mac Ginty, *No War, No Peace*, 148.
38 Atlantic Council of the United States, *Saving Afghanistan: An Appeal and Plan for Urgent Action* (Washington: International Security Program, 2008), 1.
39 Mac Ginty, *No War, No Peace*, 143.
40 Weiss, *Humanitarian Intervention*, 143.
41 Naomi Klein, 'The Rise of Disaster Capitalism', *The Nation*, 2 May 2005, 2.
42 Chris Alden, 'A Separate Peace: Mozambique, State Reconstruction and the Search for Sustainable Democracy', in Furley and May (eds), *Ending Africa's Wars*, 157.
43 Porter, *The Elusive Quest*, 32.
44 Rev. Ian Paisley, First Minister of Northern Ireland, speech given on 8 May. Full text available from CAIN website at *http://cain.ulst.ac.uk/issues/politics/docs/dup/ip080507.htm* (last accessed 25 April 2008).

CONCLUSION

1 Thomas Weiss, *Humanitarian Intervention: Ideas in Action* (Cambridge: Polity Press, 2007), 137.
2 Kofi Annan, 'Two Concepts of Sovereignty', *The Economist*, 18 September 1999, *http://www.un.org/News/ossg/sg/stories/ articleFull.asp?TID=33&Type=Article* (last accessed 28 April 2008). See Chapter 2, p. 64.

3 Mary Anderson, *Do No Harm: How Can Aid Support Peace or War?* (Boulder, CO: Lynne Rienner, 1999).

4 Peter Wallensteen, *Understanding Conflict Resolution: War, Peace and the Global System* (2nd edn; London: Sage, 2007), 12.

5 'UK Britons "Support NATO Strikes" ', BBC News Online, 28 March 1999, *http://news.bbc.co.uk/1/hi/uk/306010.stm* (last accessed 28 April 2008).

Bibliography

Abbas, M., *Through Secret Channels* (Reading: Garnet Publishing, 1995)

Abbot, C., P. Rogers and J. Sloboda, *Beyond Terror: The Truth about the Real Threats to Our World* (London: Rider, 2007)

Alberts, D.S., J.J. Garstka and F.P. Stein, *Network Centric Warfare: Developing and Leveraging Information Superiority* (2nd edn; Washington: CCRP Publication Series, 1999)

Alden, C., 'A Separate Peace: Mozambique, State Reconstruction and the Search for Sustainable Democracy', in O. Furley and R. May (eds), *Ending Africa's Wars* (Aldershot: Ashgate, 2006)

Anderson, M., *Do No Harm: How Can Aid Support Peace or War?* (Boulder, CO: Lynne Rienner, 1999)

Annan, K., 'Two Concepts of Sovereignty', *The Economist*, 18 September 1999, *http://www.un.org/News/ossg/sg/stories/articleFull.asp?TID=33&Type=Article* (last accessed 28 April 2008)

Atlantic Council of the United States, *Saving Afghanistan: An Appeal and Plan for Urgent Action* (Washington: International Security Program, 2008)

Baker, B., 'Post-Settlement Governance Programmes: What Is Being Built in Africa?' in O. Furley and R. May (eds), *Ending Africa's Wars* (Aldershot: Ashgate, 2006)

Ballentine, K. and H. Nitzschke, *The Political Economy of Civil War and Conflict Transformation* (Bonn: Berghof Research Center, 2005)

Banfield, J., C. Gunduz and N. Killick, 'The Confederation of British Industry and the Group of Seven: A Marathon Walk to Peace in Northern Ireland', in J. Banfield, C. Gunduz and N. Killick (eds), *Local Business, Local Peace: The Peacebuilding Potential of the Local Private Sector* (London: International Alert, 2006)

Bass, G., '*Jus Post Bellum*', *Philosophy & Public Affairs* 32 (4), 2004

BBC News Online, 'UK Britons "Support NATO Strikes" ', 28 March
1999, *http://news.bbc.co.uk/1/hi/uk/306010.stm* (last accessed 28
April 2008)
BBC News Online, 'Bush: The First 100 Days', 30 April 2001,
http://news.bbc.co.uk/1/hi/world/americas/1302232.stm (last
accessed 17 April 2008)
BBC News Online, 'Report Condemns Sudan over Darfur', 12 March
2007, *http://news.bbc.co.uk/1/hi/world/africa/6440719.stm* (last
accessed 21 April 2008)
BBC News Online, 'Middle East Fears Broken Iraq', 22 March 2007,
http://news.bbc.co.uk/1/hi/world/middle_east/6476907.stm (last
accessed 21 April 2008)
Bellamy, A.J., *Just Wars: From Cicero to Iraq* (Cambridge: Polity Press,
2006)
Bennis, P. and E. Lever, *Ending the US War in Iraq: How to Bring the
Troops Home and Internationalize the Peace* (Washington: Institute
for Policy Studies, 2005), *http://www.tni.org/achives/bennis/
endingwar.pdf* (last accessed 25 April 2008)
Blair, T., 'Doctrine of the International Community', Chicago, 24 April
1999, *http://www.number10.gov.uk/output/Page1297.asp* (last
accessed 17 April 2008)
Bloomfield, D., T. Barnes and L. Huyse (eds), *Reconciliation after Violent
Conflict: A Handbook* (Stockholm: International IDEA, 2003)
Bloomfield, Sir K., *We Will Remember Them* (Belfast: HMSO, 1998)
Bojicic-Dzelilovic, V. and M. Kaldor, 'The Political Economy of the War
in Bosnia-Hercegovina', in M. Kaldor and B. Vashee (eds), *New
Wars: Restructuring the Global Military Sector* (London: Pinter, 1997)
Bose, S., 'Flawed Mediation, Chaotic Implementation: The 1987 Indo-
Sri Lanka Peace Agreement', in S.J. Stedman, D. Rothchild and
E.M. Cousens (eds), *Ending Civil Wars: The Implementation of
Peace Agreements* (London: Lynne Rienner, 2002)
Bradol, J.H., 'The Sacrificial International Order and Humanitarian
Action', in F. Weissman (ed.), *In the Shadow of 'Just Wars':
Violence, Politics and Humanitarian Action* (London: Hurst: 2004)
Brzezinski, Z., 'Terrorized by "War on Terror" ', *Washington Post*, 25
March 2005, *http://www.washingtonpost.com/wp-dyn/content/
article/2007/03/23/AR2007032301613.html* (last accessed 28 April
2008)
Burton, M., 'The South African Truth and Reconciliation Commission:
Looking Back, Moving Forward – Revisiting Conflicts, Striving for

Peace', in B. Hamber (ed.), *Past Imperfect: Dealing with the Past in Northern Ireland and Societies in Transition* (Derry: INCORE, 1998), *http://www.brandonhamber.com/publications/Chap%202%20-%20TRC%20Mary%20Burton.pdf* (last accessed 25 April 2008)

Bush, G.W., Address to Joint Session of Congress and the American People, 20 September 2001, *http://www.whitehouse.gov/news/releases/2001/09/20010920-8.html* (last accessed 25 April 2008)

Bush, G.W., 'President's Radio Address', White House Radio, 29 July 2006, *http://www.whitehouse.gov/news/releases/2006/07/20060729.html* (last accessed 25 April 2008)

Cabrera, R., 'Should We Remember? Recovering Historical Memory in Guatemala', in B. Hamber (ed.), *Past Imperfect: Dealing with the Past in Northern Ireland and Societies in Transition* (Derry: INCORE, 1998), *http://www.brandonhamber.com/publications/Chap%203%20-%20Guatemala%20Roberto%20Cabrera.pdf* (last accessed 25 April 2008)

Calas, F. and P. Salignon, 'Afghanistan: From Militant Monks to Crusaders', in F. Weissman (ed.), *In the Shadow of 'Just Wars': Violence, Politics and Humanitarian Action* (London: Hurst, 2004)

CBI Northern Ireland, *Peace – A Challenging New Era* (Belfast: CBI, 1994)

Chan, S., *Out of Evil* (London: I.B. Tauris, 2005)

Chandler, D., 'Building Trust in Public Institutions? Good Governance and Anti-corruption in Bosnia-Herzegovina', *Ethnopolitics* 5 (1), 2006

Clapham, C., 'Rwanda: The Perils of Peace-Making', *Journal of Peace Research* 35 (2), 1998

Cochrane, F., 'Beyond the Political Elites: A Comparative Analysis of the Roles and Impacts of Community-Based NGOs in Conflict Resolution Activity', *Civil Wars* 3 (2), Summer 2000

Cochrane, F., 'Unsung Heroes? The Role of Peace and Conflict Resolution Organisations in the Northern Ireland Conflict', in J. McGarry (ed.), *Northern Ireland and the Divided World* (Oxford: Oxford University Press, 2001)

Cochrane, F. and S. Dunn, *People Power? The Role of the Voluntary and Community Sector in the Northern Ireland Conflict* (Cork: Cork University Press, 2002)

Collier, P., *Breaking the Conflict Trap: Civil War and Development Policy* (Washington: The World Bank, 2003)

Collier, P. and A. Hoeffler, *Greed and Grievance in Civil Wars*, Policy Research Paper no. 2355 (Washington: The World Bank, 2000)

Cornell, S., 'International Reactions to Massive Human Rights Violations: The Case of Chechnya', *Europe-Asia Studies* 51 (1), 1999

Cox, M., 'American Power before and after 11 September: Dizzy with Success?', *International Affairs* 78 (2), 2002

Daalder, I., 'The United States and Military Intervention in Internal Conflict', in M.E. Brown (ed.), *The International Dimensions of Internal Conflict* (Cambridge, MA: MIT Press, 1996)

Daalder, I. and J. Lindsay, *America Unbound: The Bush Revolution in Foreign Policy* (Hoboken, NJ: Wiley, 2005)

Dannrauther, R., *International Security: The Contemporary Agenda* (Cambridge: Polity Press, 2007)

Darby, J., *The Effect of Violence on Peace Processes* (Washington: United States Institute of Peace Press, 2001)

De Silva, K.M., 'Sri Lanka's Prolonged Ethnic Conflict: Negotiating a Settlement', *International Negotiation* 6, 2001

Doyle, M., 'Kant, Liberal Legacies and Foreign Affairs', *Philosophy & Public Affairs* 12 (3), 1983

du Toit, P., *South Africa's Brittle Peace* (Basingstoke: Palgrave, 2001)

Ellis, S., 'The Historical Significance of South Africa's Third Force', *Journal of Southern African Studies* 24 (2), 1998

Ellis, S., 'Interpreting Violence: Reflections on West African Wars', in N. Whitehead (ed.), *Violence* (Oxford: James Currey, 2004)

Evans, G., 'Foreword', in T. Weiss, *Humanitarian Intervention* (Cambridge: Polity Press, 2007)

Fierke, K., *Diplomatic Interventions: Conflict and Change in a Globalizing World* (Basingstoke: Palgrave Macmillan, 2005)

Fisk, R., *The Great War for Civilisation: The Conquest of the Middle East* (London: Harper Perennial, 2006)

Fourie, A. and T. Eloff, 'Exploring the Contributions of the Private Sector to the Social, Economic and Political Transformation Process in South Africa', in J. Banfield, C. Gunduz and N. Killick (eds), *Local Business, Local Peace: The Peacebuilding Potential of the Local Private Sector* (London: International Alert, 2006)

Freedman, L. (ed.), *War* (Oxford: Oxford University Press, 1994)

Friedman, T., *The Lexus and the Olive Tree* (New York: Farrar, Straus & Giroux, 1999)

Gordadze, T., 'Chechnya: Eradication of the Enemy Within', in
    F. Weissman (ed.), *In the Shadow of 'Just Wars': Violence, Politics
    and Humanitarian Action* (London: Hurst, 2004)
Gormley-Heenan, C., *From Protagonist to Pragmatist: Political
    Leadership in Societies in Transition* (Derry: INCORE, 2001)
Gormley-Heenan, C., *Political Leadership and the Northern Ireland
    Peace Process* (Basingstoke: Palgrave, 2007)
Gow, J., 'The ICTY, War Crimes Enforcement and Dayton: The Ghost
    in the Machine', *Ethnopolitics* 5 (1), 2006
Guardian, 'Dispatches from a Savage War', 15 October 2004,
    http://www.guardian.co.uk/women/story/0,,1327791,00.html (last
    accessed 21 April 2008)
Guelke, A., 'Negotiations and Peace Processes', in J. Darby and R.
    Mac Ginty (eds), *Contemporary Peacemaking: Conflict, Violence and
    Peace Processes* (Basingstoke: Palgrave, 2003)
Halliday, F., *The World in 2000* (Basingstoke: Palgrave, 2001)
Hampson, F.O., *Nurturing Peace: Why Peace Settlements Succeed or Fail*
    (Washington: United States Institute of Peace, 1996)
Harbom, L., S. Hogbladh and P. Wallensteen, 'Armed Conflict and
    Peace Agreements', *Journal of Peace Research* 43 (5), 2006
Harris, P. and B. Reilly (eds), *Democracy and Deep-Rooted Conflict:
    Options for Negotiators* (Stockholm: International IDEA Handbook
    Series 3, 1998)
Hoffman, E., 'Introduction', in M. Meredith, *Coming to Terms: South
    Africa's Search for Truth* (Oxford: Public Affairs, 1999)
Hoglund, K., 'Violence and the Peace Process in Sri Lanka', *Civil Wars*
    7 (2), 2005
International IDEA, *Democracy, Conflict and Human Security: Pursuing
    Peace in the 21st Century* (Stockholm: International IDEA, 2006)
Iraq Study Group Report (Washington: United States Institute of Peace,
    2006), *http://www.usip.org/isg/iraq_study_group_report/report/1206/
    iraq_study_group_report.pdf* (last accessed 25 April 2008)
Jackson, R.J. and P. Towle, *Temptations of Power: The United States in
    Global Politics after 9/11* (Basingstoke: Palgrave, 2006)
Jackson, S., *Fortunes of War: The Coltan Trade in the Kivus* (New York:
    Overseas Development Institute, 2003)
Jewish Virtual Library, 'Israeli Cabinet Announces Measures in
    Reaction to Hamas Election Victory', 19 February 2006, *http://
    www.jewishvirtuallibrary.org/jsource/Peace/cabinet021906.html* (last
    accessed 24 April 2008)

Jezequel, J.-H., 'Liberia: Orchestrated Chaos', in F. Weissman (ed.), *In the Shadow of 'Just Wars': Violence, Politics and Humanitarian Action* (London: Hurst, 2004)

Kaldor, M., *New and Old Wars: Organized Violence in a Global Era* (Cambridge: Polity Press, 2001)

Kaldor, M., *Global Civil Society* (Cambridge: Polity Press, 2003)

Karon, T., 'Condi in Diplomatic Disneyland', *Time*, 26 July 2006, *http://www.time.com/time/world/article/0,8599,1219325,00.html* (last accessed 24 April 2008)

Keen, D., 'War and Peace: What's the Difference?' *International Peacekeeping* 7 (4), 2001

Keen, D., 'Liberalization and Conflict', *International Political Science Review* 26 (1), 2005

Keen, D., 'How to Sell an Endless War', *Counterpunch*, 21 July 2007, *http://rmf.net/keen07212007.html* (last accessed 25 April 2008)

Khadiagala, G., 'Implementing the Arusha Peace Agreement on Rwanda', in S.J. Stedman, D. Rothchild and E.M. Cousens (eds), *Ending Civil Wars: The Implementation of Peace Agreements* (London: Lynne Rienner, 2002)

Klein, N., 'The Rise of Disaster Capitalism', *The Nation*, 2 May 2005

Knox, C. and P. Quirk, *Peace Building in Northern Ireland, Israel and South Africa* (Basingstoke: Macmillan, 2000)

Landman, T., *Democracy, Conflict and Human Security: Further Readings* (Stockholm: International IDEA, 2007)

Large, J., 'Global Governance and Resistance in Post-War Transition: The Case of Eastern Slavonia and Bosnia', in F. Cochrane, R. Duffy and J. Selby (eds), *Global Governance, Conflict and Resistance* (Basingstoke: Palgrave, 2003)

Lederach, J.P., 'The Challenge of Terror: A Traveling Essay', 16 September 2001, *http://www.nd.edu/~krocinst/sept11/ledtrav.shtml* (last accessed 25 April 2008)

Lederach, J.P., 'Cultivating Peace: A Practitioner's View of Deadly Conflict and Negotiation', in J. Darby and R. Mac Ginty (eds), *Contemporary Peacemaking: Conflict, Violence and Peace Processes* (Basingstoke: Palgrave, 2003)

Licklider, R., 'The Consequences of Negotiated Settlements in Civil Wars 1945–1993', *American Political Science Review* 89 (3), 1995

McCandless, F., 'Funding and Sustaining the Sector', *Scope*, March 2003

Mac Ginty, R., *No War, No Peace* (Basingstoke: Palgrave, 2006)

Machiavelli, N., *The Florentine History* (New York: Harper & Row, 1960)

Mack, A., *War and Peace in the 21st Century, Human Security Report 2005* (New York: Oxford University Press, 2005)

McQueen, N., *Peacekeeping and the International System* (London: Routledge, 2006)

Major, J., *House of Commons Hansard Debates*, 1 November 1993, Column 35, *http://www.publications.parliament.uk/pa/cm199293/cmhansrd/1993-11-01/Debate-2.html* (last accessed 21 April 2008)

Major, J., *The Autobiography* (London: HarperCollins, 2000)

Mallie, E. and D. McKittrick, *Endgame in Ireland* (London: Hodder & Stoughton, 2001)

Miall, M., *The Peacemakers: Peaceful Settlement of Disputes since 1945* (London: Macmillan, 1992)

Miall, H., O. Ramsbotham and T. Woodhouse, *Contemporary Conflict Resolution* (Cambridge: Polity Press, 1999)

Mitchell, G., *Making Peace* (London: William Heinemann, 1999)

Mowlam, M., *Momentum* (London: Hodder & Stoughton, 2002)

Newman, E. and O. Richmond, *Challenges to Peace Building: Managing Spoilers during Conflict Resolution* (New York: United Nations University Press, 2006)

Nye, J., *Soft Power: The Means to Success in World Politics* (New York: Public Affairs, 2004).

Nye, J., *Power in the Global Information Age* (London: Routledge, 2004)

O'Malley, P., 'Northern Ireland and South Africa: "Hope and History at a Crossroads" ', in J. McGarry (ed.), *Northern Ireland and the Divided World* (Oxford: Oxford University Press, 2001)

Orend, B., '*Jus Post Bellum*', *Journal of Social Philosophy* 31 (1), 2001

Ottaway, M., 'Eritrea and Ethiopia: Negotiations in a Transitional Conflict', in I.W. Zartman (ed.), *Elusive Peace: Negotiating an End to Civil Wars* (Washington: Brookings Institution, 1995)

Pankhurst, D., 'Issues of Justice and Reconciliation in Complex Political Emergencies: Conceptualizing Reconciliation, Justice and Peace', *Third World Quarterly* 20 (1), 1995

Paris, R., 'International Peacebuilding and the "Mission Civilisatrice" ', *Review of International Studies* 28, 2002

Paris, R., *At War's End: Building Peace after Civil Conflict* (Cambridge: Cambridge University Press, 2004)

Peter, T.A., 'National Intelligence Estimate: Al Qaeda Stronger and a Threat to US Homeland', *Christian Science Monitor*, 19 July 2007, *http://www.csmonitor.com/2007/0718/p99s01-duts.html* (last accessed 25 April 2008)

Porter, N., *The Elusive Quest: Reconciliation in Northern Ireland* (Belfast: Blackstaff Press, 2003)

Prunier, G., *The Rwanda Crisis: History of a Genocide* (New York: Columbia University Press, 1995)

Ramsbotham, O., T. Woodhouse and H. Miall, *Contemporary Conflict Resolution* (2nd edn; Cambridge: Polity Press, 2005)

Reiss, M., 'Lessons of the Northern Ireland Peace Process', Press Release, US Department of State, 9 September 2005, *http://www.state.gov/p/eur/rls/rm/54869.htm* (last accessed 22 April 2008)

Reno, W., *Corruption and State Politics in Sierra Leone* (Cambridge: Cambridge University Press, 1995)

Report of the International Commission on Intervention and State Sovereignty (ICISS), *The Responsibility to Protect* (Ottawa: International Development Research Centre, 2001)

Rettberg, A., 'El Salvador: A Firm Grip on the Peace Process', in J. Banfield, C. Gunduz and N. Killick (eds), *Local Business, Local Peace: The Peacebuilding Potential of the Local Private Sector* (London: International Alert, 2006)

Rice, C., 'Special Briefing on Travel to the Middle East and Europe', 21 July 2006, *http://www.state.gov/secretary/rm/2006/69331.htm* (last accessed 24 April 2008)

Richardson, L.F., *Statistics of Deadly Quarrels* (Pittsburgh: Boxwood Press, 1960)

Rieff, D., 'Kosovo: The End of an Era?' in F. Wiessman (ed.), *In the Shadow of 'Just Wars': Violence, Politics and Humanitarian Action* (London: Hurst, 2004)

Rigby, A., 'Civil Society, Reconciliation and Conflict Transformation in Post-War Africa', in O. Furley and R. May (eds), *Ending Africa's Wars* (Aldershot: Ashgate, 2006)

Rogers, P., *Losing Control: Global Security in the 21st Century* (London: Pluto Press, 2000)

Rogers, P., *A War on Terror: Afghanistan and After* (London: Pluto Press, 2004)

Rothstein, R. (ed.), *After the Peace: Resistance and Reconciliation* (London: Lynne Rienner, 1999)

Ryan, S., *The United Nations and International Politics* (London: Macmillan, 2000)

Said, E., *Peace and Its Discontents* (London: Vintage, 1995)

Sandole, D., *Capturing the Complexity of Conflict: Dealing with Violent Ethnic Conflicts of the Post-Cold War Era* (London: Pinter, 1999)

Sisk, T., *Democratisation in South Africa: The Elusive Social Contract* (Princeton: Princeton University Press, 1994)

Slater, R., *Rabin of Israel: Warrior for Peace* (New York: HarperCollins, 1996)

Smith, D., 'Trends and Causes of Armed Conflict' (Berlin: Berghof Research Center for Constructive Conflict Management, 2004)

Stedman, S.J., 'Negotiation and Mediation in Internal Conflict', in M.E. Brown (ed.), *The International Dimensions of Internal Conflict* (Cambridge, MA: MIT Press, 1996)

Stedman, S.J., 'Spoiler Problems in Peace Processes', *International Security* 22 (2), 1997

Stedman, S.J. 'Peace Processes and the Challenges of Violence', in J. Darby and R. Mac Ginty (eds), *Contemporary Peacemaking: Conflict, Violence and Peace Processes* (Basingstoke: Palgrave, 2003)

Stedman, S.J., D. Rothchild and E.M. Cousens (eds), *Ending Civil Wars: The Implementation of Peace Agreements* (London: Lynne Rienner, 2002)

Taylor, R., 'South Africa: The Role of Peace and Conflict Resolution Organizations in the Struggle against Apartheid', in B. Gidron, S. Katz and Y. Hasenfeld (eds), *Mobilizing for Peace* (Oxford: Oxford University Press)

van Tongeren, P., M. Brenk, M. Hellema and J. Verhoeven (eds), *People Building Peace II: Successful Stories of Civil Society* (London: Lynne Rienner, 2007)

Wallensteen, P., *Understanding Conflict Resolution: War, Peace and the Global System* (London: Sage, 2002)

Wallensteen, P., *Understanding Conflict Resolution: War, Peace and the Global System* (2nd edn; London: Sage, 2007)

Wallensteen, P. and M. Sollenberg, 'The End of International War? Armed Conflict 1989–95', *Journal of Peace Research* 33 (3), Aug. 1996

Weiss, T., *Humanitarian Intervention: Ideas in Action* (Cambridge: Polity Press, 2007)

Welch, D.A., *Justice and the Genesis of War* (New York: Cambridge University Press, 1993)

Wiggins, H., 'Sri Lanka: Negotiations in a Secessionist Conflict', in
I.W. Zartman (ed.), *Elusive Peace* (Washington: Brookings
Institution, 1995)

Williams, A., *Liberalism and War: The Victors and the Vanquished*
(London: Routledge, 2006)

Wright, Q., *A Study of War* (Chicago: University of Chicago Press,
1966)

Zahar, M.J., 'Reframing the Spoiler Debate in Peace Processes', in J.
Darby and R. Mac Ginty (eds), *Contemporary Peacemaking:
Conflict, Violence and Peace Processes* (Basingstoke: Palgrave, 2003)

Zartman, I.W., 'The Unfinished Agenda: Negotiating Internal
Conflicts', in R. Licklider (ed.), *Stopping the Killing: How Civil
Wars End* (New York: New York University Press, 2003)

Zartman, I.W. (ed.), *Elusive Peace: Negotiating an End to Civil Wars*
(Washington: Brookings Institution, 1995)

Zartman, I.W., 'Negotiating Internal Conflict: Incentives and
Intractability', *International Negotiation* 6, 2001

Zartman, I.W., 'The Timing of Peace Initiatives: Hurting Stalemates
and Ripe Moments', *The Global Review of Ethnopolitics* 1 (1),
September 2001

Index

Abbas, Mahmoud 84–5
Abu Ghraib prison 134, 140, 142
Adams, Gerry
    first meeting with Paisley 70–1
    and Major 78, 83
    position change 122–3
    role in negotiations 95
Afghanistan
    mutually hurting stalemate in 128
    reconstruction 176, 179, 181
    war in 134–5, 190
African National Congress (ANC)
    and business community 50–1
    and Inkatha Freedom Party 123
    negotiations with National Party
        50–1, 88, 96, 114, 123
    pre-negotiations 82
    and security services 107
    Senegal meeting 52
    unbanning 51
Ahern, Bertie 92–3, 98–9
Al-Qaeda
    belief system 137
    as enemy in GWOT 130, 135
    political agenda 126, 141, 144–5
    power 184–5
    recruitment 138, 140
    strengthening 139
    structure 133
Alden, Chris 181–2
Amir, Yigal 100, 115
ANC see African National Congress
Anderson, Mary 188
Angola 102, 103, 108
Annan, Kofi
    on humanitarian action 64
    on humanity 187
    in Kenya 43–4
    on Rwanda 57–8
    on sovereignty 56
    on terrorism 66
Annan Plan 60
apartheid 50, 96

Aquinas, St Thomas 20
Arafat, Yasser 85, 90–1, 95, 99
ARENA 52
Arkan 108
armed conflict, quantification 15
arms industry 104–6
Arusha peace agreement 102, 108,
    119–21
atrocities 31
Augustine, St 20

back-channels 83–5
Baker, Bruce 171
Baker, James 143–4
Ballentine, Karen 102–3
bargaining 91–4
Bass, Gary 23–4
Bellamy, Alex 24–5
Beslan 66, 133
Bin Laden, Osama 140, 146, 174
bi-polar world 29
black economy 106
Blair, Tony
    election of (1997) 92, 97
    and GWOT 66
    and Iraq 140
    on just wars 19, 21–2, 23
    and Kosovo 21–2
    and Middle East 147
    and Northern Ireland 92–3, 98–9
Bojicic-Dzelilovic, Vesna 31
Bose, Sumantra 86
Bosnia 87
    ICTY effect in 160
    intervention in 49, 55
    post-war reconstruction 170, 171–3
    way of war in 31
    see also Dayton agreement
Botha, P.W. 96
Bowen, Jeremy 39
Bradol, Jean-Hervé 176
brinkmanship 91–3
Brzezinski, Zbigniew 137–8

Burton, Mary 166
Bush, George W.
  foreign policy agenda 25–6
  and Global War on Terror 9, 66,
    129–30, 134, 135
  and Iraq 140, 143–4
  Presidency of 126

Cabrera, Roberto 150
Calas, François 152–3
Camp David Agreement 85
Carter, Jimmy 77, 137
CBI, Northern Ireland 47–8
cease-fire agreements 26, 74, 115
Chan, Stephen 19–20
Chandler, David 170
Chapter VI interventions 59
Chapter VII interventions 41–2, 64
Chapultepec Peace Accords 52
Chechnya 64–9, 133, 134
Cheney, Dick 174
Chile 159
civilians
  direct targeting of 20, 22
  proportion of fatalities 32
Clapham, Christopher 121
Clinton, Bill 85
Clinton, Hillary 142
Clinton administration 49
Clonard Monastery 46
'coalition of the willing' 127, 130
Coetsee, Kobie 82
Collier, Paul 102
Colombia 103
constructive ambiguity 94–5
Consultative Business Movement
  (CBM) 50–1
Convention for a Democratic South
  Africa (CODESA) 51
Cornell, Svante 68–9
Council of Europe, Parliamentary
  Assembly 66–7
counter-insurgency strategies 133–4
Cox, Michael 129
Cristiani, Alfredo 52
Cromwell, Oliver 19
Cyprus 36, 60

Daalder, Ivo 129, 131
Dannrauther, Roland 128, 135
Darby, John 110
Darfur 58
Dayton agreement 49, 55, 87, 160,
  171–2
de Klerk, F.W. 96
'dealers' 110

Declaration of Palestinian
  Independence 80
Declaration of Principles (DOP)
  89–91
defence spending 106
Democratic Party (US) 142
democratic peace 16–18, 171, 191
  policy drivers 23
Democratic Republic of Congo (DRC)
  104, 185
Democratic Unionist Party (DUP) 92,
  123
democratization 17, 59–60, 171–3
Donaldson, Denis 107
Doyle, Michael 16–17
DRC 104, 185
du Toit, Pierre 82, 88

East Timor 163
ECOMOG 31
Egypt, and Israel 85
El Salvador 52–3, 163
  negotiation 73
Ellis, Stephen 31, 107
EPLF 77
Eritrea 61, 76–7
Ethiopia 61, 76–7
ethnic cleansing 189
'ethnic outbidding' 79
ethnic violence 128–9
European Union (EU)
  interventionism 168
  and Palestinian Authority 111
  peace-keeping forces 63
Evans, Gareth 56–7
'extraordinary renditions' 134, 142,
  147

FAFO 85
Falk, Richard 143
Fatah party 111
Fierke, Karin 55
'filtration camps' 65
Fisk, Robert 12
FMLN 52
forgiveness 163, 165, 166
France, arms trade 105
Franklin, Benjamin 1
Frelimo 62
Freud, Sigmund 1
Friedman, Thomas 18
FUSADES 52–3

Gandhi, Rajiv 85–6
Germany 105, 168, 189
Global Policy Forum 136

Global War on Terror (GWOT) 9, 66,
    126–49
  boundaries 130–1
  cornerstones to ending 139–41
  ending 144–8
  ending war in Iraq 141–4
  failure 138–9
  and Middle East crisis 146–7
  understanding 128–38
  'Golden Arches Theory' 18
Good Friday Agreement
  beliefs in 122–3
  destabilization attempt 116
  implementation problems 93–4
  leadership roles in 98–9
  negotiations leading to 49
  reconciliation initiatives 155
  referendum 48
  suspension of structures 107
Gordadze, Thornike 65
Gormley-Heenan, Cathy 97
Gow, James 160
'greed or grievance' 102
Grotius, Hugo 20
Grozny 65
Guantánamo Bay 134, 140, 147
Guatemala 163–4
Gulf War, first (1991) 131, 139–40
GWOT see Global War on Terror

Habyarimana, Juvénal 119–20
Halliburton 174
Halliday, Fred 16, 22
Hamas 111–12
Hezbollah 118
Hitler, Adolf 168, 189
Ho Chi Minh 83
Hoeffler, Anke 102
Hoffman, Eva 155
Hoglund, Kristine 116
Holbrooke, Richard 49
human rights, state sovereignty vs 21, 159
Human Security Report 2005 3, 17, 32
humanitarian aid 152–3, 176–7
humanitarian intervention 56, 188
  growth 21
humanitarian war 16
Hume, John 46
Hussein, Saddam 135, 138, 146, 161, 175
Hutus 119–21

IMF 181–2
imperialism 176
India, as mediator 85
Indo-Sri Lanka Peace Agreement
    (ISPA) 86

Inkatha Freedom Party (IFP) 50–1,
    123
Institute for Policy Studies 141–2
institutional mechanisms, post-
    settlement 154–7
inter-state conflicts, reduction in 3, 28
Interahamwe 120
interests, war over 130
International Commission on
    Intervention and State Sovereignty
    53–4
International Committee of the Red
    Cross (ICRC) 176–7
International Criminal Tribunal for the
    Former Yugoslavia (ICTY) 158, 159,
    160
International IDEA 26, 28, 154
  definition of third-party intervention
    40
international non-governmental
    organizations (INGOs) 44
intervention gap 64
interventionism 139, 168
intifada, Palestinian 89, 90
intra-state conflicts
  increase in 3, 28
  negotiations within see negotiation
  way fought 72
IRA see Provisional IRA
Iran 143
Iraq
  Government of National Unity 138
  reconstruction 174–7, 181
  trial of Saddam Hussein 161
Iraq Study Group 143–4, 175
Iraq war 4, 71, 134–5, 136–8, 139–40
  casualties 138
  ending 141–4
  mutually hurting stalemate 143
Irish Business and Employers
  Confederation 47
Israel
  and Egypt 85
  and Lebanon 118
  UN peace-keeping mission 42
Israel/Palestine conflict
  bargaining 94
  final-status issues 91
  and GWOT 146–7
  leadership role 99–100
  mutually hurting stalemate 90
  negotiations 89–91
  pre-negotiations 79–80, 82–3
  'road map for peace' 110, 136
  US policy stance 135–6
  see also Oslo agreement

Jackson, General Sir Mike 106
Jackson, Robert 148
jus post bellum 23–5, 158
'just cause' 20
Just War Theory (JWT) 19, 23
    updating 23–5
justice
    order over 178
    in war 19–23
    see also restorative justice; retributive
        justice

Kabila, Laurent 185
Kaldor, Mary 29, 30, 131–2, 170
Karadžić, Radovan 160
Karzai, Hamid 180
Keen, David 18, 104–5, 127
Kenya 43–4
Khadiagala, Gilbert 120
Khan, Sadiq 134
Kissinger, Henry 25
Klein, Naomi 181
Knox, Colin 51
Kosovo 21–2, 55, 63, 108, 189
Kurds, in Iraq 136

Labour Party (Israel) 90
'land for peace' model 89, 90, 100, 117
Landman, Todd 17
Large, Judith 172–3
leadership
    chameleonic 97
    importance in negotiations 95–100
Lebanon 118, 135
Lederach, John Paul 48, 77
legalization, of direct actors 74
legitimacy 156–7
legitimate authority 20
liberalization 17–18, 168–9, 171–3
Liberia 31, 104
Licklider, Roy 5
Likud Party 90, 100, 135
Lindsay, James 129
'link, the' 84
Liverpool, University of 99
London attacks (July 2005) 133
Lorenz, Konrad 1
LTTE 85–6

Mac Ginty, Roger 18, 26, 170, 174, 177, 180
Macedonia 63
Machiavelli, Niccolò 101
McQueen, Norrie 60–1, 62
Madrid conference 89
Madrid train bombings 133
Major, John 77–8, 83–4, 97

Mandela, Nelson 51, 82, 96, 161–2
Mandela Initiative 82
Marshall Plan 151, 168
'mavericks' 110
Meredith, Martin 155
Miall, Hugh 37
Middle East 85
    relations with West 147
    US policy 143
    see also Israel/Palestine conflict
Milošević, Slobodan 160–1, 189–90
Mitchell, George 49, 92–3, 99
Mladić, General 160
Morgenthau, Hans 25
Moscow hostage crisis 133
Mowlam, Mo 97–9
Mozambique 61–2, 181–2
    negotiation 73
multilateralism 147
mutually assured destruction (MAD) 29
mutually hurting stalemate (MHS) 33,
    35, 74

Namibia, negotiation 73
National Party
    leadership 96
    negotiations with ANC 50–1, 88, 96,
        114, 123
    pre-negotiations 82
national self-determination struggles 29
Nationalist Republican Alliance
    (ARENA) 52
NATO
    in Afghanistan 179
    in former Yugoslavia 55
    in Kosovo 21–2, 63, 189
    purpose 21
negotiation
    incentives as dynamic 74
    leadership importance 95–100
    location 80–1
    making first move 81–5
    obstacles 75–6
    pattern 73–4
    political 87–95
    pre-negotiations 76–81
    rules of engagement 87
neo-liberalism, policy shift to 21
Netanyahu, Benjamin 100, 115
Network-Centric War (NCW) 132
network war 131–2
'new wars' 29
Newman, Edward 103, 112
Nicaragua 73
9/11 attacks 128–9, 132–4
Nitzschke, Heiko 102–3

Northern Ireland 44–9
  bargaining 91–4
  business sector 47–8
  cease-fires 46
  church intermediaries 46
  leadership role 96–9
  negotiation 88, 91–4
  peace process beginnings 77–8
  power-sharing 94
  pre-negotiations 77–8, 81, 83–4
  reconciliation 183
  security services 107
  Victims' Commission 155–6
  violent resistance to peace process
    115–16
  see also Good Friday Agreement
Norway, as mediator 85
Nye, Joseph 12, 49

Obama, Barack 142
Olmert, Ehud 111
Omagh bombing 116
ONUMOZ 61–2
'Operation Concordia' 63
'Operation Enduring Freedom' 152
'Operation Iraqi Freedom' 136
'opportunists' 110
order, over justice 178
Orend, Brian 24
Organization of African Unity (OAU)
    119–20
OSCE 63, 65
Oslo agreement 84–5, 89, 90–1, 99–100
  opposition 110, 115, 124
Ottaway, Marina 77

Paisley, Ian
  first meeting with Gerry Adams 70–1
  position change 122–3
  and reconciliation 183
  role in negotiations 95
  withdrawal from talks 92
Palestine
  Declaration of Palestinian
    Independence 80
  statehood 91, 146
  see also Israel/Palestine conflict; PLO
Palestinian Authority (PA) 90, 111
Palestinian Legislative Council (PLC) 111
Pankhurst, Donna 165
paramilitary factions
  consolidation 80
  political recognition 79
Paris, Roland 17, 59–60, 169, 171
peace constituency 48
peace dividend 47–8, 52

peace-enforcement operations,
    development 41
peace-keeping operations 41
  before Cold War 42
  since Cold War 42
Peres, Shimon 99, 100
Pinochet, Augusto 159
PLO 79–80, 84–5, 89–91
Politkovskaya, Anna 67–8
Porter, Norman 153, 182–3
  'predatory disaster capitalism' 181
Provisional IRA 77–8
  as beyond the pale 145
  cease-fire 46, 92
  Downing Stret mortar attack 84
  spying charge 107
  weapons decommissioning 93
Prunier, Gerard 120–1
Putin, Vladimir 65–6, 67–8

Quirk, Padraic 51

Rabin, Yitzhak
  assassination 100, 115
  election 82, 90
  leadership role 99–100
  and Oslo process 85, 90–1, 95,
    99–100
  peace initiative 82–3
Ramsbotham, Oliver 37
rational actor model 122
Ražnatović, Željko (Arkan) 108
Real IRA 116
realpolitik 64
rebuilding
  politicization 169–77
  through reconciliation 153–67
  through reconstruction 167–9
reconciliation
  evolution of term 153
  individual vs collective aspects 165
  institutional response 154–7
  rebuilding through 153–67
  and restorative justice 162–3
reconstruction
  and armed conflict 173–4, 179–80
  credibility requirements 179–82
  need for 177–82
  politicization 169–77
  rebuilding through 167–9
Record of Understanding 114, 123
Red Cross 176–7
Reid, Father Alec 46
Reiss, Mitchell 94
Renamo 62
Reno, William 4

resistance to peace 101–25
  peaceful resisters 117–25
  reasons 104–8
  violent resisters 113–16
  see also spoilers
Responsibility to Protect (R2P) 56–7, 58
restorative justice 158, 161–7
  and reconciliation 162–3
retributive justice 158–61
Revolution in Military Affairs (RMA)
  22, 132
Rice, Condoleezza 118
Richardson, Lewis Fry 29
Richmond, Oliver 103, 112
Rieff, David 22
Rigby, Andrew 157–8
'ripe moments' 33, 35–7, 45, 76–7, 186
RMA 22, 132
'road map for peace' 110, 136
Robertson, George 189
Rogers, Paul 136–7
Rothstein, Robert 95
Russia
  arms trade 105
  and Chechnya 64–9
Rwanda 54, 57–8, 102, 108, 119–21
  tribunal 158, 160, 161
Rwandan Patriotic Front (RPF) 119

Sachs, Albie 164
Said, Edward 110, 124
Salignon, Pierre 152–3
Salvadoran Foundation for
  Development (FUSADES) 52–3
Sandole, Dennis 14–15, 28
Savimbi, Jonas 108
SDLP 46
security, national and international 149
'securocrats' 107
September 11 attacks 128–9, 132–4
shadow state 4
Shamir, Yitzhak 99–100, 117
Sharon, Ariel 135, 136–7
Shi'a Arabs, in Iraq 136
Sierra Leone 18
Sinn Fein 46, 83–4, 92, 97, 107
  exclusion from negotiations 115–16
Sisk, Tom 114
Skinner, Dennis 78
Slabbart, Fredrick van Zyl 52
Smith, Dan 34–5
social engineering 118–19
Sollenberg, Margareta 3, 27
South Africa 44, 49–52
  business community 50–1
  church 50, 51

leadership role 96
National Peace Accord 114
negotiation 73, 88
pre-negotiations 82
race relations 166
Record of Understanding 114, 123
security services 107
Truth and Reconciliation
  Commission 155, 162–3, 164–5
South African Council of Churches 51
South African Defence Force (SADF) 50
sovereignty of states see state
  sovereignty
spoilers 8, 75, 101, 108–13
  conflict resolution process as 121
  greedy 109
  invisible 106
  limited 109
  total 109
Srebrenica 55
Sri Lanka 85–6, 102, 116
Staehlin, Balthasar 176–7
state
  emergence of system 29
  evolution 28
  subversion for personal gain 4
state sovereignty 56
  human rights vs 21, 159
Stedman, Stephen 8, 108–9, 113
sub-state warfare 9
Sudan 58
Sunni Arabs, in Iraq 136
surveillance 132, 133–4

Tajikistan, pre-negotiations 81
Taliban 127, 134–5, 137, 179
Tamils 85–6
Tanzania 119
Taylor, Charles 104
Taylor, Rupert 50
terrorism 66–7, 147–9
  spectaculars 133
  see also Global War on Terror
Thatcher, Margaret 97
'Third Force' 107
third-party intervention 39–69
  conflict prevention 62–3
  definition 40
  development 40–3
  limits 63–9
  macro interventions 53–63
  micro interventions 44–53
  non-coercive international 59
  roles of third parties 43–4
Thucydides 12, 25
torture 134, 142, 147

Towle, Philip 148
trade-offs 89
transnational organizations, in
    reconstruction 175
Trimble, David 93, 95, 98
trust, building of 75–6, 92–3
truth and reconciliation commissions
    (TRCs) 154, 155, 162–7
Turkey 143
Tutsis 119–21
Tutu, Archbishop Desmond 153–4,
    162–3, 165

Uganda 119
UK see United Kingdom
Ulster Unionist Party 93, 97
UN see United Nations
United Kingdom, arms trade 105
United Nations
    and Chechnya 68
    failures 53–4, 57–8
    in former Yugoslavia 55
    interventionism 168–9
    and Iraq 143
    non-coercive interventions 61–2
    post-Cold War evolution 53–8
    purpose 21
    and Rwanda 161
    as spoiler 110–11
    strengthening 147
United Nations Charter 21, 59
    see also Chapter VI interventions;
        Chapter VII interventions
United Nations Security Council
    and arms trade 105
    before Cold War 42
    during Cold War 41–2
    permanent members 68, 105
    since Cold War 42
United Nations Truce Supervision
    Organization (UNTSO) 42
United States
    arms trade 105–6
    Atlantic Council 179
    foreign policy 141, 146, 147
    homeland security 141, 146, 147, 148
    and Iraq reconstruction 175
    as mediator 85
    Middle East policy 143
    National Intelligence Council 139
    public opinion on Iraq 185
    as spoiler 110–12
UNMEE 61
UNPREDEP 63
UNPROFOR 63
Uppsala Conflict Data Program 27
US see United States

values
    core 20–2
    war between 130
Versailles Treaty 168
victims, defining 156–7
victory
    conflicts ended through 71
    as outcome of armed conflict 35
Vietnam 83, 88, 131
violence
    categorizations 13
    as inevitable 2
    in resistance to peace 113–16
    suspension vs ending 34–5

Wallensteen, Peter 2, 3, 27, 35, 53, 61, 71,
    110, 188
Walzer, Michael 20
war
    circumstances for ending 33–4
    definition 13, 15
    limits of 25–7
    modern trends in 27–32
    as necessity 190
    social meaning 15–25
    way of 30–1
war crimes tribunals (WCTs) 154,
    158–9, 160–1
war economies 104
'war entrepreneurs' 109
war on terror see Global War on
    Terror
warfare
    decentralization 132
    phrases to describe 6
    weapons of mass destruction 131, 175
Weiss, Thomas 21, 55, 56, 58, 64, 109,
    159, 180–1, 185
Welch, David 22
Williams, Andrew 139, 145, 153, 159,
    161, 169, 173
Williams, Jody 58
Woodhouse, Tom 37
World Bank 168–9, 181
World War I 34, 168
World War II 34, 168
Wright, Quincy 13, 29

Yeltsin, Boris 65
Yugoslavia 55, 108

Zahar, Marie-Joelle 121
Zartman, William 8, 35–7, 40, 45, 74,
    76
'zealots' 110
Zimbabwe 104
'zones of civility' 170–1